KOVELS' DICTIONARY OF MARKS ∾

POTTERY

AND

PORCELAIN

by

Ralph and Terry Kovel

CROWN PUBLISHERS, INC.
New York

To Rix and Dorothy,

OUR MOTHERS

Published by Crown Publishers, Inc., 201 East 50th Street, New York, New York 10022. Member of the Crown Publishing Group.

Random House, Inc. New York, Toronto, London, Sydney, Auckland
http://www.randomhouse.com/

CROWN and colophon are trademarks of Crown Publishers, Inc.

Printed in the United States of America

Library of Congress Cataloging-in-Publication Data
Kovel, Ralph
[Dictionary of marks]
Kovels' dictionary of marks : pottery and porcelain / by Ralph and
Terry Kovel.—1st ed.
Rev. ed. of: Kovels' dictionary of marks : pottery and porcelain. 1953.
Includes bibliographical references and index.
1. Pottery—Marks. 2. Porcelain—Marks. I. Kovel, Terry.
II. Kovel, Ralph. Kovels' dictionary of marks.
III. Title. IV. Title: Dictionary of marks.
NK4215.K68   1995   738'.0275—dc20   95-3361

ISBN 0-517-70137-5

10 9 8 7 6

CONTENTS

FOREWORD

Every collector knows that the least reliable but the quickest way to identify a piece of porcelain is to identify the mark. This book was written to make this identification easier. We warn the reader that marks are often forged and changed and that this book does not attempt to tell you that all porcelain marked in a certain way came from a certain factory. We give you a listing of the better-known marks and enough information so that you can learn more about your porcelains, if you wish to do so. Research and experience will tell you if the color, texture, weight, design, or general "feel" of the piece is right. This book will help you identify the mark. It is quite different from any other book of marks that the reader may have seen and, therefore, in order to use it properly it is necessary to explain the actual layout of the pages.

The book is divided into two parts. We have arranged the marks according to their shapes. The first half contains those marks that look like letters or words. Often a mark may resemble a C or a crescent or some other letter or shape. There are subheadings for each section suggesting other parts of the book that may contain the mark you seek. The second half of the book contains marks that look like a circle, square, bird or animal shape, etc. The Contents and the Index of Marks give the complete listing of these sections; the Index of Marks also gives additional cross references, such as specific animals, associated shapes, etc.

We have tried to put the simple shapes at the beginning of the book. For example, if your mark is the picture of an anchor with an A beneath it, look under Section A. A would be the easiest part of the mark to recognize. If the mark is a circle with a bird and writing inside, look under Section Circle and Sign. (Marks will often be blurred and sometimes it is impossible to read the writing, so we have, whenever possible, listed the mark by its outer outline.) If you cannot find the mark in that particular Section, look through the Index of Marks, for there you will find a complete listing of all marks that contain birds, regardless of the outer shape.

The explanation of each mark listed in this book is as follows:

(1) The first word, that in capitals, is the name of the city in which the factory is located. If the city is not known then the country is listed in capital letters.

(2) The next word is, if not already given, the name of the country.

(3) The factory name or the name of some person intimately connected with the factory, such as the founder or the most famous potter or artist, is the next part of the explanation.

(4) The type of ware is listed next, if it is known.

(5) The method of producing the mark on the object is described next.

(6) The color of the mark is next.

(7) The date when the mark was used is at the end of the description.

Often only part of this information is available. For example, the first mark listed in the book is as follows: (1) ALCORA, city; (2) *Spain*, country; (3) unknown; (4) *Porcelain*, type of ware; (5) *Incised*, how the mark is produced; (6) *Red, gold, black*, color of mark; (7) *From 1784*, date when the mark was used. In areas where boundaries changed frequently we have tried to list the name of the country during the years the mark was used. This system will become clear to the reader quite quickly.

Many American marks and twentieth century marks are included but very few are listed from the sixteenth century or earlier. No majolica has been discussed in this book because that is a separate problem in identification for the collector. No Chinese or Japanese marks are included because our new method of classification would add nothing in this field. If you wish to find out about these marks we suggest your read *The Book of Pottery and Porcelain*, by Warren E. Cox, or *Marks and Monograms on European and Oriental Pottery and Porcelain*, by William Chaffers.

There is some confusion in any reference book containing Delft marks. The Delft factories had a special way of registering their marks and the factory names which were registered are often misspelled. In this book each factory name is written in Dutch and then translated into English, so the reader will be able to find these names in other source books. Because each writer spells these names a little differently and each century saw a change in the actual way the Dutch language was written, we have written each name in its modern-day Dutch spelling. Do not be upset if this spelling is different from the one you are accustomed to using. Often, for the Delft factory, you may find a person's name listed instead of a factory name. This is usually an artist or the factory owner and is also important for further research.

There are two important marks that need separate explanations to the reader. The first is the Sevres mark, which can be found under Section Lines. For the accurate date of this mark consult the following table:

A	–	1753
B	–	1754
C	–	1755
D	–	1756
E	–	1757
F	–	1758
G	–	1759
H	–	1760
I	–	1761
J	–	1762
K	–	1763
L	–	1764
M	–	1765
N	–	1766
O	–	1767
P	–	1768
Q	–	1769
R	–	1770
S	–	1771
T	–	1772
U	–	1773
V	–	1774

X	–	1775
Y	–	1776
Z	–	1777
AA	–	1778
BB	–	1779
CC	–	1780
DD	–	1781
EE	–	1782
FF	–	1783
GG	–	1784
HH	–	1785
II	–	1786
JJ	–	1787
KK	–	1788
LL	–	1789
MM	–	1790
NN	–	1791
OO	–	1792
PP	–	1793
To July 17		
Tg	–	1801
X	–	1802

XI	–	1803
÷	–	1804
ǁ	–	1805
⚓	–	1806
7	–	1807
8	–	1808
9	–	1809
10	–	1810
o.z. (onze)	–	1811
d.z. (douze)	–	1812
t.z. (treize)	–	1813
q.z. (quatorze)		1814
q.n. (quinze)	–	1815
s.z. (seize)	–	1816
d.s. (diz sept)		1817

After 1817 the year is shown by the last two figures only:

18	–	1818
19	–	1819
etc.		

The other mark is that used in England from 1842 to 1883. To understand this mark completely, notice the tables below. This mark was often used with other marks that designated the factory or pattern name.

Mark A

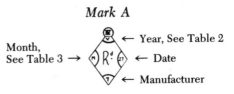

Month, See Table 3 →

← Year, See Table 2
← Date
← Manufacturer

The mark above (A) was used from 1842 to 1867. The Roman numerals in the circle at the top of the mark indicate the type of ware manufactured.

Table 1

I — metal	III — glass
II — wood	IV — earthenware

The letter below this circle tells the year of manufacture, as follows:

Table 2

X — 1842	P — 1851	Z — 1860
H — 1843	D — 1852	R — 1861
C — 1844	Y — 1853	O — 1862
A — 1845	J — 1854	G — 1863
I — 1846	E — 1855	N — 1864
F — 1847	L — 1856	W — 1865
U — 1848	K — 1857	Q — 1866
S — 1849	B — 1858	T — 1867
V — 1850	M — 1859	

The letter in the left-hand corner of the diamond-shaped mark (A) indicates the month of the year in which the object was manufactured.

Table 3

C — January	E — May	D — September
G — February	M — June	B — October
W — March	I — July	K — November
H — April	R — August	A — December

The number in the right-hand corner of the diamond indicates the day of the month in which the object was manufactured. The number in the bottom corner of the mark tells the manufacturer of the object.

The mark below (B) was used from 1868 to 1883.

Mark B

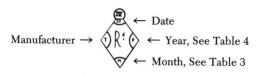

The Roman numerals in the circle at the top of the mark indicate the type of ware manufactured, as it did in the other diamond-shaped mark (see *Table 1*). The number in the circle below the Roman numeral indicates the day of the month. The letter in the lower corner of the diamond-shaped mark (B) indicates the month of the year in which the object was manufactured. The same table of letters applies to this mark (B) as to the other mark (A) (*see Table 3*). The number in the left-hand corner tells the manufacturer of the object. The letter in the right-hand corner indicates the year of manufacture, as follows:

Table 4

X	—	1868	U	—	1874	Y	—	1879
H	—	1869	S	—	1875	J	—	1880
C	—	1870	V	—	1876	E	—	1881
A	—	1871	P	—	1877	L	—	1882
I	—	1872	D	—	1878	K	—	1883
F	—	1873						

RALPH M. KOVEL
TERRY H. KOVEL

BIBLIOGRAPHY

The following is a list of books that we would like to recommend to the reader who wishes to learn more about pottery and porcelain:

Marks and Monograms on European and Oriental Pottery and Porcelain, by William Chaffers
The Book of Pottery and Porcelain, by Warren E. Cox
The Practical Book of Chinaware, by Everlein and Ramsdell
Pottery and Porcelain, by Frederick Litchfield
American Potters and Pottery, by John Ramsay
Early American Pottery and China, by John Spargo

a   b   c   d   e   f

Section A
See also Sections
H, Lines

(a) ALCORA, Spain. Porcelain. Incised red, gold, black. From 1784.
(b) PARIS, France. Hard paste. Painted red, gold. From 1793.
(c) BOW, Great Britain. Porcelain. 1744-1776. (d) BOW, Great
Britain. Porcelain. 1740-1775. (e) BOW, Great Britain. Porcelain.
Circa 1744. (f) HOLLAND. Oude Amstel. Porcelain. 1782.

g   h   i   j   k   l

(g) ST. AMAND-LES-EAUX, France. Fayence. Est. 1740. (h)
HOLLAND. Arnheim. Fayence. 1780. (i) HOLLAND. Oude Amstel. Porcelain. 1784-1800. (j) KIEL, Germany. Fayence. Circa 1770.
(k) ALCORA, Spain. Porcelain. Painted or incised red, gold, black.
From 1784. (l) PARIS, France. Hard paste. Painted red. 1770-1780.

m   n   o   p   q   r

(m) ANSBACH, Germany. Porcelain. Est. 1758. (n) BOW, Great
Britain. Porcelain. 1740-1775. (o) BOW, Great Britain. Porcelain.
1744-1776. (p) PARIS, France. Sometimes with a crown. 1775-1869.
(q) PARIS, France. Hard paste. Painted red. Est. 1778. (r) ST.
CLOUD, France. Porcelain. 1670-1773.

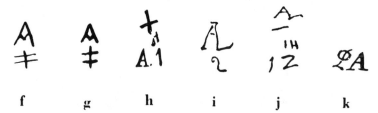

a   b   c   d   e

(a) PARIS, France. Hard paste. Painted. 1773. (b) ALCORA,
Spain. Porcelain. Painted red, gold, or black; or incised. From 1784.
(c) PERSIA, TURKEY, SYRIA. Fayence. 19th century. (d) CO-
PENHAGEN, Denmark. Fayence. Mark under glaze. 1903. (e)
WEDGWOOD, Great Britain. Mark of a painter, Thomas Allen.
1875-1905.

f   g   h   i   j   k

(f) HOLLAND. Weesp. 1764-1771. (g) ANSBACH, Germany. Porcelain. Circa 1759. (h) BRISTOL, Great Britain. Pottery and porcelain. Blue, or gold overglaze. 18th century. (i) ROTTERDAM, Holland. A. Luffen, artist. Fayence. 1700. (j) HOLLAND. De Griekse
A (The Greek A). Fayence. 1765. (k) MOUSTIERS, France. Joseph Olery. Fayence. 18th century.

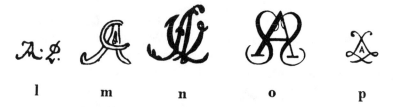

l   m   n   o   p

(l) MOUSTIERS, France. Joseph Olery. Fayence. 18th century.
(m) NYMPHENBERG, Germany. Porcelain. Impressed or incised.
Est. 1747. (n) BORDEAUX, France. Est. circa 1783. (o) St.
AMAND-LES-EAUX, France. Soft paste. Est. 1800. (p) SEVRES,
France. Soft paste. Painted blue. 1753. (Often copied.)

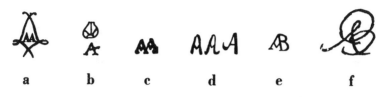

a   b   c   d   e   f

(a) SEVRES, France. Soft or hard paste. 1777-1778. (b) FRANCE. Painted red. 18th century. (c) ARRAS, France. Hard paste. Est. 1782. (d) ANSBACH, Bavaria. Hard Paste. Painted blue. Early 18th century. (e) LILLE, France. Fayence. Painted. 18th century. (f) MOUSTIERS, France. Fayence. 18th century.

g   h   i   j

(g) ITALY. Porcelain. 1752. (h) FONTAINEBLEAU, France. Fayence. 17th century. (i) ITALY. Porcelain. 1752. (j) MOUSTIERS, France. Fayence. 18th century.

k   l   m   n   o   p

(k) BURTON-ON-TRENT, Great Britain. Ashby Potter's Guild. Pottery. Circa 1909. (l) DAEHMEL, Germany. Est. 1854. (m) PARIS, France, Advenir Lamarre. Hard paste. Painted 1773. (n) AMSTERDAM, (Amstel), Holland. Daeuber, director. Hard paste. Painted blue. 1783. (o) PARIS, France. Gros Caillou. 1773. (p) HOLLAND. Delft. Painted blue. 1774.

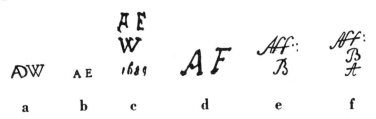

a   **b**   **c**   **d**   **e**   **f**

(**a**) ANDENNES, France. Pottery. Impressed. Early 19th century.
(**b**) LIMOGES, France. 1842-1898. (**c**) SWITZERLAND. Fayence.
1689. (**d**) BOW, Great Britain. Porcelain. 1744-1776. (**e**) ROR-
STAND, Sweden. Fayence. Est. 1727. (**f**) RORSTAND, Sweden.
Fayence. From 1758.

g   **h**   **i**   **j**   **k**

(**g**) TOULOUSE, France. Fouqué Arnoux and Company. Fayence.
Painted. 1820. (**h**) SAVONA, Italy. Pottery. 17th century. (**i**)
ROCKHILL, Pennsylvania, U.S.A. Charles Headman. 1840-1870.
(**j**) BRISTOL, Great Britain. 1703-1803. (**k**) HOLLAND. De
Griekse A (The Greek A). Fayence. 1765.

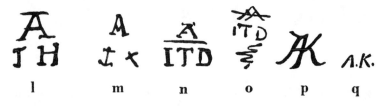

l   **m**   **n**   **o**   **p**   **q**

(**l**) HOLLAND. De Griekse A (The Greek A). Fayence. 1765. (**m**)
BOW, Great Britain. Porcelain. 1744-1776. (**n**) HOLLAND. De
Griekse A (The Greek A). Fayence. 1759. (**o**) HOLLAND. De
Griekse A (The Greek A). Fayence. Painted blue. 1764. (**p**) HOL-
LAND. De Ster (The Star). A Kiell, artist. Delft. 1764. (**q**) HOL-
LAND. De Witte Ster (The White Star). A. Kiell, artist. Delft.
Painted blue. 1764.

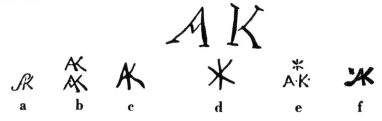

a   b   c   d   e   f

(a) HOLLAND. Samuel Piet Roerder, artist. Delft. Painted. 1650.
(b) HOLLAND. De Witte Ster (The White Star). A Kiell, artist.
Delft. Painted blue. 1764. (c) HOLLAND. De Oude Moriaan's
Hooft (The Old Moor's Head). Delft. 1759. (d) HOLLAND. De
Ster (The Star). A. Kiell, artist. Delft. 1763. (e) HOLLAND. De
Witte Ster (The White Star). Delft. Painted blue. 1764. (f) HOL-
LAND. A Kiell, artist. Delft. Painted blue. 1764.

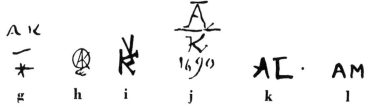

g   h   i   j   k   l

(g) HOLLAND. De Ster (The Star). A. Kiell, artist. Delft. 1764.
(h) HOLLAND. Q. Kleynoven. artist. Delft. Painted blue. 1680.
(i) HOLLAND. A. Kiell, artist. Delft. Painted blue. 1764. (j) HOL-
LAND. De Griekse A (The Greek A). A. Korks, artist. Delft. 1687.
(k) ALCORA, Spain. Porcelain. Painted red, gold black, or incised.
From 1784. (l) AICH. Germany. Porcelain. 1849-1860.

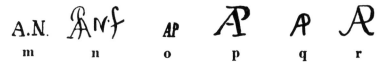

m   n   o   p   q   r

(m) ALT-ROHLAU, Bohemia. A. Nowotny, artist. Pottery and hard
paste porcelain. Impressed blue. Circa 1823. (n) MOUSTIERS,
France. Fayence. 18th century. (o) MOSCOW, Russia. 1806-1872.
(p) HOLLAND. De Twee Scheepjes (The Two Ships). A. Pennus.
Delft. 1759. (q) APREY, France. Pottery. Painted black. 1750.
(r) APREY, France. Fayence. 1750.

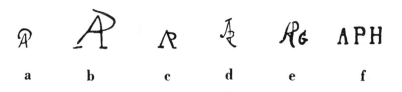

a   b   c   d   e   f

(a) APREY, France. Pottery. Painted black. 1750. (b) HOLLAND. De Twee Scheepjes (The Two Ships). A. Pennus. Fayence. Delft. Circa 1760. (c) MOSCOW, Russia. A. Popoff. Hard paste. Painted. 1805-1872. (d) ANSBACH, Bavaria. J. A. Hannong. Hard paste. Painted blue. 1718. (e) APREY, France. Fayence. Est. 1750. (f) BOHEMIA. Hegewald. 1850.

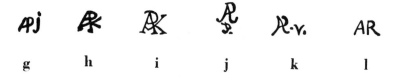

g   h   i   j   k   l

(g) APREY, France. Fayence. Est. 1750. (h) HOLLAND. Keyser and Pynaker. Pottery. Fayence. Delft. Painted blue. 1680. (i) HOLLAND. Keyser and Pynaker. Fayence. Delft. Painted color. 1680. (j) APREY, France. Fayence. Est. 1750. (k) APREY, France. Fayence. Est. 1750. (l) ARRAS, France. Soft paste. Est. 1770.

m   n   o   p   q   r

(m) ARRAS, France. Soft paste. Est. 1770. (n) PARIS, France. Claude Reverend. Fayence. 1664. (o) MEISSEN, Germany. Hard paste. Painted blue underglaze. Circa 1725. (p) MEISSEN, Germany. Helene Wolfsohn, decorator. Circa 1860. (q) MEISSEN, Germany. Helene Wolfsohn, decorator. Hard paste. Painted blue. Circa 1860. (r) PARIS, France. Pottery. Painted blue. 1664.

a   **b**   **c**   **d**   **e**

(**a**) MEILLONAS, France. Fayence. Est. 1745. (**b**) HOLLAND. Fayence. Delft. Painted blue. 1680. (**c**) ANSBACH, Bavaria. J. A. Hannong. Hard paste. Painted blue. Circa 1700. (**d**) EISENACH, Germany. A. Saeltzer. Circa 1858+. (**e**) HOLLAND. A. J. v. d. Meer. Fayence. Delft. 1671.

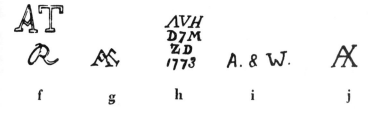

f   **g**   **h**   **i**   **j**

(**f**) GREAT BRITAIN. Don Pottery. Pottery. 1790. (**g**) HOLLAND. A. Kiell. Delft. Painted blue. 1764. (**h**) HOLLAND. Fayence. Delft. Painted. Circa 1700. (**i**) NORWICH, Connecticut, U.S.A. Armstrong and Wentworth. Impressed. 1812-1834. (**j**) AICH, Germany. Porcelain. Artist's initials. Circa 1849.

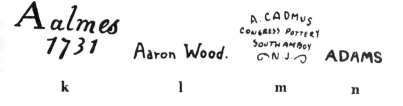

k   **l**   **m**   **n**

(**k**) HOLLAND. De Ster (The Star). J. Aalmes. Fayence. Delft. Est. 1690. (**l**) BURSLEM, Great Britain. Pottery. Impressed. 1750. (**m**) SOUTH AMBOY, New Jersey, U.S.A. Cadmus. Impressed. Circa 1850. (**n**) STOKE-ON-TRENT, Great Britain. U.S.A. William Adams II. 1829.

ADAMS   ADAMS & Co.   Adams & Co.

a   b   c

(a) TUNSTALL, Great Britain. Printed ware, stoneware, jaspers.
1787-1810. (b) TUNSTALL, Great Britain. Jasper ware. Impressed.
Circa 1790. (c) TUNSTALL, Great Britain. Creamware. Impressed.
Circa 1790.

ADAMS   ADAMS   A.D. HIGGINS
ENGLAND   TUNSTALL   CLEVELAND
                                       OHIO

d   e   f

(d) TUNSTALL, Great Britain. Printed. 19th century. (e) TUN-
STALL, Great Britain. Impressed. 19th century. (f) CLEVELAND,
Ohio, U.S.A. A. D. Higgins. Impressed. 1837-1850.

ADMIRAL   A.J. BUTLER & Co.
———————— A.G.C. DIPPLE   Aich   NEW BRUNSWICK
V. P.CO. LEWISBURG, PA.   N. J.

g   h   i   j

(g) EAST LIVERPOOL, Ohio, U.S.A. Vodrey Brothers. 1857-1885.
(h) LEWISBURG, Pennsylvania, U.S.A. A. G. Dipple. Impressed.
Circa 1890. (i) AICH, Germany. Porcelain. Impressed. Circa 1849-
1860. (j) NEW BRUNSWICK, New Jersey, U.S.A. A. J. Butler and
Company. Impressed. Circa 1850.

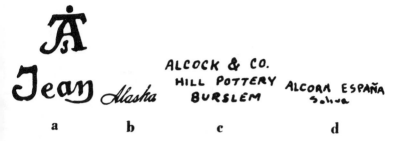

a   b   c   d

(a) PARIS, France. A. Jean. Fayence. 1859. (b) EAST LIVER-
POOL, Ohio, U.S.A. East End Pottery Company. 20th century. (c)
BURSLEM, Great Britain. Staffordshire. 1830. (d) ALCORA, Spain.
Soliva, painter. Fayence. Est. 1750.

e   f   g

(e) GREENSBORO, Pennsylvania, U.S.A. Alexander Boughner.
Impressed. 1812-1850. (f) LIMOGES, France. Est. 1774. (g) EAST
LIVERPOOL, Ohio, U.S.A. William Brunt Pottery Company. 1850-
1894.

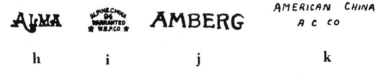

h   i   j   k

(h) EVANSVILLE, Indiana, U.S.A. Crown Pottery Company. Est.
1891. (i) EAST LIVERPOOL, Ohio, U.S.A. William Brunt Pottery
Company. 1850-1894. (j) AMBERG, Germany. Late 19th century.
(k) TRENTON, New Jersey, U.S.A. American Crockery Company.
Est. 1876.

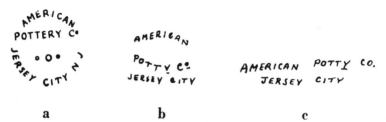

a   b   c

(**a**) JERSEY CITY, New Jersey, U.S.A. American Pottery Company. Printed. 1833-1845. (**b**) JERSEY CITY, New Jersey, U.S.A. American Pottery Company. Printed. Circa 1830. (**c**) JERSEY CITY, New Jersey, U.S.A. American Pottery Company. Impressed or printed. Circa 1830.

a moulins   Amstel   Amstel.   ANCHOR JEN

d   e   f   g

(**d**) MOULINS, France. Fayence. 18th century. (**e**) HOLLAND. Amstel Niewer. Hard paste. Painted blue. Circa 1800. (**f**) HOLLAND. Oude Amstel. Hard paste. Painted blue. 1782. (**g**) TRENTON, New Jersey, U.S.A. Anchor Pottery Company. Printed. Circa 1890.

ANTHONY SCOTT   ANTHONY SHAW
& SONS   BURSLEM   A PEYRAU

h   i   j

(**h**) SUNDERLAND, Great Britain. Anthony Scott and Sons. Circa 1835. (**i**) BURSLEM, Great Britain. 1850. (**j**) NEW YORK CITY, New York, U.S.A. A. Peyrau. 1891.

a   b   c   d

(a) CAPO-DI-MONTE, Italy. Soft paste. Incised. Circa 1760. (b) GLOUCESTER, New Jersey. U.S.A. American Porcelain Manufacturing Company. Soft paste. Impressed. 1855. (c) EAST LIVERPOOL, Ohio, U.S.A. Vodrey Brothers. 1857-1885. (d) HOLLAND. A. D. Haak. Fayence. Delft. 1780.

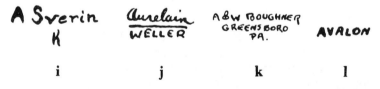

e   f   g   h

(e) NORWICH, Connecticut, U.S.A. Armstrong and Wentworth. Impressed. 1814-1834. (f) ASHFIELD, Massachusetts, U.S.A. Hastings and Belding. Impressed. 1850-1855. (g) SHELTON, Great Britain. Astbury Pottery. Impressed. Circa 1830. (h) HOLLAND. De Drie Astonnen (The Three Ash Barrels). G. P. Kam. Fayence. Delft. 1674.

A Sverin
K   Aurelain
               WELLER   A &W BOUGHNER
                                   GREENSBORO
                                   PA.   AVALON

i   j   k   l

(i) SCHWERIN, Germany. Fayence. 1760. (j) ZANESVILLE, Ohio, U.S.A. S. A. Weller. Late 19th century. (k) GREENSBORO, Pennsylvania, U.S.A. A. and W. Boughner. Impressed, blue. 1850-1890. (l) EAST LIVERPOOL, Ohio, U.S.A. Cartwright Brothers. 1880-1900.

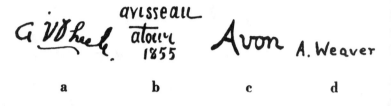

a   b   c   d

(a) HOLLAND. De Lampetkan (The Ewer). Fayence. Delft. 1780.
(b) TOURS, France. Est. 1842. (c) CINCINNATI, Ohio, U.S.A.
Avon Pottery. 1886-1888. (d) NOCKAMIXON, Pennsylvania, U.S.A.
Abraham Weaver. 1824-1844.

SECTION B
See also Sections
H, E, Lines

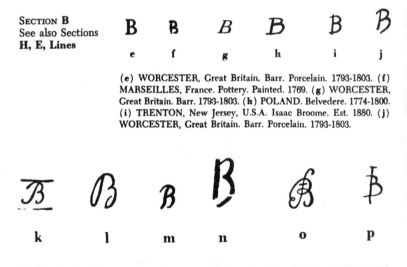

e   f   g   h   i   j

(e) WORCESTER, Great Britain. Barr. Porcelain. 1793-1803. (f)
MARSEILLES, France. Pottery. Painted. 1769. (g) WORCESTER,
Great Britain. Barr. 1793-1803. (h) POLAND. Belvedere. 1774-1800.
(i) TRENTON, New Jersey, U.S.A. Isaac Broome. Est. 1880. (j)
WORCESTER, Great Britain. Barr. Porcelain. 1793-1803.

k   l   m   n   o   p

(k) KIEL, Germany. Fayence. Circa 1770. (l) BOISSETTE,
France. Circa 1777. (m) WORCESTER, Great Britain. Flight and
Barr. Incised. 1792-1807. (n) BOW, Great Britain. Porcelain. 1744-
1776. (o) LILLE, France. Fayence. 1720-1778. (p) HOLLAND.
De Porceleyne Byl (The Porcelain Hatchet). J. Brouwer. Fayence.
Delft. 1759.

$\overset{\infty}{B}$ $\overset{+}{B}$ $\overset{*}{B}$ $\mathcal{B}$ **B:** $\mathcal{B}..$

a   b   c   d   e   f

(**a**) FRANKENTHAL, Germany. Est. 1755. (**b**) BRISTOL, Great Britain. Hard paste. Painted. 1773. (**c**) HOLLAND. J. Brouwer. Pottery. Painted blue. 1750. (**d**) BOISSETTE, France. Underglaze blue. Circa 1778. (**e**) BUDAU, Germany. 1825. (**f**) BOISSETTE, France. 1777.

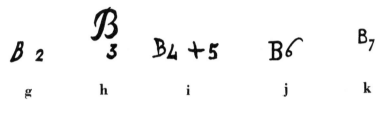

g   h   i   j   k

(**g-h**) BRISTOL, Great Britain. Pottery or porcelain. Blue or gold. 18th century. (**i**) BRISTOL, Great Britain. Porcelain. 1765-1782. (**j**) BRISTOL, Great Britain. Pottery or porcelain. Blue or gold. 18th century. (**k**) BRISTOL, Great Britain. Hard paste. Blue or gold. 1773.

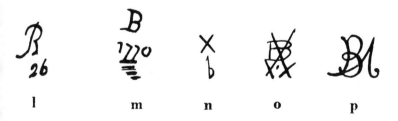

l   m   n   o   p

(**l**) PINXTON, Great Britain. Soft paste. 1796. (**m**) TOURNAY, France. Est. 18th century. (**n-o**) BRISTOL, Great Britain. Porcelain. 1773. (**p**) NIDERVILLER, France. Hard paste. Circa 1758.

a   b   c   d

(a) BRUSSELS, Belgium. 1780. (b) NIDERVILLER, France. Circa 1758. (c) MOUSTIERS, France. Fayence. 1778. (d) HO-HENSTEIN, Germany. Porcelain. Circa 1850.

e   f   g   h   i

(e) ST. CLOUD, France. J. B. Chicaneau, founder. Porcelain. Painted. Circa 1700. (f) NIDERVILLER, France. Hard Paste. Est. 1758. (g) ROUEN, France. Duprey. Fayence. 1800. (h) ROUEN, France. Duprey. 1800. (i) ST. AMAND-LES-EAUX, France. Fayence. Est. 1718.

j   k   l   m

(j) LILLE, France, Francois Boussemart. Fayence. 1729-1773. (k) BAYREUTH, Germany. Frankel and Schreck. Circa 1745. (l) COPENHAGEN, Denmark. Bing and Grondahl. 1895+. (m) BAYREUTH, Germany, Knöller. Fayence. Circa 1730.

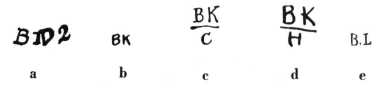

a   b   c   d   e

(**a**) ROUEN, France. Duprey. Fayence. 1800. (**b**) BAYREUTH, Germany. Porcelain. Circa 1800. (**c-d**) BAYREUTH, Germany. Knoller. Fayence. Circa 1745. (**e**) LUXEMBOURG. Belgium. Porcelain. Painted. 1806.

f   g   h   i   j   k

(**f**) LIMBACH, Germany. Porcelain. Est. 1773. (**g-h**) LUXEMBOURG, Belgium. Boch, director. Pottery and hard paste. Painted. 1806. (**i-j**) ALENCELON, France. Brancas. Hard paste. Circa 1763. (**k**) LIMBACH, Germany. Porcelain. Est. 1773.

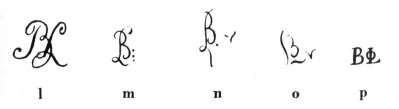

l   m   n   o   p

(**l**) ORLEANS, France. Gold or blue. Benoist le Brun. 1808-1811. (**m-n-o**) LIMBACH, Germany. Porcelain. Est. 1773. (**p**) MOUSTIERS, France. Joseph Olery. Fayence. 1738.

a   b   c   d   e

(**a**) ORLEANS, France. Benoist Le Brun. 1808-1811. (**b-c**) TREN-TON, New Jersey, U.S.A. Burroughs and Mountford. 1879-1882. (**d**) HOLLAND. De Vergulde Bloompot (The Golden Flowerpot). Fayence. Delft. 1759. (**e**) HOLLAND. De Vergulde Bloompot (The Golden Flowerpot). Fayence. Delft. 1761.

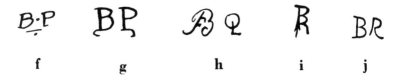

f   g   h   i   j

(**f-g**) BAYREUTH, Germany. Pfeiffer. Fayence. 1760-1767. (**h**) ALCORA, Spain. Porcelain. Est. 1727. (**i**) MARANS, France. Jean Pierre Roussencq. Pottery. Est. 1740. (**j**) BOURG-LA-REINE, France. Est. 1773.

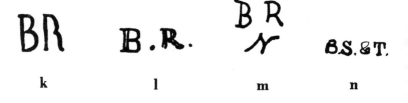

k   l   m   n

(**k-l-m**) BOURG-LA-REINE, France. Soft paste. Est. 1773. (**n**) BURSLEM, Great Britain. Barker, Sutton, and Till. 1830-1850.

B. V. $\mathcal{B}$ $\mathcal{B}$ $\mathcal{B}$ B·∇·S $1702\frac{6}{1}$

a   b   c   d   e

(a) PARIS, France. M. Victor Barbizet. Fayence, 1850. (b-c) NI-
DERVILLER, France. Baron de Beyerle, founder. Hard Paste.
Painted. 1754. (d) LIMBACH, Germany. Porcelain. Est. 1772 (e)
HOLLAND. De Klauw (The Claw). Fayence. Delft. 1702.

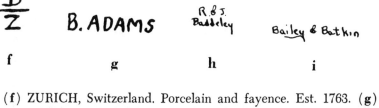

$\dfrac{B}{Z}$ B. ADAMS   R.&J.
Baddeley   Bailey & Batkin

f   g   h   i

(f) ZURICH, Switzerland. Porcelain and fayence. Est. 1763. (g)
TUNSTALL, Great Britain. Benjamin Adams. 1805-1820 (h) SHEL-
TON, Great Britain. Pottery. Impressed. Circa 1760. (i) LONG-
TON, Great Britain. Bailey and Batkin. Est. 1751.

BAKER, BEVANS & IRWIN   Balmoral B&C Royal Blue   BARKER   BARNABAS EDMUNDS & CO. CHARLESTOWN

j   k   l   m

(j) SWANSEA, Great Britain. Baker, Bevans and Irwin. 1813-1839.
(k) TRENTON, New Jersey, U.S.A. Burgess and Campbell. Est.
1870. (l) FENTON, Great Britain. Pottery. Circa 1790. (m)
CHARLESTOWN, Massachusetts, U.S.A. Edmunds and Company.
Impressed. Circa 1856.

FRANCE
LIMOGES

Barr Flight & Barr

BARR FLIGHT & BARR.
Royal Porcelain Works.
WORCESTER.
London House.
N°1 Coventry Street.

a   b   c

(**a**) LIMOGES, France. Circa 1870. (**b-c**) WORCESTER, Great Britain. Hard paste. Printed. 1807-1813.

Barr Flight & Barr
Royal Porcelain Works
Worcester
London House
No 1 Coventry Street

BARTOL   AMEO Botero   BATHWELL GOODFELLOW

d   e   f

(**d**) WORCESTER, Great Britain. Hard paste. Printed. 1807-1813.
(**e**) SAVONO, Italy. 1728. (**f**) BURSLEM, Great Britain. Impressed. Circa 1810.

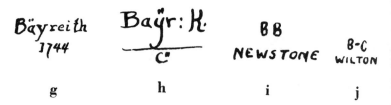

Bäyreith
1744

Bayr: K.
C°

BB
NEWSTONE

B-C
WILTON

g   h   i   j

(**g**) BAYREUTH, Germany. J. F. Metzsch, decorator. 1744. (**h**) BAYREUTH, Germany. Knoller. Fayence. 1728-1744. (**i**) STOKE-ON-TRENT, Great Britain. Minton. Hard paste. 1845-1861. (**j**) TRENTON, New Jersey, U.S.A. International Pottery Company. Est. 1870.

BELL

BELL CHINA
B P C?
Findlay, Ohio

BELPER POTTERY
DENBY

a   b   c

(a) STRASBURG, Virginia, U.S.A. Samuel and Solomon Bell. 1852-1883. (b) FINDLAY, Ohio, U.S.A. Bell Pottery Company. 19th century. (c) DERBYSHIRE, Great Britain. Belper Pottery. Stoneware. 1812.

BENNETT & CHOLLAR
HOMER

Berlin
ANCHOR POTTERY
ALL

BERLIN
C A V SONS
ENGLAND.

d   e   f   g

(d) HULL, Great Britain. Bellevue Pottery Company. 1825. (e) HOMER, New York, U.S.A. Bennett and Chollar. Impressed. 1843. (f) TRENTON, New Jersey, U.S.A. Anchor Pottery Company. Circa. 1895. (g) Charles Allerton & Sons, Longton, England. Circa 1860-present (mark used after 1891).

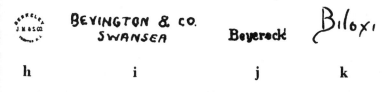

BEVINGTON & CO.
SWANSEA

Beyereck

Biloxi

h   i   j   k

(h) TRENTON, New Jersey, U.S.A. Glasgow Pottery Company. Circa 1870. (i) SWANSEA, Wales. Porcelain. 1814-1822. (j) BEY-ERECK, Germany. Stoneware. Circa 1824. (k) EAST BILOXI, Mississippi, U.S.A. George Ohr. 1890-1900.

a   **b**   **c**   **d**

(**a**) HANLEY, Great Britain. E. J. Birch. Staffordshire. Circa 1800.
(**b**) NEWARK, New Jersey, U.S.A. B. J. Krumeich. Circa 1850.
(**c**) CORTLAND, New York, U.S.A. Sylvester Blair. 1828-1836.
(**d**) BOURG-LA-REINE, France. Soft paste and pottery. Painted
blue. 1773.

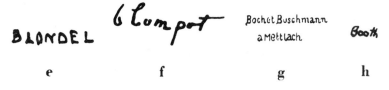

e   **f**   **g**   **h**

(**e**) DOUAI, France. Est. 1781. (**f**) HOLLAND. De Vergulde
Bloompot (The Golden Flowerpot). Fayence. Delft. Circa 1693.
(**g**) METTLACH, Germany. Fayence. 19th century. (**h**) TUN-
STALL, Great Britain. Enoch Booth. Pottery. Impressed. 1750.

BOOTH & SONS   *Bordeaux*   *Borgano*   *Borne*
                      Mercer   *Pinxit*
                                                             Anno
                                                             1738

i   **j**   **k**   **l**

(**i**) STOKE-ON-TRENT, Great Britain. Booth and Sons. 1803. (**j**)
TRENTON, New Jersey, U.S.A. Mercer Pottery Company. Circa
1870. (**k**) TURIN, Italy. Fayence. 18th century. (**l**) ROUEN,
France. Claude Borne. Fayence. 1738.

BOSS BROS.
MIDDLEBURY
OHIO

BOOTKWELL
GOODFELLOW

BOTT & CO

a   b   c

(**a**) AKRON, Ohio, U.S.A. Boss Brothers. Impressed. Circa 1875.
(**b**) TUNSTALL, Great Britain. 1828. (**c**) GREAT BRITAIN. Bott
and Company. Staffordshire. Early 19th century.

J. Boulard a Nevers
1622

BOURNE'S
POTTERIES

BOURNE'S POTTERIES
DENBY & CODNOR PARK
DERBYSHIRE

d   e   f

(**d**) NEVERS, France. J. Boulard, potter. 1622. (**e**) DERBYSHIRE,
Great Britain. Stoneware. Circa 1800. (**f**) DERBYSHIRE, Great
Britain. Stoneware. 19th century.

BOURNE, NIXON & CO   BOUTET   B. Plant

B
Potter
42

g   h   i   j

(**g**) TUNSTALL, Great Britain. Bourne, Nixon, and Company.
Circa 1830. (**h**) AUXERRE, France. (Yonne.) Est. 1799. (**i**) LANE
END, Great Britain. Pottery. Impressed. 1777. (**j**) PARIS, France.
Christopher Potter. Circa 1790.

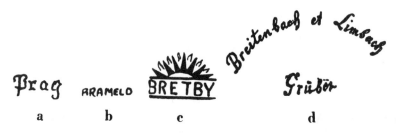

a   b   c   d

(a) PRAGUE, Bohemia. Prager. Lead-glazed earthenware. 1810-1862. (b) SWINTON, Great Britain. (Rockingham factory.) John and William Brameld, potters. Late 18th and 19th centuries. (c) BURTON-ON-TRENT, Great Britain. Tooth and Company. 20th century. (d) LIMBACH, Germany. Porcelain. Est. 1722.

e   f   g   h   i

(e) BRISTOL, Great Britain. Porcelain. Circa 1750. (f) EAST LIVERPOOL, Ohio, U.S.A. Cartwright Brothers. Circa 1900. (g) TRENTON, New Jersey, U.S.A. Isaac Broome. 1880-1882. (h) EAST HAMPTON, New York, U.S.A. Middle Lane Pottery. Circa 1900. (i) ROUEN, France. Brument. 1699.

j   k   l   m   n   o

(j) BRUSSELS, Belgium. Fayence. 1705. (k-l-m-n) EAST LIVERPOOL, Ohio, U.S.A. Burford Brothers Pottery Company. 1879-1904. (o) CROOKSVILLE, Ohio, U.S.A. Burley and Winters. Circa 1850.

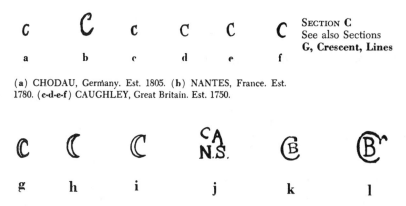

a	b	c	d	e	f

(a) CHODAU, Germany. Est. 1805. (b) NANTES, France. Est. 1780. (c-d-e-f) CAUGHLEY, Great Britain. Est. 1750.

g	h	i	j	k	l

(g-h-i) CAUGHLEY, Great Britain. Est. 1750. (j) DOCCIA, Italy Est. 1737. (k) BAYREUTH, Germany. Hard Paste. Painted. 1744 (l) BAYREUTH, Germany. Hard Paste. Painted. 1744.

m	n	o	p	q

(m) CASTEL-DURANTE, Italy. Est. 1570. (n) HOLLAND. De Ster (The Star). C. D. Berg. Fayence. Delft. 1720. (o) COAL-BROOKDALE, Great Britain. Hard Paste. Painted blue. Circa 1825-1850. (p) HOLLAND. De Ster (The Star). C. D. Berg. Fayence. Delft. 1720. (q) HOLLAND. De Jonge Moriaan's Hooft (The New Moor's Head). H. Strale. 1764.

a b c d e

(a) ST. PETERSBURG, Russia. Hard Paste. Painted blue. 1765.
(b) TERVUEREN, Belguim. Fayence. 1720. (c-d) LIMOGES,
France. Hard Paste. Painted red. 1773. (e) LIMOGES, France.
Hard paste. 1773.

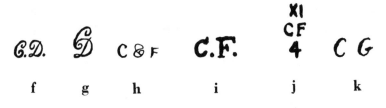

f g h i j k

(f-g) COALBROOKDALE, Great Britain. Hard paste. Painted
blue. 1787. (h) SCOTLAND. Circa 1850. (i-j) PIRKENHAMMER,
Germany. Christian Fischer. Hard paste. 1846-1853. (k) LEEDS,
Great Britain. Est. 1760.

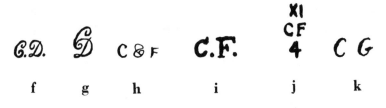

l m n o p q

(l) STOKE-ON-TRENT, Great Britain. Copeland and Garrett.
1833-1847. (m) LEEDS, Great Britain. Est. 1760. (n) STRAS-
BOURG, France. Fayence. Incised. 1721-1739. (o) PARIS, France.
Hard paste. Painted red. 1784. (p) ROCKHILL, Pennsylvania,
U.S.A. Charles Headman. 1840-1870. (q) PARIS, France. Chanou.
1746-1779.

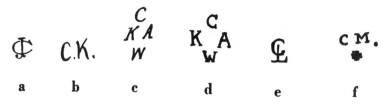

a   b   c   d   e   f

(a) NEW YORK, New York, U.S.A. Carr and Morrison. Circa 1853.
(b) BUCKSVILLE, Pennsylvania, U.S.A. Christian Klinker. Circa
1780. (c) MORRISVILLE, Pennsylvania, U.S.A. Robertson Art Tile
Company. 19th century. (d) CHELSEA, Massachusetts, U.S.A.
Chelsea Keramic Art Works. Impressed. 1875–1889. (e) HOL-
LAND. De Metale Pot (The Metal Pot). L. Cleffius. Fayence. Delft.
1667. (f) PARIS, France. Marie-Anne Chicaneau. 1741.

g   h   i   j   k   l

(g) ST. CLOUD, France. Fayence. Porcelain. Circa 1711. (h)
FLORSHEIM, Germany, Fayence. Circa 1780. (i) NYON, Switzer-
land. Hard paste. Painted blue. 1780. (j) NEW ORLEANS, Louisi-
ana, U.S.A. Newcomb Pottery. 1896-1945. (k) NIDERVILLE,
France. Custine. Hard paste. 1770-1793. (l) TELECHANY, Poland.
Count Michael Oginski. Late 18th century.

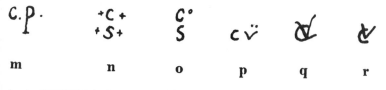

m   n   o   p   q   r

(m) CREPY-EN-VALOIS, France. 1762. (n) SINCENY, France.
Pottery. Painted color. 1733. (o) MARSEILLES, France. Savy.
Fayence. 1770. (p-q) THURINGIA. Germany. Kloster Veilsdorf.
Porcelain. Est. 1760. (r) GREENPOINT, New York, U.S.A. Volk-
mar Keramic Company. Circa 1880.

| a | b | c | d | e |

(**a-b**) HOLLAND. De Oude Moriaan's Hooft (The Old Moor's Head). G. Verstelle. Fayence. Delft. 1764. (**c**) HOLLAND. De Klauw (The Claw). C. V. Schoonhove. Fayence. Delft. 1668. (**d**) CAEN, France. Hard paste. Painted red. 1793. (**e**) CAEN, France. Hard paste. 1793.

| f | g | h | i |

(**f**) LIMOGES, France. 1842-1898. (**g**) PORTLAND, Maine, U.S.A. Caleb Crafts. Impressed. Circa 1840. (**h**) SWANSEA, Great Britain. John F. Calland. Circa 1845. (**i**) SWANSEA, Great Britain. Hard paste. Painted color. 1765.

| j | k | l |

(**j**) AKRON. Ohio, U.S.A. Camp and Thompson. Impressed. 1870-1880. (**k**). STEUBENVILLE, Ohio, U.S.A. Steubenville Pottery Company. Est. 1879. (**l**) APREY, France. Fayence, Est. 1744.

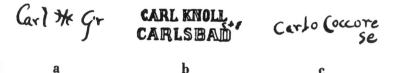

a   b   c

(**a**) BUEN RETIRO, Spain. Soft paste. 1759-1808. (**b**) FISCHERN, Bohemia. 1848. (**c**) NAPLES, Italy. Circa 1785.

CARLSBAD   **CAULDON**   CAULDON England

d   e   f

(**d**) FISCHERN, Bohemia. Porcelain. 1848. (**e**) SHELTON, Great Britain. Ridgways. Circa 1850. (**f**) SHELTON, Great Britain. Circa 1905-1920.

C. CROLIUS
MANUFACTURER
NEW YORK   GDale   C DILLON & Cº
ALBANY   CFH
GDM

g   h   i   j

(**g**) NEW YORK. New York, U.S.A. Clarkson Crolius, Senior. Circa 1840. (**h**) COALBROOKDALE, Great Britain, Circa 1830. (**i**) ALBANY, New York, U.S.A. C. Dillon and Company. Circa 1830. (**j**) FRANCE. E. Gerard Dufraissein et Morel, Charles F. Haviland. 1882-1898.

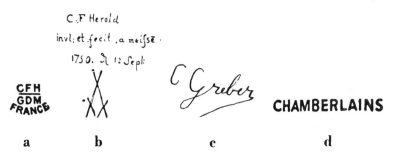

a   **b**   **c**   **d**

(**a**) FRANCE. E. Gerard Dufraissein et Morel. Whiteware. 1882-1898. (**b**) MEISSEN, Germany. 1750. (**c**) HANOVER, Pennsylvania. Greber Pottery. Circa 1850. (**d**) WORCESTER, Great Britain. Impressed, printed. 1847-1850.

♔
Chamberlain's
Regent China
Worcester
& 155
New Bond Street,
London.

Chamberlain & Co.,
Worcester

Chamberlain's

e   **f**   **g**

(**e**) WORCESTER, Great Britain. 1788-1808. (**f**) WORCESTER. Great Britain. 1847. (**g**) WORCESTER, Great Britain. 1814-1820.

Chamberlain's
Worcester.
& 63. *Piccadilly.*
London

CHAMBERLAIN & CO.
WORCESTER
155 NEW BOND STREET
& NO 1
COVENTRY ST
LONDON

♔
Chamberlains
Worcester
& 155
New Bond Street,
London
—
Royal Porcelain Manufacturers

h   **i**   **j**

(**h**) WORCESTER, Great Britain. 1814. (**i**) WORCESTER, Great Britain. 1840-1845. (**j**) WORCESTER, Great Britain. 1820-1840.

CHAS ALLERTON B SONS
ENGLAND

Chas. Headman

a   b   c

(a) EAST LIVERPOOL, Ohio, U.S.A. United States Pottery. Est.
1846. (b) LONGTON, Great Britain, Charles Allerton. Circa 1900.
(c) ROCKHILL, Pennsylvania, U.S.A. Charles Headman. Circa
1825.

Chatillon

Chelfea
1745

CHELSEA KERAMIC
ART WORKS
ROBERTSON B SONS

d   e   f

(d) CHATILLON, France. Hard paste. Est. 1775. (e) CHELSEA,
Great Britain. Soft paste. 1745. (f) CHELSEA, Massachusetts,
U.S.A. Chelsea Keramic Art Works. Circa 1875-1880.

Chester   CHETHAM   Chetham & Woolley
Lane End 1798

CHICAGO

g   h   i   j

(g) EAST LIVERPOOL, Ohio, U.S.A. William Brunt Pottery Company. Circa 1875. (h) LANE END, Great Britain. Staffordshire.
1795. (i) LANE END, Great Britain. Staffordshire. 1798. (j) EAST
LIVERPOOL, Ohio, U.S.A. William Brunt Pottery Company. Circa
1875.

CHILD　　　　　　　　　　　　　Chodau　　CHOLLAR & DARBY
　　　　　　　　　　　　　　　　　　　　　　HOMER, N.Y.

a　　　　　　　b　　　　　　c　　　　　　　d

(a) TUNSTALL, Great Britain. Smith Child, potter. Cream-colored ware. Impressed. Late 18th century. (b) PARIS, France. Porcelain. 1795. (c) CHODAU, Germany. Est. 1805. (d) HOMER, New York, U.S.A. Chollar and Darby. Impressed. Circa 1845.

C H. PILLIVUY
& Cie PARIS　　　Christian　　CHRISTIAN LINK　　CLEM HAMILTON
　　　　　　　　　　　　　　　STONETOWN

e　　　　　　f　　　　　　g　　　　　　　h

(e) FOECY, France. Pillivuyt family, potters. 19th and 20th centuries. (f) LIVERPOOL, Great Britain. Pottery. Impressed. 1765. (g) STONETOWN, Pennsylvania, U.S.A. Christian Link. Impressed. Circa 1870. (h) TUSCARAWAS COUNTY, Ohio, U.S.A. Clem Hamilton. Impressed. Circa 1870.

CLOSE & Co
Late
C.LINK　　W. ADAMS & SONS
C.LINK　　EXETER　　STOKE-UPON-TRENT　　Coalport.

i　　　　　　j　　　　　　k　　　　　　　l

(i-j) STONETOWN, Pennsylvania. U.S.A. Christian Link. Impressed. Circa 1870. (k) STOKE-ON-TRENT, Great Britain. Impressed. Circa 1829. (l) COALBROOKDALE, Great Britain. Hard paste. Painted blue. 1810-1825.

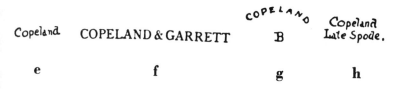

a **b** **c** **d**

(**a**) GLASGOW, Scotland. Cochran and Fleming. Circa 1860. (**b**) TRENTON, New Jersey, U.S.A. Columbian Art Pottery. Est. 1875. (**c-d**) CORLEAR'S HOOK, New York, U.S.A. Thomas Commeraw. Circa 1810.

Copeland   COPELAND & GARRETT   COPELAND   Copeland
                                      B   Late Spode.

e **f** **g** **h**

(**e**) STOKE-ON-TRENT, Great Britain. Hard paste and pottery. Impressed. 1847. (**f**) STOKE-ON-TRENT, Great Britain. 1833-1847. (**g**) STOKE-ON-TRENT, Great Britain. 1847. (**h**) STOKE-ON-TRENT, Great Britain. W. T. Copeland and Sons. 1847-1867.

CORLEAR'S HOOK   CORTLAND   C. P. CO.   C. P. Co.
                                           CHINA

i **j** **k** **l**

(**i**) CORLEAR'S HOOK, New York, U.S.A. Impressed. Circa 1800. (**j**) CORTLAND, New York, U.S.A. Sylvester Blair. Circa 1830. (**k**) GREENOCK, Scotland. Clyde Pottery Company. 1900. (**l**) CHITTENANGO, New York, U.S.A. Chittenango Pottery Company. Circa 1900.

a   b   c   d   e

(a) CHITTENANGO, New York, U.S.A. Chittenango Pottery Company. Circa 1900. (b) PHOENIXVILLE, Pennsylvania, U.S.A. Chester Pottery Company. Est. 1894. (c-d) EVANSVILLE, Indiana, U.S.A. Crown Pottery Company. Circa 1895. (e) BALTIMORE, Maryland, U.S.A. Maryland Pottery Company. Circa 1880.

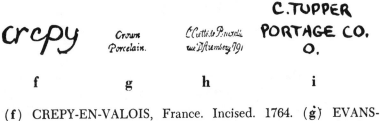

f   g   h   i

(f) CREPY-EN-VALOIS, France. Incised. 1764. (g) EVANSVILLE, Indiana, U.S.A. Crown Pottery Company. Circa 1895. (h) BRUSSELS, Belguim. Louis Cretté. Hard paste. Painted color. 1791-1803. (i) PORTAGE COUNTY, Ohio, U.S.A. C. Tupper. Impressed. Circa 1870.

CYFFLÉ
A LUNÉVILLE.   Cyples   CYPLES & BARKER

j   k   l

(j) LUNEVILLE, France. Fayence. 1758. (k) LONGTON, Great Britain. Cyples, potter. Late 18th and early 19th centuries. (l) LONGTON, Great Britain. Staffordshire. Circa 1800.

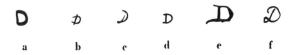

a   b   c   d   e   f

SECTION **D**
See also Sections
O, Lines

(**a**) DAVENPORT, Great Britain. Impressed. 1793-1882. (**b**) DERBY, Great Britain. 1770-1784. (**c**) CAUGHLEY, Great Britain. Hard paste. Painted blue. Est. 1750. (**d**) DALLWITZ, Bohemia. W. W. Lorenz. Circa 1832. (**e**) HOLLAND. De Griekse A (The Greek A). J. T. Dextra. Fayence. Delft. 1759. (**f**) NORD, France. Valenciennes. Louis Dorez. Fayence. 1735.

g   h   i   j   k

(**g**) NORD, France. Valenciennes. Louis Dorez. 1735. (**h**) DERBY, Great Britain. Soft paste. Painted red. 1756. (**i**) DRYVILLE, Pennsylvania, U.S.A. John Dry (Drey). Circa 1825. (**j**) WORCESTER, Great Britain. John Donaldson, painter. Porcelain. 1737-1810. (**k**) DERBY, Great Britain. 1782.

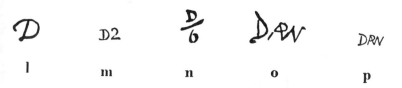

l   m   n   o   p

(**l**) DERBY, Great Britain. 1770. (**m**) LILLE, France. Pottery. Painted color. Circa 1745. (**n**) HOLLAND. De Griekse A (The Greek A). J. T. Dextra. Fayence. Delft. 1759. (**o**) HOLLAND. De Paauw (The Peacock). D. Kam. Fayence. Delft. 1697. (**p**) HOLLAND. De Paauw (The Peacock). Jacobus de Milde. Fayence. Delft. 1651.

a   b   c   d   e

(a) HOLLAND. Fayence. Delft. 1764. (b) HOLLAND. De Paauw
(The Peacock). Jacobus de Milde. Registered 1764. (c) MEN-
NECY-VILLEROY, France. Soft paste. 1734. (d) TRENTON, New
Jersey, U.S.A. Prospect Hill Pottery Company. Circa 1880. (e)
NEVERS, France. Denis Lefebvre. Pottery. Painted. 17th century.

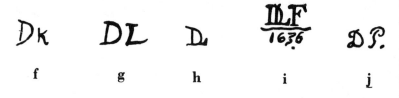

f   g   h   i   j

(f) HOLLAND. De Paauw (The Peacock). D. Kam. Fayence.
Delft. 1697. (g) LONGTON HALL, Great Britain. William Littler,
potter. Staffordshire. 1750-1760. (h) NORD, France. Valenciennes.
Louis Dorez. 1735. (i) NEVERS, France. Denis Lefebvre. 1636.
(j) SILESIA, Germany. Proskau. Fayence. Dietrichstein period.
1770-1783.

k   l   m   n   o

(k) HOLLAND. De Paauw (The Peacock). Fayence. Delft. 1701.
(l-m) HOLLAND. De Dubbelde Schenkkan (The Double Jug).
Fayence. Delft. 1764. (n) MENNECY-VILLEROY, France. Soft
paste. Painted and incised. Est. 1734. (o) HOLLAND. De Roos
(The Rose). Fayence. Delft. 1759.

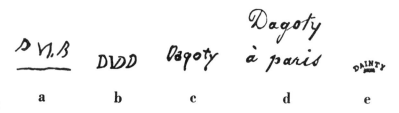

a   b   c   d   e

(**a**) HOLLAND, De Fortuyn (The Fortune). P. V. D. Briel. Fayence. Delft. 1759. (**b**) HOLLAND. D. van der Does. Fayence. Delft. Registered 1764. (**c-d**) PARIS, France. Dagoty, potter. Hard paste. Painted red. 1822. (**e**) TRENTON, New Jersey, U.S.A. Crescent Pottery Company. Est. 1881.

DALTON POTTERY   **DALWITZ**   **DARTE FRERES A' PARIS**

f   g   h

(**f**) DALTON, Ohio, U.S.A. Dalton Pottery Company. Impressed. 1875. (**g**) DALLWITZ, Germany. Circa 1804. (**h**) PARIS, France. Darte brothers, porcelain-makers. Stenciled red. 1795-1840.

DAVENPORT LONGPORT   David Spinner   **DAWSON**

i   j   k

(**i**) LONGPORT, Great Britain. Pottery. Impressed. 1793. (**j**) MELFORD, Pennsylvania, U.S.A. Circa 1810. (**k**) SUNDERLAND, Great Britain. Ford Pottery. Est. 1800.

a   b   c   d

(a) LIMOGES, France. Circa 1875. (b) CASTLEFORD, Great Britain. Pottery. Impressed. 1790. (c) CASTLEFORD, Great Britain. Pottery. Circa 1800. (d) DRYVILLE, Pennsylvania, U.S.A. Dry Brothers. Circa 1850.

e   f   g   h   i

(e) HOLLAND. De Vergulde Bloompot (The Golden Flowerpot). P. Verberg. Pottery. 1764. (f) HAVILAND, France. Decorated ware. Red. 1915. (g) DERBY, Great Britain. 1750. (h) HOLLAND. De Griekse A (The Greek A). T. Dextra. Fayence. Delft. 1764. (i) HARTFORD, Connecticut, U.S.A. Daniel Goodale. Impressed. Circa 1825.

DICKENS WARE
WELLER.   Oihl   **DILLWYN & CO.**   Dixon & Co.

j   k   l   m

(j) ZANESVILLE, Ohio, U.S.A. S. A. Weller. Circa 1890. (k) PARIS, France. Hard paste. Painted red. 1780. (l) SWANSEA, Wales. Circa 1840. (m) SUNDERLAND, Great Britain. Sunderland Pottery. Printed. 1805.

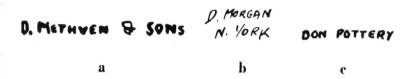

a   b   c

(a) SCOTLAND. D. Methven and Sons. Circa 1875. (b) NEW YORK, New York, U.S.A. D. Morgan. Impressed. Circa 1880. (c) DON, Great Britain. Don Pottery. Pottery. Est. 1790.

d   e   f   g

(d) LAMBETH, Great Britain. Doulton. Circa 1891. (e) LAMBETH, Great Britain. Doulton. Circa 1886-1914. (f) EAST LIVERPOOL, Ohio, U.S.A. Potters Cooperative Company. Est. 1876. (g) EAST LIVERPOOL, Ohio, U.S.A. Potters Cooperative Company. Circa 1892.

Dᵣ Frāc
Ant'Gruef
Neap
1710   DUCROZ & MILLIDGE   DUDSON BROTHERS
HANLEY, ENGLAND   Duÿn

h   i   j   k

(h) NAPLES, Italy. Francesco Antonio Grue. 1731-1806. (i) LANE END, Great Britain. Ducroz and Millidge. Circa 1850. (j) HANLEY, Great Britain. Dudson Brothers. Circa 1891. (k) HOLLAND, De Porceleyne Schootel (The Porcelain Dish). J. van Duyn. Fayence. Delft. Painted blue. 1764.

SECTION E
See also Sections
B, Lines

$\mathcal{E}$ $\underset{1779}{\overset{\mathcal{E}}{}}$ **EB**   E B S $\mathcal{E}f$ E. I. B.

a   b   c   d   e   f

(a) ST. PETERSBURG, Russia, 1762-1796. (b) DERBY, Great
Britain. 1779. (c) PARIS, France. Circa 1800. (d) HOLLAND. De
Jonge Moriaan's Hooft (The New Moor's Head). Fayence. Delft.
1764. (e) MOUSTIERS, France. Fayence. 18th century. (f) HAN-
LEY, Great Britain. Impressed. 18th century.

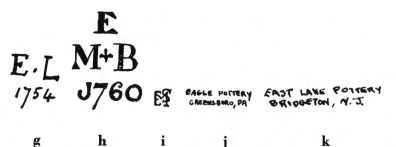

g   h   i   j   k

(g) BOW, Great Britain. 1754. (h) BRISTOL, Great Britain. Pottery. 1760. (i) HOLLAND. Johannes Mesch. Fayence. Delft. 1680.
(j) GREENSBORO, Pennsylvania, U.S.A. James Hamilton. Stoneware. 1844-1890. (k) BRIDGETON, New Jersey, U.S.A. George
Hamlyn. Impressed. Circa 1835.

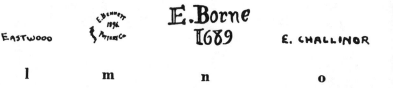

l   m   n   o

(l) HANLEY, Great Britain. W. Baddeley, Pottery. Impressed.
1795. (m) BALTIMORE, Maryland, U.S.A. Edwin Bennett. Circa
1870. (n) NEVERS, France. 1689. (o) BURSLEM, Great Britain.
1819.

EDGE & GROCOTT

EDWARD NORTON CO.
BENNINGTON
V. T

EDWARDS
D. H.

a

b

c

(**a**) GREAT BRITAIN. Edge and Grocott. Impressed. Circa 1825.
(**b**) BENNINGTON, Vermont, U.S.A. Edward Norton and Company. Impressed. Circa 1890. (**c**) FENTON, Great Britain. James
Edwards. Circa 1850.

E.&G. NASH
UTICA

E. HALL
NEWTON TOWNSHIP
TUSCARAWAS CO.
O.

E.H. MERRILL
SPRINGFIELD
O.

ELECTRIC

d

e

f

g

(**d**) UTICA, New York, U.S.A. E. and G. Nash. Impressed. Circa
1820. (**e**) NEWTON, Tuscarawas, Ohio, U.S.A. W. P. Harris. Impressed. Circa 1840. (**f**) SPRINGFIELD, Ohio, U.S.A. Edwin H.
Merrill. Impressed. Circa 1835. (**g**) EAST LIVERPOOL, Ohio,
U.S.A. Burford Brothers Pottery Company. Circa 1890.

E. & L.P. NORTON
BENNINGTON, VT.

Elsmere

Elton

E Lycett

h

i

j

k

(**h**) BENNINGTON, Vermont, U.S.A. E. and L. P. Norton. Impressed. Circa 1875. (**i**) EAST LIVERPOOL, Ohio, U.S.A. Cartwright Brothers. Circa 1890. (**j**) CLEVEDON, Great Britain. Sunflower Pottery Company. 1879-1930. (**k**) ATLANTA, Georgia, U.S.A.
Edward Lycett. Circa 1900.

E. Mayer   E. MAYER & SON   ENGLAND

a   b   c

(**a**) HANLEY, Great Britain. Stoneware. Before 1820. (**b**) HAN-
LEY, Great Britain. E. Mayer and Son. 1820. (**c**) Word added to
all wares imported into the U.S.A. from England after 1891.

ENOCH BOOTH
1757

Enoch Wood

E. NORTON
BENNINGTON
VT.

d   e   f

(**d**) TUNSTALL, Great Britain. Enoch Booth. 1757. (**e**) BURS-
LEM, Great Britain. 1783-1790. (**f**) BENNINGTON, Vermont,
U.S.A. Edward Norton. Impressed. Circa 1882.

E. NORTON & CO.
BENNINGTON, VT.

ENTERPRISE
POTTERY
CO.

Erosian
WELLER

ESTE ✦ 1783 ✦

g   h   i   j

(**g**) BENNINGTON, Vermont, U.S.A. Edward Norton and Com-
pany. Impressed. Circa 1890. (**h**) TRENTON, New Jersey, U.S.A.
Enterprise Pottery Company. Circa 1900. (**i**) ZANESVILLE, Ohio,
U.S.A. S. A. Weller. Circa 1890. (**j**) ESTE, Italy. Porcelain. 1783.

ESTE
G

Etiolles
1768
Pelleve

ETRUSCAN

a   **b**   **c**

(**a**) ESTE, Italy. Franchini. Impressed. After 1782. (**b**) ETOILLES,
France. Porcelain. 1770. (**c**) PHOENIXVILLE, Pennsylvania,
U.S.A. Griffen, Smith, and Hill. Impressed. Circa 1879.

ETRUSCAN   MATOLICA

EVAN B. JONES
PITTSTON
PENNA

EVANS & GLASSON
SWANSEA
BEST GOODS
CUBA

d   **e**   **f**

(**d**) PHOENIXVILLE, Pennsylvania, U.S.A. Griffin, Smith, and
Hill. Impressed. Est. 1879. (**e**) PITTSTON, Pennsylvania, U.S.A.
Evan B. Jones. Impressed. Circa 1880. (**f**) SWANSEA, Great Brit-
ain. Evans and Glasson. Circa 1855.

E & W BENNETT
CANTON AVE.
BALTIMORE, MARYLAND

E. WENTWORTH
NORWICH

E. Wood

g   **h**   **i**

(**g**) BALTIMORE, Maryland, U.S.A. E. and W. Bennett. Impressed.
Circa 1850. (**h**) NORWICH, Connecticut, U.S.A. Armstrong and
Wentworth. Impressed. Circa 1820. (**i**) BURSLEM, Great Britain.
Enoch Wood. 1783-1840.

SECTION **F**
See also Sections
P, Lines

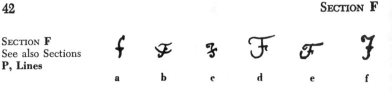

a   b   c   d   e   f

(**a**) ROUEN, France. Fayence. 1644. (**b**) PARIS, France. Feuillet, decorator. Hard paste. 1820-1850. (**c**) FURSTENBERG, Germany. Est. 1747. (**d**) FURSTENBERG, Germany. Porcelain. Est. 1747. (**e**) FURSTENBERG. Germany. Hard paste. Painted blue. Est. 1747. (**f**) COPENHAGEN, Denmark. Jacob Fortling. Fayence. 1755-1762.

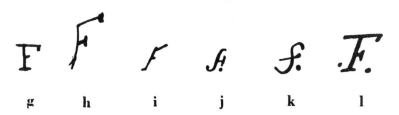

g   h   i   j   k   l

(**g**) FRANKFORT-ON-MAIN, Germany. Fayence. Est. 1666. (**h**) LONGTON, Great Britain. Circa 1750. (**i**) BOW, Great Britain. Porcelain. Circa 1760. (**j**) MOUSTIERS, France. Hard paste and soft paste. Circa 1775. (**k**) MOUSTIERS, France. Fayence. Circa 1775. (**l**) BOW, Great Britain. Thomas Frye. Porcelain. 1744.

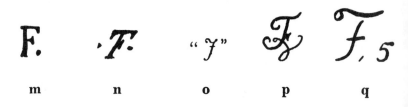

m   n   o   p   q

(**m**) MARSEILLES, France. Joseph Fauchier II. Fayence. 17th and 18th centuries. (**n**) BOW, Great Britain. Est. 1750-1760. (**o**) COPENHAGEN, Denmark. Jacob Fortling. Fayence. 1755-1762. (**p**) BERNBURG, Germany. Fayence. 1725. (**q**) COPENHAGEN, Denmark. Fournier. Soft paste. Painted blue. 1759-1765.

a   b   c   d   e

(a) HOLLAND. F. M. Byckloh. Fayence. Delft. 1680. (b) GREIN-STADT, Germany. Franz Baroto. Circa 1850. (c) PARIS, France. Francois Briat. Fayence. Circa 1600. (d) LILLE, France. Francois Boussemart. Fayence. Circa 1750. (e) LILLE, France. Francois Boussemart. Circa 1750.

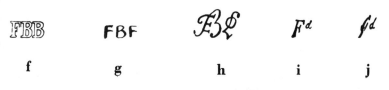

f   g   h   i   j

(f) WORCESTER, Great Britain. Flight, Barr, and Barr. 1813-1840. (g) FAENZA, Italy. Fayence. 18th century. (h) MOUS-TIERS, France. Joseph Olery. Fayence. 18th century. (i) MOUS-TIERS, France. Pottery. Painted. 1780. (j) MOUSTIERS, France. Fayence. 18th century.

k   l   m   n   o

(k) NAPLES, Italy. 18th-19th century. (l) MOUSTIERS, France. Fayence. 18th century. (m) ALCORA, Spain. Fayence. 18th century. (n) DALLWITZ, Bohemia. Est. 1804. (o) ISLEWORTH, Great Britain. Joseph Shore. 1760.

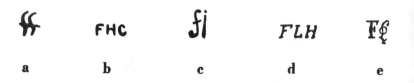

a   b   c   d   e

(**a**) ROUEN, France. 16th century. (**b**) HARRISBURG, Pennsylvania, U.S.A. Cowden and Wilcox. Impressed. Circa 1880. (**c**) MOUSTIERS, France. Fayence. 18th century. (**d**) FLORSHEIM, Germany. Fayence. Est. 1765. (**e**) MOUSTIERS, France. Joseph Olery. Fayence. 18th century.

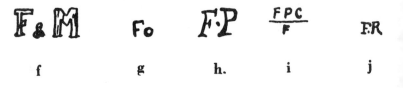

f   g   h.   i   j

(**f**) PIRKENHAMMER, Bohemia. Hard paste. 1857-1875. (**g**) ALCORA, Spain. Fayence. Est. 1727. (**h**) MOUSTIERS, France. Fayence. 18th century. (**i**) FRANKLIN, Ohio, U.S.A. Franklin Pottery Company. Impressed. Circa 1880. (**j**) NEVERS, France. Pottery. Painted. 1730.

F·R·   F&R   (⁺⁺F&R   ·F·R·1734

k   l   m   n

(**k**) RATO, Portugal. Fayence. Est. 1767. (**l**) PIRKENHAMMER, Germany. Fischer and Reichenbach. Hard paste. Painted. 1811-1846. (**m**) PIRKENHAMMER, Germany. Fischer and Reichenbach. Hard paste. 1802. (**n**) NEVERS, France. Fayence, 1734.

F & U

F
Z

ℋℋ

Fabbrica Magrin
Pesaro

a   b   c

(a) DALLWITZ, Bohemia. 1845. (b) BUEN RETIRO, Spain. Soft paste. 1759. (c) PESARO, Italy. Circa 1870.

FABRICA REAL DE
ALCORA AÑO 1735

Fabrique du Pont-
aux-Choux

faicte le 5 May
1642
par edme Brion.

dement a St Verain

d   e   f

(d) ALCORA, Spain. Fayence. Est. 1727. (e) PARIS, France. Pont-aux-Choux. 1794. (f) SAINT VERAIN, France. 1764.

faict a Rouen
1647

faite à Martres
18 septembre
1775

fait par
Lebrun à Lille

g   h   i

(g) ROUEN, France. Fayence. 1644. (h) MARTRES, France. Fayence. 1775. (i) LILLE, France. Porcelain. 19th century.

1789
fait Par Pierre
à mony

F. and R. PRATT & CO.
FENTON

Fatto en Torino

a   b   c

(**a**) ROUEN, France. Fayence. 1789. (**b**) FENTON, Great Britain. F. and R. Pratt and Company. Pottery. After 1810. (**c**) TURIN, Italy. Fayence. 16th century.

FELL   **FELL & Co.**   FENIX
FENTON & HANCOCK
ST. JOHNSBURY
VT.

d   e   f   g

(**d-e**) NEWCASTLE-ON-TYNE, Great Britain. Thomas Fell, potter, 18th-19th century. (**f**) EAST LIVERPOOL, Ohio, U.S.A. Smith-Phillips China Company. 19th century. (**g**) ST. JOHNSBURY, Vermont, U.S.A. Fenton and Hancock, Impressed. Circa 1870.

FENTON STONE WORKS
C. J. M. & Co.

ferrat moustiers

FERRYBRIDGE

h   i   j

(**h**) FENTON, Great Britain. Charles J. Mason and Company. Before 1856. (**i**) MOUSTIERS, France. Fayence. 1760. (**j**) FERRY-BRIDGE, Great Britain. Pottery. Est. 1792.

F. F.

Feuillet

Trevifo. 1799

Fo Grangol

a · b · c

(**a**) PARIS, France. Hard paste. Painted red. 1790. (**b**) VENEZIA, Italy. Treviso. 1799. (**c**) MOUSTIERS, France. Fayence. 1745.

F.H.COWDEN
HARRIS BORG

F.J. CAIRE

Fletcher & Co.
Shelton

Fleury

d · e · f · g

(**d**) HARRISBURG. Pennsylvania, U.S.A. Cowden and Wilcox. 1880. (**e**) HUNTINGTON, New York, U.S.A. Frederick J. Caire. Circa 1860. (**f**) SHELTON, Great Britain. Circa 1786. (**g**) PARIS, France. M. F. Fleury. 1773.

Flight

FLIGHTS

Flight Barr & Barr

h · i · j

(**h**) WORCESTER, Great Britain. Blue. 1782-1791. (**i**) WORCES-TER, Great Britain. 1782-1791. (**j**) WORCESTER, Great Britain. 1813-1840.

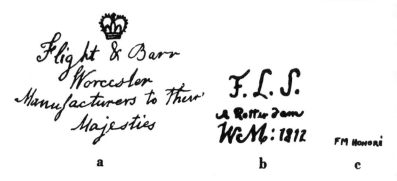

a	**b**	**c**

(**a**) WORCESTER, Great Britain. Flight and Barr. 1792-1807. (**b**) Rotterdam, Holland. 1812. (**c**) PARIS, France. Porcelain. 1785-1820.

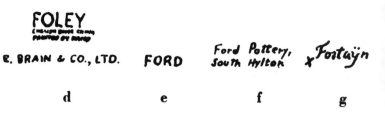

d	**e**	**f**	**g**

(**d**) STOKE-ON-TRENT, Great Britain. E. Brain and Company. Foley China. 1936+. (**e-f**) SUNDERLAND, Great Britain. Ford Pottery Company. Est. 1800. (**g**) HOLLAND. De Fortuyn (The Fortune). Pieter van der Briel. Fayence. Delft. Painted blue. 1691.

Fossé   FOWLER, THOMPSON & Co.   FULPER BROS FLEMINGTON, N.J.   FREDERICK MEAR

h	**i**	**j**	**k**

(**h**) ROUEN, France. 16th century. (**i**) PRESTONPANS, Scotland. Fowler, Thompson, and Company. Circa 1825. (**j**) FLEMINGTON, New Jersey, U.S.A. Fulper Brothers. Impressed. After 1805. (**k**) BOSTON, Massachusetts, U.S.A. Frederick Mear. Impressed. Circa 1840.

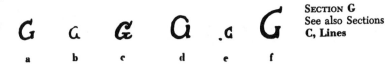

a   b   c   d   e   f

(a) BOW, Great Britain. Porcelain. 1744-1776. (b) BUEN RE-
TIRO, Spain. Soft paste. 1759-1808. (c-d) GOTHA, Germany.
Painted blue. 1805-1830. (e) ST. PETERSBURG, Russia. Blue.
Circa 1760. (f) TAVERNES, France. Fayence. 1760-1780.

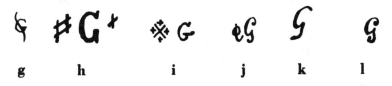

g   h   i   j   k   l

(g) FAENZA, Italy. Fayence. 15th century. (h) TAVERNES,
France. Fayence. 1760-1780. (i) TOURNAY, Belgium. Boch Brothers. 1850. (j) MOUSTIERS, France, Joseph Olery. Fayence. 18th
century. (k) MOUSTIERS, France. Fayence. 18th century. (l)
GOTHA, Germany. Hard paste. Painted blue. 1757-1927.

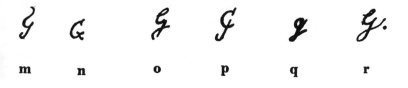

m   n   o   p   q   r

(m-n) GERA, Germany. Hard paste. Painted blue. 1780. (o) BOW,
Great Britain. Porcelain. 1750-1770. (p) BERLIN, Germany. Gotz-
kowsky. 1761-1763. (q) ST. PETERSBURG, Russia. Painted blue.
Circa 1758. (r) NYON, Switzerland. Porcelain. 1780.

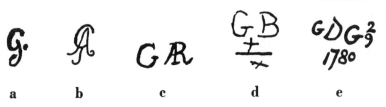

a   **b**   **c**   **d**   **e**

(**a**) TAVERNES, France. Fayence. 1760-1780. (**b**) PARIS, France.
Dihl and Guerhard. Duc d'Angouleme, patron. Hard paste. Painted
red. 1780. (**c**) ROUEN, France. Guillebaud. 1730. (**d**) HOLLAND.
De Lampetkan (The Ewer). G. Brouwer. Fayence. 1756. (**e**)
RENNES, France. Est. 18th century.

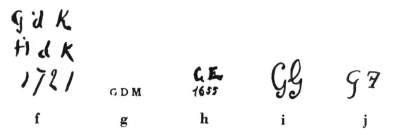

f   **g**   **h**   **i**   **j**

(**f**) HOLLAND. De Dubbelde Schenkkan (The Double Jug). Fayence. Delft. 1721. (**g**) LIMOGES, France. 1842-1898. (**h**) WIN-
TERTHUR, Switzerland. Fayence. 1655. (**i**) NAPLES, Italy. Guis-
tini Brothers. 18th century. (**j**) BUEN RETIRO, Spain. Soft paste.
1759-1808.

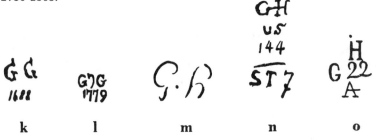

k   **l**   **m**   **n**   **o**

(**k**) WINTERTHUR, Switzerland. Pfaum. 1688. (**l**) HOLLAND.
Fayence. Delft. Painted. Circa 1700. (**m**) PARIS, France. Guy and
Housel, potters. Late 18th and early 19th centuries. (**n**) HOLLAND.
De Dubbelde Schenkkan. (The Double Jug). Fayence. Delft. 1721.
(**o**) STRASBURG, France. Joseph Hannong. Circa 1771.

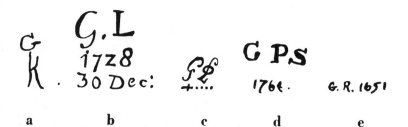

a   b   c   d   e

(**a**) HOLLAND. De Griekse A (The Greek A). G. L. Kruyk.
Fayence. Delft. 1645. (**b**) MEISSEN, Germany. Hard paste. 1728.
(**c**) MOUSTIERS, France. Joseph Olery. Fayence. 18th century.
(**d**) HOLLAND. De Porceleyne Schootel (The Porcelain Dish).
Fayence. Delft. 1764. (**e**) WROTHAM, Great Britain. 1651.

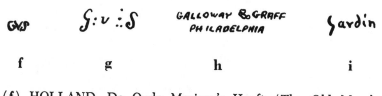

f   g   h   i

(**f**) HOLLAND. De Oude Moriaan's Hooft (The Old Moor's
Head). Fayence. Delft. Painted blue. 1764. (**g**) HOLLAND. De
Oude Moriaan's Hooft (The Old Moor's Head). Fayence. Delft.
1764. (**h**) PHILADELPHIA, Pennsylvania, U.S.A. Galloway and
Graff. Est. 1868. (**i**) ROUEN, France. Nicolas Gardin. 1760.

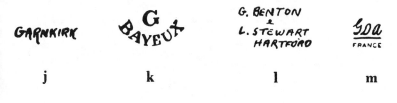

j   k   l   m

(**j**) SCOTLAND, Garnkirk Company. Circa 1870. (**k**) BAYEUX,
France. F. Gosse, proprietor. 1849. (**l**) HARTFORD, Connecticut,
U.S.A. G. Benton and L. Stewart. Circa 1818. (**m**) LIMOGES,
France. 1842-1898.

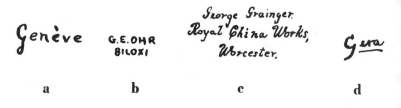

a   b   c   d

(**a**) NYON, Switzerland. Porcelain. 1781-1813. (**b**) EAST BILOXI, Mississippi, U.S.A. George Ohr. Circa 1900. (**c**) WORCESTER, Great Britain. Porcelain. Circa 1830. (**d**) GERA, Germany. Blue underglaze. Est. 1779.

G:G
pesaro
1765

G. F. BOWERS   G. H. & CO.   G. H. Kittredge.

e   f   g   h

(**e**) TUNSTALL, Great Britain, G. F. Bowers. Circa 1850. (**f**) PESARO, Italy. 1765. (**g**) SWANSEA, Wales. 1765-1870. (**h**) TRENTON, New Jersey, U.S.A. Glasgow Pottery Company. Circa 1875.

Gide 1789   GEISSHÜBEL   Giordano   GINORI

i   j   k   l

(**i**) NYON, Switzerland. Porcelain. 1789. (**j**) GIESSHUBEL, Germany. Porcelain. Circa 1815. (**k**) NAPLES, Italy. Michele Giordano and son, modelers. Late 18th and early 19th centuries. (**l**) DOCCIA, Italy. Soft paste. Impressed. 1821.

a b c d

(a) BUEN RETIRO, Spain. Guiseppe Fumo, modeler. Soft paste. 1759-1808. (b-c) TRENTON, New Jersey, U.S.A. Glasgow Pottery Company. Circa 1875. (d) PROSKAU, Germany. Fayence. 1817.

e f g

(e) GOGGINGEN, Germany. Fayence. H. Simon, painter. Est. 1748. (f) HARTFORD, Connecticut, U.S.A. Goodale and Stedman. 1822. (g) HARTFORD, Connecticut, U.S.A. Goodwin and Webster. Circa 1825.

h i j k

(h) LIVERPOOL, Ohio, U.S.A. John Goodwin. Stoneware. 1893-circa 1906. (i) GOTHA, Germany. Circa 1805. (j) TRENTON, New Jersey, U.S.A. Greenwood Pottery. Printed. Est. 1864. (k) WORCESTER, Great Britain. Hard paste. Painted red. 1800.

GRAINGER, WOOD & CO.
WORCESTER,
WARRENTED'

GREEN

GREEN
DON POTTERY

GREEN,
LEEDS

a   b   c   d

(a) WORCESTER, Great Britain. Porcelain. 1800. (b) LIVER-POOL, Great Britain. Guy Green. Late 18th century. (c) SWIN-TON, Great Britain. Don Pottery. 1790. (d) LEEDS, Great Britain. Circa 1760.

GREEN, LIVERPOOL

GREENWOOD CHINA
TRENTON, N.J.

GREENWOOD
POTTERY

GR et Cie

e   f   g   h

(e) LIVERPOOL, Great Britain. Guy Green. Late 18th century. (f) TRENTON, New Jersey, U.S.A. Greenwood Pottery Company. Printed. Circa 1904. (g) TRENTON, New Jersey. U.S.A. Greenwood Pottery Company. Printed. Circa 1870. (h) LIMOGES, France. Circa 1773.

Grofs my

GROS

GROSVENOR & SON

GRUEBY

i   j   k   l

(i) ISLE ST. DENIS, France. Porcelain. Est. 1778. (j) ALCORA, Spain. Fayence, porcelain. Est. 1750. (k) SCOTLAND. Grosvenor and Son. Circa 1870. (l) BOSTON, Massachusetts, U.S.A. Grueby Faience Company, 1897-1911.

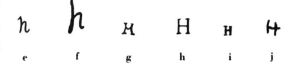

a	b	c	d

(**a**) GREAT BRITAIN. Wincanton Pottery. 1737. (**b**) PARIS,
France. Hard paste. Stenciled red. 1780. (**c**) ROUEN, France.
Guillibaud, potter. 1720-1750. (**d**) HOLLAND. Gysbert Verhaast.
Fayence. Delft. Circa 1760.

SECTION **H**
See also Section
Lines

e	f	g	h	i	j

(**e**) PARIS, France. 18th century. (**f**) FAUBOURG ST. LAZARE,
France. Hannong. Porcelain. 1773. (**g**) STRASBURG, Germany.
Fayence, porcelain. Circa 1750. (**h**) STRASBURG, Germany.
Pierre Hannong. Fayence. Circa 1750. (**i**) PARIS, France. Han-
nong. Hard paste and pottery. Painted color. 1773. (**j**) HOLLAND.
De Ster (The Star). D. Hofdick. Fayence. Delft. 1705.

k	l	m	n	o

(**k**) STRASBURG, Germany. J. Hannong. Hard paste and pottery.
Painted blue. 1752. (**l**) ALT-ROHLAU, Bohemia. Benedict Hass-
lacher, proprietor. 1813-1823. (**m**) NEVERS, France. Fayence. 17th
century. (**n-o**) STRASBURG, Germany. Joseph Hannong. Fayence,
porcelain. 1752.

a   b   c   d   e

(**a**) HOLLAND. De Drie Porceleyne Fleschen (The Three Porcelain Bottles). Hugo Brouwer. Fayence. Delft. Painted blue. 1764.
(**b**) HOLLAND. De Drie Porceleyne Fleschen (The Three Porcelain Bottles). Hugo Brouwer. Fayence. Delft. 1764. (**c**) QUIMPER, France. Antoine de la Hubaudiere. 1782. (**d**) NEVERS, France. Henri Borne. Fayence. Painted color. 1680. (**e**) HERREBOE, Norway. Hosenfeller. 1762.

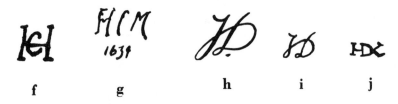

f   g   h   i   j

(**f**) GOULT, France. Fayence. Est. 1740. (**g**) SWITZERLAND. Fayence. 1634. (**h**) PARIS, France. Fayence. Circa 1850. (**i**) TURIN, Italy. Fayence. 18th century. (**j**) HOLLAND. Fayence. Delft. 17th century.

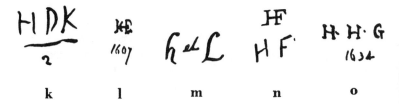

k   l   m   n   o

(**k**) HOLLAND. De Dubbelde Schenkkan (The Double Jug). Fayence. 1721. (**l**) WINTERTHUR, Switzerland. Fayence. 1607. (**m**) VINCENNES, France. Hannong and Laborde. Porcelain. 1765. (**n**) NAPLES, Italy. 18th century. (**o**) WINTERTHUR, Switzerland. Fayence. 17th century.

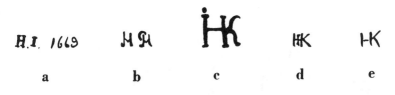

a   b   c   d   e

(a) WROTHAM, Great Britain. Slipware. 1669. (b) STRASBURG, Germany. J. and P. Hannong. Fayence, hard paste. Painted blue. 1700. (c) STRASBURG, Germany. Hannong. Fayence, hard paste. 18th century. (d) HOLLAND. Jan Zoon Kuylich. Fayence. Delft. 1680. (e) PRAGUE, Germany. Prager. Porcelain. 1810-1835.

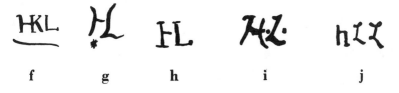

f   g   h   i   j

(f) HERREBOE, Norway. Peter Hofnagel, founder. Fayence. 1762. (g) STRASBURG, Germany. Hannong. Fayence, porcelain. 18th century. (h) HOLLAND. De Porceleyne Fles (The Porcelain Bottle). J. Harlees. 1770. (i) VINCENNES, France. Hard paste. 1764. (j) VINCENNES, France. Hannong and Laborde. Hard paste. 1765.

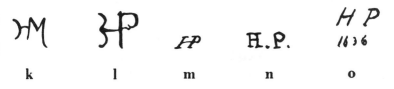

k   l   m   n   o

(k) ZANESVILLE, Ohio, U.S.A. American Encaustic Tiling Company. 19th century. (l) PARIS, France. Fayence. 1862. (m) BRUGES, Flanders. Fayence. Est. 1751. (n) HANLEY, Great Britain. Humphrey Palmer, potter. Staffordshire. 1760. (o) WINTERTHUR, Switzerland. Fayence. 17th century.

a   b   c   d

(**a**) MONTGOMERY, Pennsylvania, U.S.A. Henry Roudebuth. 19th
century. (**b**) MORRISVILLE, Pennsylvania, U.S.A. Robertson Tile
Company. 19th century. (**c**) STRASBURG, France. Hannong. Fayence, hard paste. Painted blue. 1709. (**d**) HOLLAND. F. v. Hesse.
Fayence. 1730.

e   f   g   h

(**e**) HOLLAND. De Roos (The Rose). Fayence. Delft. 1732. (**f**)
DERBY, Great Britain. H. S. Keys, painter. Hard paste. Late 18th–
early 19th century. (**g**) STRASBURG, France. Hannong. Fayence,
porcelain. 1709. (**h**) Holland. De Roos (The Rose). H. v. d. Bosch.
1803.

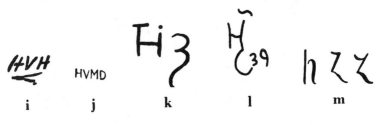

i   j   k   l   m

(**i**)HOLLAND. Fayence. Delft. Painted blue. Hendrick Van Hoorn.
1764. (**j**) HOLLAND. T'Hart (The Stag). Hendrick van Mid-
deldijk. 1764. (**k**) STRASBURG, France. Hannong. Fayence, porcelain. 1709. (**l**) PARIS, France. Samson, the imitator. Circa 1875.
(**m**) VINCENNES, France. Hard paste. 1800.

Haas & Czjzek
in
Schlaggenwald   Hackwood   HACKWOOD & CO.

a   b   c

(a) SCHLAGGENWALD, Germany. Porcelain. 1840. (b) SHEL-
TON, Great Britain. Fayence. Impressed. 1842. (c) SHELTON,
Great Britain. 1842.

HADDONFIELD, N.J.   Haidinger   halley
C.W. & BRO.

d   e   f

(d) HADDONFIELD, New Jersey, U.S.A. Charles Wingender and
brother. Impressed. Circa 1890. (e) ELBOGEN, Germany. Earthenware, porcelain. 1815. (f) PARIS, France. Halley, decorator. Early
19th century.

HAMILTON & JONES   HAMPSHIRE   H&C°
GREENSBORO, PA.   POTTERY   H&C°

g   h   i   j

(g) GREENSBORO, Pennsylvania, U.S.A. Hamilton and Jones.
Impressed. Circa 1870. (h) KEENE, New Hampshire, U.S.A.
Hampshire Pottery Company. Painted red. Circa 1875. (i) HAVI-
LAND, France. Whiteware for presidential sets. Painted green.
Circa 1879. (j) HAVILAND, France. Whiteware. Painted green.
Circa 1880.

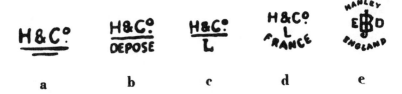

a   **b**   **c**   **d**   **e**

(a) HAVILAND, France. Whiteware. Painted green. Circa 1880.
(b) HAVILAND, France. Whiteware. Painted green. 1887. (c)
HAVILAND, France. Painted red, black, blue or green on decorated
ware; painted green on whiteware. 1876. (d) HAVILAND, France.
Whiteware. Painted green. 1891. (e) HANLEY, Great Britain.
E. J. Bodley. Late 19th century.

HARDMUTH   Harley   HARTLEY, GREEN & CO.

f   **g**   **h**

(f) BUDWEIS, Germany. Carl Hardmuth. Porcelain. 1846. (g)
LANE END, Great Britain. Pottery and hard paste. Impressed.
1809. (h) LEEDS, Great Britain. Pottery. Circa 1781-1820.

i   **j**   **k**

(i) LEEDS, Great Britain. Circa 1781-1820. (j) LEEDS, Great Britain. Pottery. Circa 1781-1820. (k) ASHFIELD, Massachusetts,
U.S.A. Hastings and Belding. Impressed. Circa 1855.

HAVILAND & CO.

Haviland & Co
Limoges

Haviland's
Chantilly

a   b   c

(a) HAVILAND, France. Decorated ware. Painted red, green, black, blue. 1876. (b) HAVILAND, France. Red. 1876-1930. (c) HAVILAND, France. Decorated ware. Painted red, green. 1948-1953.

Haviland
France   HAWLEY

HAXTUN & CO.
FORT EDWARD
N.Y.

HAYNES DILLWYN
& CO
CAMBRIAN POTTERY
SWANSEA

d   e   f   g

(d) HAVILAND, France. Whiteware. Painted green. 1893-1930, 1941-1962. (e) LEEDS, Great Britain. Hawley, potter. Kilnhurst. Circa 1800. (f) FORT EDWARD, New York, U.S.A. Haxton and Company. Impressed. Circa 1875. (g) SWANSEA, Wales. 1790-1802.

H. BOOTH   *H. CANS*

H&CO
L
FRANCE

Heath

h   i   j   k

(h) STOKE-ON-TRENT, Great Britain. Hugo Booth. Circa 1785. (i) LANCASTER, Pennsylvania, U.S.A. H. Gans. Circa 1870. (j) LIMOGES, France. Est. 1840. (k) DERBY, Great Britain. Pottery. Impressed. 1760.

Heindering Waanders
1781

HELEN   HELSINBERG

a   b   c

(**a**) HOLLAND. H. Waanders. Fayence. Delft. 1781. (**b**) EVANS-
VILLE, Indiana, U.S.A. Crown Pottery Company. Est. 1891. (**c**)
HELSINBERG, Sweden. 1770.

HENDERSON'S FLINT
STONEWARE   HENRI   HENRY LEWIS
MANUFACTORY   DEUX

d   e   f

(**d**) JERSEY CITY, New Jersey, U.S.A. Jersey City Pottery Com-
pany. 1830. (**e**) ZANESVILLE, Ohio, U.S.A. J. B. Owens Pottery
Company. Circa 1890. (**f**) HUNTINGTON, New Hampshire,
U.S.A. Impressed. Circa 1825.

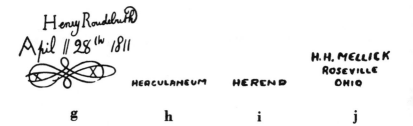

HERCULANEUM   HEREND   H.H. MELLICK
ROSEVILLE
OHIO

g   h   i   j

(**g**) MONTGOMERY, Pennsylvania, U.S.A. Henry Roudebuth.
19th century. (**h**) LIVERPOOL, Great Britain. Pottery. Impressed.
1796. (**i**) HEREND, Hungary. Moritz Fischer. Hard paste. Painted
blue. After 1839. (**j**) ROSEVILLE, Ohio, U.S.A. H. H. Mellick.
Impressed. Circa 1875.

HICKS & MEIGH   HIRAM SWANK & SONS JOHNSTOWN, PA.   HOBSON   HOLLITSCH

a   b   c   d

(**a**) SHELTON, Great Britain. Hicks and Meigh. 1806-1820. (**b**) JOHNSTOWN, Pennsylvania, U.S.A. Hiram Swank and Sons. Impressed. Circa 1875. (**c**) EVANSVILLE, Indiana, U.S.A. Crown Pottery Company. Est. 1891. (**d**) HOLLITSCH, Hungary. Impressed. Circa 1800.

Hooren   HOTEL G P CO.   HOTEL V. P. Co.   Housel   H & R DANIEL

e   f   g   h   i

(**e**) HOLLAND, De Drie Porceleyne Astonnen (The Three Porcelain Ash Barrels). Fayence. Delft. Painted blue. 1764. (**f**) EAST LIVERPOOL, Ohio, U.S.A. Globe Pottery Company. Est. 1888. (**g**) EAST LIVERPOOL, Ohio, U.S.A. Vodrey Brothers. Circa 1875. (**h**) PARIS, France. Hard paste. Painted. 1799. (**i**) STOKE-ON-TRENT, Great Britain. Circa 1830.

H. Stofflet   H V' hvorn   H. WORES   DMVETJM

j   k   l   m

(**j**) BERKS, Pennsylvania, U.S.A. Heinrich Stofflet. Circa 1815. (**k**) Holland, De Drie Astonnen (The Three Ash Barrels). H. V. Hoorn. Fayence. Delft. 1759. (**l**) DOVER, Ohio, U.S.A. H. Wores. Impressed. Circa 1830. (**m**) HOLLAND. H. Zieremans. Fayence. Delft. 1757.

a   b   c   d   e   f

(a) ALTHALDENSLEBEN, Germany. Hard paste. Impressed. 1810. (b) ILMENAU, Germany. Porcelain. Est. 1777. (c) BOW, Great Britain. Painted red, blue. Est. 1744. (d) ST. CLOUD, France. Fayence, porcelain. 1678-1766. (e) LISBON, Portugal. Est. 1773. (f) BRISTOL, Great Britain. Painted blue, gold. 18th century.

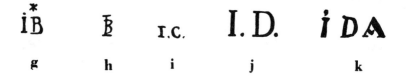

g   h   i   j   k

(g) HOLLAND. De Ster (The Star). Fayence. Delft. Painted blue. 1764. (h) HOLLAND. De Porceleyne Byl (The Porcelain Hatchet). J. Brouwer. 1759. (i) NEW YORK, New York, U.S.A. John Crolius. Impressed. Circa 1790. (j) PARIS, France. M. J. Devers. Fayence. 1850. (k) HOLLAND. De Vergulde Boot (The Golden Boat). Johannes der Appel. Fayence. Delft. 1764.

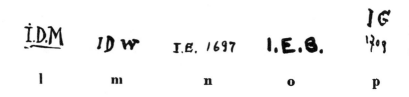

l   m   n   o   p

(l) HOLLAND. De Paauw (The Peacock). Jacobus de Milde. Fayence. Delft. 1764. (m) HOLLAND. J. d. Weert. Fayence. Delft. 1663. (n) WROTHAM, Great Britain. Slipware. 17th and 18th centuries. (o) SHELTON, Great Britain. Ralph and John Baddeley. Circa 1772. (p) WINTERTHUR, Switzerland. Pfau. 17th century.

H I.H. 1764 I.H.D *IK* I K

a b c d e

(a) STRASBURG, France. Paul Hannong. 1752. (b) WORCES-
TER, Great Britain. 1764. (c) HOLLAND. Fayence. Delft. Painted
blue. 1765. (d) MORTLAKE, Great Britain. Late 18th century.
(e) HOLLAND. De Oude Moriaan's Hooft (The Old Moor's
Head). J. Kool. 1676.

I K JK I&K I.L. 1638 $\frac{ITD}{7}$

f g h i j

(f) HOLLAND, De Dubbelde Schenkkan (The Double Jug). 1714.
(g) HOLLAND. Jan Kuylich, the younger. Fayence. Delft. Painted
blue. 1680. (h) HOLLAND. Jan Kuylich. Fayence. Delft. Painted
blue. 1680. (i) WROTHAM, Great Britain. 17th century. (j) HOL-
LAND. De Griekse A (The Greek A). J. T. Dextra. Fayence. Delft.
1764.

L T D 12 ITD DEX '' I V IVH 1728 I V K

k l m n o

(k) HOLLAND. De Griekse A (The Greek A). J. T. Dextra. Fayence. Delft. 1764. (l) HOLLAND. De Griekse A (The Greek A).
1764. (m) HOLLAND. De Fortuyn (The Fortune). Fayence.
Delft. 1691. (n) HOLLAND. De Jonge Moriaan's Hooft (The New
Moor's Head). Fayence. Delft. 1728. (o) HOLLAND. De Drie
Astonnen (The Three Ash Barrels). J. P. v. Kessel. Fayence. Delft.
1655.

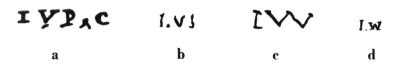

a   b   c   d

(a) HOLLAND. De Klauw (The Claw). J. Van Putten and Company. Fayence. Delft. 1830-1850. (b) HOLLAND. De Oude Moriaan's Hooft (The Old Moor's Head). G. Verstelle. Fayence. Delft. 1764. (c) HOLLAND. De Oude Moriaan's Hooft (The Old Moor's Head). 1661. (d) WROTHAM, Great Britain. Slipware. 17th-18th century.

e   f   g

(e) ROTTERDAM, Holland. Pieter Janz Aelmis, potter. Fayence. 1691-1707. (f) FAIRFAX, Vermont, U.S.A. Isaac Farrar. Circa 1800. (g) LANE END, Great Britain. Cyples, potter. Staffordshire. Late 18th-early 19th century.

h   i   j   k

(h) BURSLEM, Great Britain. J. Dale, potter. Staffordshire. Late 18th-early 19th cenutry. (i) WROTHAM, Great Britain. Slipware. 1699. (j) GREAT BRITAIN. John Hall and Sons. Staffordshire. Circa 1810. (k) OLEANS, New York, U.S.A. I. H. Wands. Impressed. Circa 1860.

I. MEAD   İh·DE-OELF
SE·VIN·KEL.
:T·D.   INDIAN CHINA   INTᴿNATIONAL Cₕᵢₙₐ TRENTON·N·J

    a   b   c·   d

(a) ATWATER, Ohio, U.S.A. I. Mead and Company. Impressed. Circa 1850. (b) HOLLAND. De Dessel (The Axe). Fayence. Delft. 1696. (c) TRENTON, New Jersey, U.S.A. Ceramic Art Company. Est. 1879. (d) TRENTON, New Jersey, U.S.A. Burgess and Campbell. 1860-1868.

I Perdv
1734   I P·S
ALYON
1773   IRONSTONE CHINA
BURGESS & CAMPELL

    e   f   g

(e) ROUEN, France. J. Perdu, painter. 1734-1756. (f) LYONS, France. Fayence. 1773. (g) TRENTON, New Jersey, U.S.A. Burgess and Campbell. Est. 1879.

I·R·Palvdev·   ISAAC HEWETT
EXCELSIOR WORKS
PRICES LANDING
PENNA.   I. Smith

    h   i   j

(h) NANTES, France. Fayence. 1634. (i) PRICE'S LANDING, Pennsylvania, U.S.A. Isaac Hewitt. Painted blue. Circa 1875. (j) WRIGHTSTOWN, Pennsylvania, U.S.A. Joseph Smith. Circa 1775.

a   b   c   d   e

(a) WINCANTON, Great Britian. Nathaniel Ireson. potter. 1740-1750. (b) HANLEY, Great Britain. Job Ridgway, owner. 1802. (c) BURSLEM, Great Britain. Bagshaw and Maier. Circa 1800. (d) GREAT BRITAIN. Old Hall Works. Earthenware. Est. 1790. (e) TROY, New York, U.S.A. Israel Seymour. Impressed. Circa 1825.

SECTION J
See also Sections
L, Lines

f   g   h   i   j

(f) THURINGIA, Germany. Ilmenau. Fayence, porcelain. Est. 1777. (g) LONGTON, Great Britain. William Littler, potter. Porcelain, stoneware. 1750-1760. (h) APREY, France. Fayence. Est. 1750. (i) LA ROCHELLE, France. J. Briqueville. Est. 1743. (j) HOLLAND. De Boot (The Boot) J. d. Appel. Fayence. 1759.

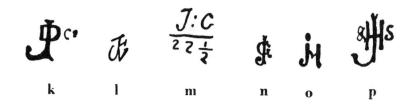

k   l   m   n   o   p

(k) HANLEY, Great Britain. J. Dimmock and Company. 1878-1904. (l) KREUSSEN, Germany. Caspar and H. C. Vest. Stoneware. Painted color. Circa 1623. (m) Holland. Jan Gaal, potter. 1707-1725. (n) STOKE-ON-TRENT, Great Britain. G. Jones and Sons. Late 19th-early 20th century. (o) STRASBURG, France. P. Hannong. Fayence, porcelain. 1709-1780. (p) WORCESTER, Great Britain. James Hadley and Sons. Porcelain. 1896-1897.

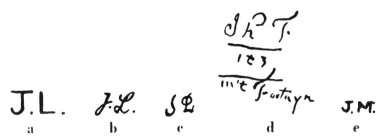

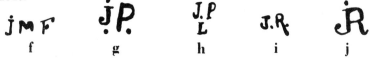

a   b   c   d   e

(a) SOUTH AMBOY. New Jersey, U.S.A. Warns and Letts. Circa 1805. (b) COTE-D'OR, France. Premieres, factory. Fayence. Stenciled blue. 19th century. (c) MOUSTIERS, France. Joseph Olery. Fayence. 18th century. (d) HOLLAND. De Fortuyn (The Fortune). Fayence. Delft. 1706. (e) AUSSIG, Bohemia. Jon Maresch. 1840.

f   g   h   i   j

(f) ST. CLOUD, France. Soft paste. 1678-1766. (g) FONTAINE-BLEAU, France. Jacob Petit, potter. Soft paste. Painted blue. Circa 1830. (h) LIMOGES, France. J. Pouyat, potter. Painted red. 1842. (i) NEW YORK, New York, U.S.A. John Remney. Stoneware. Circa 1775. (j) MARSEILLES, France. Joseph Robert, potter. Porcelain. 1754-1793.

k   l   m   n   o

(k) LIONVILLE, Pennsylvania, U.S.A. J. Vickers. Circa 1805. (l) HOLLAND. De Griekse A (The Greek A). Fayence, Delft. 1701. (m) WEISBADEN, Germany. Circa 1780. (n) BURTON-ON TRENT, Great Britain. Ashby Potter's Guild. Pottery. Est. 1909. (o) POUGHKEEPSIE, New York, U.S.A. Jacob Caire. Impressed. Circa 1850.

JACOB DICK
TUSCARAWAS Co.
OHIO

Jacob Medinger   *Jacob Taney*

a   b   c

(a) TUSCARAWAS COUNTY, Ohio, U.S.A. Jacob Dick. Impressed. 1835. (b) NEIFFER, Pennsylvania, U.S.A. Jacob Medinger. Circa 1885-1930. (c) NOCKAMIXON, Pennsylvania, U.S.A. Jacob Taney. Circa 1795.

J Albany f.

JAMES HAMILTON
GREENSBORO, PA.

J. BELL

d   e   f

(d) CASTILLE, Spain. Talavera de la Reyna, factory. Fayence. 17th-18th century. (e) GREENSBORO, Pennsylvania, U.S.A. James Hamilton. Impressed. Circa 1875. (f) WAYNESBORO, Pennsylvania, U.S.A. John Bell. Impressed. Circa 1875.

J. & E. NORTON & CO.
BENNINGTON, VT

J.A.Weber   J. BENNETT N.Y.

g   h   i

(g) BENNINGTON, Vermont, U.S.A. J. and E. Norton. Impressed. Circa 1855. (h) BARNESVILLE, Pennsylvania, U.S.A. J. A. Wever. Impressed. Circa 1875. (i) NEW YORK, New York, U.S.A. John Bennett. Circa 1875.

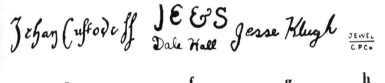

J. BENNETT,
WEST ORANGE N.J   J Boulard   a Nevers   J. BOURNE & SON   J. DICK

a   b   c   d

(a) MOULTONBORO, New Hampshire, U.S.A. James S. Bennett.
Impressed. Circa 1842. (b) NEVERS, France. J. Boulard, potter.
Fayence. 1622. (c) DENBY, Great Britain. J. Bourne, potter. 19th
century. (d) TUSCARAWAS COUNTY, Ohio, U.S.A. Jacob Dick.
Impressed. 1835.

Jehan Custode ff   JE&S   Jesse Klugh   JEWEL
                     Dale Hall   C.P.Co

e   f   g   h

(e) NEVERS. France. Pierre Custode, potter. Fayence. 1632-1656.
(f) FENTON, Great Britain. J. Edwards and Son. Circa 1875.
(g) MORGANTOWN, Pennsylvania, U.S.A. Jesse Klugh. 1874.
(h) EVANSVILLE, Indiana, U.S.A. Crown Pottery Company.
Circa 1900.

J. Feresch   J.FIGLEY   J. Fisher   J & G LOCKETT

i   j   k   l

(i) KLUM, Bohemia. Feresch. Porcelain. 1835. (j) NEWPORT,
Ohio, U.S.A. Joseph Figley. Impressed. Circa 1850. (k) HART-
FORD, Connecticut, U.S.A. J. C. Fisher. Impressed. Circa 1810.
(l) BURSLEM, Great Britain. J. Lockett, potter. Earthenware, salt-
glazed stoneware. 1802.

J & J G. LOW,
PATENT
ART TILE WORKS
CHELSEA
J. H. WEATHERBY   *MASS. U.S.A.*   J.K. CALLAND
& SONS   *COPYRIGHT 1881 BY J & J LOW*   (LANDOR POTTERY)

a   b   c

(a) HANLEY, Great Britain. J. H. Weatherby and Sons. Staffordshire. Circa 1890. (b) CHELSEA, Massachusetts, U.S.A. Low Art Tile Company. 1881. (c) SWANSEA, Great Britain. John F. Calland. Circa 1850.

J. Keeling   J. LOCKETT   J. LOCKETT & SONS

d   e   f

(d) HANLEY, Great Britain. J. Keeling. Pottery. Impressed. 1790. (e) BURSLEM, Great Britain. J. Lockett, potter. Earthenware, salt-glazed stoneware. 1800. (f) BURSLEM, Great Britain. J. Lockett, potter. Earthenware, salt-glazed stoneware. 1829.

J.M.MADDEN
RONDOUT   J. MEIGH &
J. M. & S. CO.   N.Y.   J & M P.B & C°   SONS

g   h   i   j

(g) TRENTON, New Jersey. U.S.A. John Moses and Sons. Circa 1875. (h) RANDOUT, New York, U.S.A. J. M. Madden. Impressed. Circa 1870. (i) SCOTLAND. J. and M. P. Bell and Company. Circa 1845. (j) HANLEY, Great Britain. Job Meigh and Sons, potters. Staffordshire. Impressed. Late 18th and 19th centuries.

J. NORTON
BENNINGTON
VT.

J. NORTON
EAST BENNINGTON
VT.

J. NORTON & CO.
BENNINGTON
VT.

a   b   c

(a-b) BENNINGTON, Vermont, U.S.A. Julius Norton. Impressed. Circa 1845. (c) BENNINGTON, Vermont, U.S.A. J. Norton and Company. Circa 1860.

Johannes
Leman

JONATHAN FENTON
DORSET, VT.

JOHN BELL
WAYNESBORO

JOHN BOYER

d   e   f   g

(d) TYLER'S PORT, Pennsylvania, U.S.A. Johannes Leman. Circa 1830. (e) DORSET, Vermont, U.S.A. Jonathan Fenton. Impressed. Circa 1805. (f) WAYNESBORO, Pennsylvania, U.S.A. John W. Bell. Circa 1890. (g) SCHUYLKILL COUNTY, Pennsylvania, U.S.A. John Boyer. Circa 1810.

JOHN HOPKINS

JOHN MANN
RAHWAY
N.J.

JOHN PRUDEN
ELIZABETH
N.J.

John Ridgway

h   i   j   k

(h) SENECA COUNTY, Ohio, U.S.A. John Hopkins. Impressed. Circa 1835. (i) RAHWAY, New Jersey, U.S.A. John Mann. Impressed. Circa 1835. (j) ELIZABETH, New Jersey, U.S.A. John Pruden. Impressed. Circa 1870. (k) HANLEY, Great Britain. John Ridgway, pottery owner. Staffordshire. Circa 1830-1841.

John Rose & Co.
COLEBROOK·DALE   JOHN SANDERS   JOHN W. BELL   JOHN WRIGHT

    a   b   c   d

(a) COALPORT, Great Britain. John Rose, factory founder. 1793-1841. (b) CONNECTICUT, U.S.A. John Sanders. Circa 1815. (c) WAYNESBORO, Pennsylvania, U.S.A. John W. Bell. Circa 1890. (d) GREAT BRITAIN. Jon Wright, artist. Slipware. Circa 1707.

J. OLDFIELD   JOSEPH BELL   Joseph   Glass   JOSEPH.GLASS.SY.H.GX

    e   f   g   h

(e) BRAMPTON, Great Britain. J. Oldfield, potter. Brownware. 1810. (f) PUTNAM, Ohio, U.S.A. Joseph Bell. Impressed. Circa 1835. (g-h) HANLEY, Great Britain. Joseph Glass, potter. Slipware. 1703.

José Gricci   JOSEPH MAYER & Co.   Joseph Nigg.   Jos. Hemphill Phila.

    i   j   k   l

(i) BUEN RETIRO, Spain. Guiseppe Gricci, modeler. Soft paste. 1745-1770. (j) HANLEY, Great Britain. Joseph Mayer and Company. 19th century. (k) VIENNA, Austria. Porcelain. 1800. (l) PHILADELPHIA, Pennsylvania, U.S.A. Joseph Hemphill. Painted red. Circa 1835.

J.QF
1 ₹3

JOSHUA H EATH JOSIAH WEDGWOOD J & P int Fortuyn

a	b	c	d

(a) DERBY, Great Britain. Joshua Heath, potter. Pottery. Impressed. 1760. (b) ETRURIA, Great Britain. Wedgwood, factory. Josiah Wedgwood, potter and founder. Circa 1780. (c) NEW-CASTLE-ON-TYNE, Great Britain. Jackson and Patterson. Pottery. Circa 1800. (d) HOLLAND. De Fortuyn (The Fortune). 1706.

J. P.
L.

J. PHILLIPS
HYLTON POTTERY **FRANCE.** *JP.* *J. REMMEY*
MANHATTAN WELLS
NEW YORK

e	f	g	h

(e) SUNDERLAND, Great Britain. John Phillips, potter. Late 18th-early 19th century. (f) LIMOGES, France. Jean Pouyat, potter. 1842-1898. (g) FONTAINEBLEAU, France. Jacob Petit, potter. Circa 1800. (h) NEW YORK, New York, U.S.A. John Remmey III. Brown stoneware. Impressed. Circa 1800.

J. Sadler,
Liverpl. *J.S. BENNETT* *J.S. EBERLEY*
STRASBURG
VA. *J.S.T. & Co.*
KEENE N.H

i	j	k	l

(i) LIVERPOOL, Great Britain. John Sadler, engraver for transfer printing. 1756-1770. (j) MOULTONBORO, New Hampshire, U.S.A. James S. Bennett. Impressed. Circa 1840. (k) STRASBURG, Virginia, U.S.A. J. S. Eberley. Impressed. Circa 1900. (l) KEENE, New Hampshire, U.S.A. J. S. Taft and Company. Circa 1875.

JULIUS NORTON   JULIUS NORTON
BENNINGTON   EAST BENNINGTON
VT.   VT

J VD Niet Fecit

a   b   c

(**a-b**) BENNINGTON, Vermont, U.S.A. Julius Norton. Impressed.
Circa 1845. (**c**) ROTTERDAM, Holland. Fayence. 17th-18th century.

J. VOYEZ   J. WALLEY'S WARE   J. W. R
Stone China   J. & W. R.

d   e   f   g

(**d**) HANLEY, Great Britain. John Voyez, modeler. Circa 1790.
(**e**) COBRIDGE, Great Britain. J. Walley. 1795. (**f**) SHELTON,
Great Britain. John & William Ridgway. 1814-1830. (**g**) SHELTON,
Great Britain. Bell Works. John & William Ridgway. 1814-1830.

SECTION **K**
See also Section
Lines

K   K̇   K   𝘬   𝘬   k

h   i   j   k   l   m

(**h**) KLOSTERLE, Bohemia. Porcelain, lead-glazed earthenware.
1794-1803. (**i**) HOLLAND. Jan Kuylich. Fayence. Delft. Painted
blue. 17th century. (**j**) HOLLAND. De Drie Porceleyne Fleschen
(The Three Porcelain Bottles). Fayence. Delft. 1676. (**k**) KIEL,
Germany. Fayence. Circa 1770. (**l**) HOLLAND. Jan Kuylich, the
younger. Fayence. Delft. Painted blue. Registered 1680. (**m**) HOL-
LAND. De Porceleyne Fles (The Porcelain Bottle). Fayence. Delft.
1698.

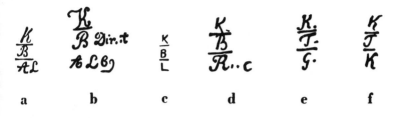

a   b   c   d   e   f

(**a**) HOLSTEIN, Germany. Kiel, factory. Fayence. Painted gold or color. 1770. (**b**) HOLSTEIN, Germany. Kiel, factory. J. Buchwald, director. Fayence. 1770. (**c-d**) HOLSTEIN, Germany. Kiel, factory. Fayence. Circa 1770. (**e-f**) HOLSTEIN, Germany. Kiel, factory. Johann Tannich, director. 1763-1768.

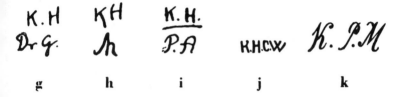

g   h   i   j   k

(**g**) HOLSTEIN, Germany. Kellinghusen, factory. Dr. Grauer, potter. Fayence. 1795-1820. (**h**) HOLSTEIN, Germany. Kellinghusen, factory. Fayence. Circa 1800. (**i**) MEISSEN, Germany. Konigliche Hof Conditorei Warschau. Hard paste. 18th century. (**j**) MEISSEN, Germany. Konigliche Hof Conditorei Warschau. Hard paste. Painted blue. 18th century. (**k**) MEISSEN, Germany. Konigliche Porzellan Manufaktur. Hard paste. Underglaze blue. Circa 1756+.

l   m   n   o   p

(**l**) KRISTER, Germany. 1831-1900. (**m**) PHILADELPHIA, Pennsylvania, U.S.A. Kurlbaum and Schwartz. Impressed. 1851-1855. (**n**) HOLLAND. De Porceleyne Fles (The Porcelain Bottle). Fayence. Delft. 1698. (**o**) HOLLAND. De Klauw (The Claw). Fayence. Delft. 1750. (**p**) HOLLAND. Fayence. Delft. Painted blue. 1700.

Keeling Toft & Co.   Kenneth   KEZONTA

a   b   c

(a) HANLEY, Great Britain. Keeling, potter. Staffordshire. Impressed. 1806-1824. (b) SEBRING, Ohio. French china. (c) CINCINNATI, Ohio, U.S.A. Cincinnati Art Pottery Company, Circa 1886.

K & G   KIEBZ   KIEBЗ
LUNEVILLE K. Herr 13   ――― Kiel   Kiel
                    II   15   ―――
                                               T

d   e   f   g·   h   i

(d) LUNEVILLE, France. Keller and Guerin, owners. Fayence. Circa 1889. (e) VIENNA, Austria. Claudius Herr, painter. Late 18th-early 19th century. (f) KIEV, Russia. Porcelain. 1798-1850. (g) KIEV, Russia. Fayence. Painted. 1798-1850. (h) KIEL, Germany. Fayence. 1758. (i) KIEL, Germany. Tannich and Kleffel, owners. Fayence. Painted gold or color. 1763.

              Kishere
Kishere   Mortlake   Klentsch   K.L.HMULLER
                                             1875

j   k   l   m

(j-k) MORTLAKE, Great Britain. Joseph Kishere, potter. Stoneware. 1800-1811. (l) KLENTSCH, Germany. Porcelain. Circa 1835. (m) NEW YORK, New York, U.S.A. Union Porcelain Works. After 1876.

KLUM KNAPPER AND BLACKHURST KODAU KOSMO K.T.& K. CHINA

a   b   c   d   e

(a) KLUM, Germany. Porcelain. 1800-1850. (b) GREAT BRITAIN.
Knapper and Blackhurst. Circa 1850. (c) CHODAU, Germany. 1834-
1845. (d) EAST LIVERPOOL, Ohio, U.S.A. Smith-Phillips China
Company. Late 19th century. (e) EAST LIVERPOOL, Ohio, U.S.A.
Knowles, Taylor, and Knowles. Est. 1854.

SECTION **L**
See also Sections
I, J, Lines

f   g   h   i   j   k

(f) ARDUS, France. Fayence. 1739-1876. (g-h) PARIS, France.
Jean-Joseph Lassia, proprietor. Porcelain. 1774-1784. (i) THURIN-
GIA, Germany. Limbach, factory. Porcelain. 1772-1788. (j) PARIS,
France. Jean-Joseph Lassia, proprietor. Porcelain. 1774-1784. (k)
THURINGIA, Germany. Limbach, factory. Hard paste. 1772-1788.

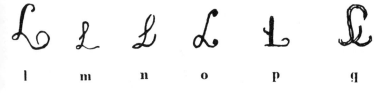

l   m   n   o   p   q

(l) PARIS, France. Jean-Joseph Lassia, proprietor. Hard paste.
1774-1784. (m) THURINGIA, Germany. Limbach, factory. Hard
paste. Painted red. 1772. (n) THURINGIA, Germany. Limbach,
factory. Hard paste. 1772. (o) NORD, France. Valenciennes, factory. Fayence. 1735-1780. (p) TOURS, France. Fayence. Est. 1750.
(q) BUEN RETIRO, Spain. Soft paste. 1759-1808.

a   b   c   d   e   f

(a) ARDUS, France. Fayence. 1739-1876. (b) HOLLAND. De Metale Pot (The Metal Pot). Fayence. Delft. 1667. (c) OIRON, France. Henri Deux ware (may have been made at Saint-Porchaire). 1676. (d) APREY, France. Fayence. Est. 1744. (e-f) THURINGIA, Germany. Limbach, factory. Hard paste. 1772-1788.

g   h   i   j   k   l

(g-h) FRANCE. Louis Brancas, Comte de Lauraguais, invented hard paste. Circa 1763. (i-j) LUXEMBOURG, Belgium. Circa 1770. (k) SEPTFONTAINES, Germany. Villeroy and Boch, potters. 1766. (l) THURINGIA, Germany Limbach, factory. Porcelain. 1772-1788.

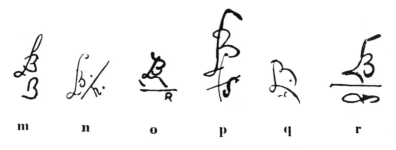

m   n   o   p   q   r

(m) LUXEMBOURG, Belgium. Circa 1770. (n-o-p-q-r) THURINGIA, Germany. Limbach, factory. Hard paste. 1772-1788.

a	b	c	d	e

(a) BRUSSELS, Belgium. L. Crette, porcelain-decorator. Hard paste. Painted. 1791-1803. (b) ROUEN, France. Hubert Lettellier, potter. Cream-colored ware. 1781. (c) SINCENY, France. Joseph Le Cerf, painter. 1773. (d) HOLLAND. Lucas van Kessel. Fayence. Delft. 1675. (e) THURINGIA, Germany. Limbach, factory. Hard paste. 1772.

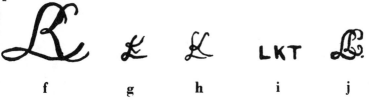

f	g	h	i	j

(f) THURINGIA, Germany. Limbach, factory. Hard paste. 1772.
(g) THURINGIA, Germany. Bernburg, factory. Fayence. 1725.
(h) THURINGIA, Germany. Limbach, factory. Hard paste. Painted red, black, purple. 1772. (i) DRYVILLE, Pennsylvania, U.S.A. Lewis K. Tomlinson. Impressed. Circa 1875. (j) NORD, France. Valenciennes, factory. Fayence, hard paste. 1785.

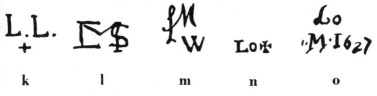

k	l	m	n	o

(k) LILLE, France. Hard paste. 1784. (l) HOLLAND. J. Mesch. Fayence. Delft. 1667. (m) WEESP, Holland. Porcelain. 1759. (n) ST. CLOUD, France. Fayence, porcelain. 1678-1766. (o) TUS-CANY, Italy. Montelupo, factory. Brown and black pottery. 17th century.

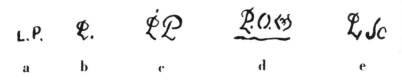

a   b   c   d   e

(**a**) LEEDS, Great Britain. Soft paste. Est. 1760. (**b-c-d-e**) MOUS-
TIERS, France. Clerissy's, factory. Joseph Olery, painter. Fayence.
1721-1749.

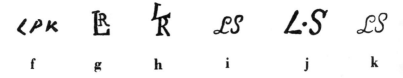

f   g   h   i   j   k

(**f**) HOLLAND. De Lampetkan (The Ewer). Widow of Gerardus
Brouwer, owner. Fayence. Delft. Painted blue. 1764. (**g**) BOR-
DEAUX, France. Lahrens and Rateau. Hard paste. Painted. 1828.
(**h**) REGENSBURG, Germany. Porcelain-decorating shop. Painted
blue. 1782. (**i-j-k**) SAINT YRIEIX, France. La Seynie, factory. Hard
paste. 1774.

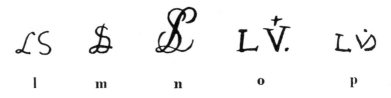

l   m   n   o   p

(**l-m**) SCEAUX, France. Jacques Chapelle, proprietor. Soft paste.
1748-1794. (**n**) SAINT YRIEIX, France. La Seynie, factory. Hard
paste. 1774. (**o**) VINOVO, Italy. Porcelain. Underglaze blue or incised. 1776-1815. (**p**) HOLLAND. De Fortuyn (The Fortune). L. v.
Dale. Fayence. Delft. 1692.

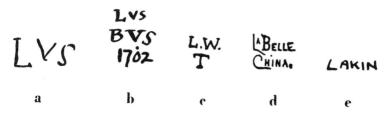

a   b   c   d   e

(**a-b**) HOLLAND. De Klauw (The Claw). Fayence. Delft. 1662.
(**c**) TEINITZ, Bohemia. Count Wrtby, founder. Lead-glazed earthenware. 1801. (**d**) WHEELING, West Virginia, U.S.A. Wheeling Pottery Company. 1893+. (**e**) HANLEY, Great Britain. Lakin, potter. Late 18th and early 19th centuries.

LAKIN & POOLE   LAMPRECHT   *Langley Ware*

f   g   h

(**f**) HANLEY, Great Britain. Lakin and Poole, potters. Late 18th and early 19th centuries. (**g**) VIENNA, Austria. Georg Lamprecht, painter. 1772-1784. (**h**) NOTTINGHAM, Great Britain. Lovatt and Lovatt. Late 19th and early 20th centuries.

Laughlin   L. & B. G. CHASE   L B   L.D. FUNKHOUSER
WHITE GRANITE   SOMERSET   orléans   STRASBURG VA.

i   j   k   l

(**i**) EAST LIVERPOOL, Ohio, U.S.A. Homer Laughlin China Company. Printed. Est. 1872. (**j**) SOMERSET, Massachusetts, U.S.A. L. and B. G. Chase. Impressed. Circa 1850. (**k**) LOIRET, France. Orleans, factory. 1753-1812. (**l**) STRASBURG, Virginia, U.S.A. L. D. Funkhouser. Impressed. Circa 1900.

LEEDS   POTTERY   LEEDS ⚹ POTTERY

a   b   c

(a-b-c) LEEDS, Great Britain. Creamware. Circa 1781-1820.

d   e   f

(d) PARIS, France. 1786. (e) CALVADOS, France. Caen, factory.
Hard paste. 1793. (f) STRASBURG, Virginia, U.S.A. Lehew and
Company. Impressed. Circa 1885.

LEHMAN ↑ RIEDINGER LELAND.

g   h   i   j

(g) POUGHKEEPSIE, New York, U.S.A. Louis, Lehman, and
Philip Riedinger (Rudinger). 1855. (h) EAST LIVERPOOL, Ohio,
U.S.A. C. C. Thompson Pottery Company. Circa 1890. (i) HOL-
LAND. L. v. Amsterdam. Fayence. Delft. 1721. (j) PARIS, France.
Lerosey, artist. Circa 1820.

a   b   c   d

(**a**) PARIS, France. Circa 1825. (**b**) HUNTINGTON, New York, U.S.A. Lewis and Gardiner (Gardner). Impressed. Circa 1840. (**c**) HUNTINGTON, New York, U.S.A. Lewis and Lewis. Impressed. Circa 1860. (**d**) UTICA, New York, U.S.A. L. F. Field. Circa 1865.

L.H. WORKS *Liberty* *lille* LIPPERT & HAAS IN SCHLAGGENWALD LISBOA

e   f   g   h   i

(**e**) NEWPORT, Ohio, U.S.A. Laban H. Works. Impressed. Circa 1845. (**f**) WELLSVILLE, Ohio, U.S.A. Pioneer Pottery Company. Circa 1890. (**g**) LILLE, France. Fayence. Painted. 1711. (**h**) SCHLAGGENWALD, Germany. Lippert and Haas, potters. 1832-1846. (**i**) LISBON, Portugal. Fayence. 1773.

L. NORTON & co. BENNINGTON VT. L. NORTON BENNINGTON VT. L. NORTON & SON BENNINGTON VT.

j   k   l

(**j**) BENNINGTON, Vermont, U.S.A. Luman Norton. Impressed. Circa 1825. (**k**) BENNINGTON, Vermont, U.S.A. Luman Norton. Impressed. Circa 1830. (**l**) BENNINGTON, Vermont, U.S.A. Luman Norton and Son. Impressed. Circa 1835.

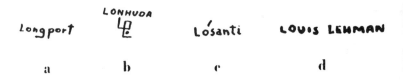

a   b   c   d

(a) LONGPORT, Great Britain. Fayence. Printed red. 1793. (b)
STEUBENVILLE, Ohio, U.S.A. Lonhuda Pottery Compnay. Est.
1892. (c) CINCINNATI, Ohio, U.S.A. M. L. McLaughlin. Est. 1876.
(d) POUGHKEEPSIE, New York, U.S.A. Louis Lehman. Impressed. Circa 1852.

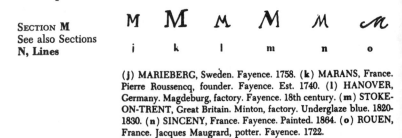

e   f   g   h   i

(e) ZANESVILLE, Ohio, U.S.A. S. A. Weller. 1895-1918. (f) NOT-
TINGHAM, Great Britain. Lovatt and Lovatt. Late 19th-early 20th
century. (g) HOLLAND. De Lampetkan (The Ewer). Widow of
Gerardus Brouwer, owner. Fayence. Delft. Painted Blue. 1764. (h)
STOKE-ON-TRENT, Great Britain. Minton, factory. L. M. Solon,
artist. Circa 1900. (i) ST. JOHNSBURY, Vermont, U.S.A. L. W. Fenton. Impressed. Circa 1840.

SECTION **M**   M   M   м   M   M   ℳ
See also Sections
N, Lines   j   k   l   m   n   o

(j) MARIEBERG, Sweden. Fayence. 1758. (k) MARANS, France.
Pierre Roussencq, founder. Fayence. Est. 1740. (l) HANOVER,
Germany. Magdeburg, factory. Fayence. 18th century. (m) STOKE-
ON-TRENT, Great Britain. Minton, factory. Underglaze blue. 1820-
1830. (n) SINCENY, France. Fayence. Painted. 1864. (o) ROUEN,
France. Jacques Maugrard, potter. Fayence. 1722.

a   b   c   d   e   f

(**a**) MARANS, France. Pierre Roussencq, founder. Fayence. Est.
1740. (**b**) MATHAULT, France. Fayence. Second half 18th century.
(**c**) OUDE LOOSDRECHT, Holland. Johannes de Mol, owner.
Hard paste. Painted blue and impressed. 1771. (**d**) MARIEBERG,
Sweden. Fayence. 1758. (**e**) HOLLAND. De Vier Helden Van
Roome (The Four Roman Heroes). Fayence. Delft. 1713. (**f**) HOL-
LAND. De Vier Helden Van Roome (The Four Roman Heroes).
Fayence. Delft. 1713.

g   h   i   j   k

(**g**) ARNOLDI, Germany. 1912+. (**h**) MOUSTIERS, France. Fayence. 18th century. (**i**) CINCINNATI, Ohio, U.S.A. M. L. Mc-
Laughlin. Est. 1876. (**j**) MENNECY, France. Porcelain. 1734-1773.
(**k**) HOLLAND. H. v. Middeldyk. Fayence. Delft. 1764.

ʃɛs   ʌF.   𝓜𝓛   MLS
1897   Mo

l   m   n   o   p

(**l**) HOLLAND. T'Hart (The Stag). J. Mes. Fayence. Delft. 1661.
(**m**) HEREND, Hungary. Moritz Fischer, founder. Hard paste.
Painted blue. 1839. (**n**) MOUSTIERS, France. Joseph Olery,
founder. Fayence. Est. 1738. (**o**) CINCINNATI, Ohio, U.S.A. Rookwood Pottery Company. Impressed. Est. 1879. (**p**) MENNECY,
France. Soft paste porcelain. 1773.

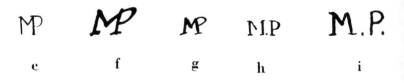

a   b   c   d

(**a**) HOLLAND. T'Hart (The Stag). Fayence. Delft. 1764. (**b-c**)
OUDE LOOSDRECHT, Holland. Johannes de Mol, founder. Hard
paste. Underglaze blue or color. 1771-1784. (**d**) ETOILLES, France.
Monier and Pelleve, founders. Hard paste. Est. 1768.

MP   **MP**   MP   M.P   M.P.

e   f   g   h   i

(**e**) HOLLAND. De Metale Pot (The Metal Pot). Fayence. Delft.
Painted blue. 1639. (**f**) HOLLAND. De Metale Pot (The Metal
Pot). Fayence. Delft. 1639. (**g**) ROUEN, France. Pierre Mouchard,
potter. 1740. (**h**) OPORTO, Portugal. Rocha Soare. Fayence.
Painted gold. 1700. (**i**) MIRAGAYA, Portugal. Fayence. Last half
18th century.

j   k   l   m   n

(**j**) ETOILLES, France. Monier and Pelleve, founders. Hard paste.
Est. 1768. (**k**) DRESDEN, Germany. Meissner Porzellan Manufak-
tur. Hard paste. 1723. (**l**) SHELTON, Great Britain. Fayence.
Printed. 1685. (**m**) PARIS, France. Pont-aux-Chaoux. 1784. (**n**)
AMUND, Germany. Fayence. 1750.

$\mathcal{MV}$ **MVB** $\frac{MVC}{4}$ M   MK

   a   b   c   d   e

(**a**) ROUEN, France. Michel-Mathieu and Michel Vallet, potters. 1757. (**b**) HOLLAND. De Twee Wildemans (The Two Savages). M. v. d. Bogarert. Fayence. Delft. 1750. (**c**) HOLLAND. Fayence. Delft. Painted blue. 1700. (**d**) ROUEN, France. Maugrard, potter. Fayence. 1722. (**e**) GERMANY. Schmidt Brothers. Est. 1847.

MACHIN & POTTS
Burslem, Staffordshire   **MACINTYRE**   MADE BY
GLOBE POTTERY CO.
E.L, O.

      f   g   h

(**f**) BURSLEM, Great Britain. Staffordshire. 1830. (**g**) GREAT BRITAIN. MacIntyre. Circa 1860. (**h**) EAST LIVERPOOL, Ohio, U.S.A. Globe Pottery Company. Circa 1890.

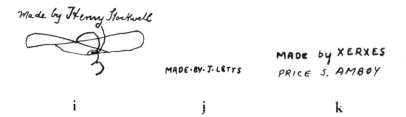

Made by Henry Stockwell

          MADE·BY· J. LETTS   MADE by XERXES
PRICE S. AMBOY

     i   j   k

(**i**) PERTH AMBOY, New Jersey, U.S.A. Henry Stockwell, artist. 1830. (**j**) CHEESEQUAKE, New Jersey, U.S.A. Joshua Letts. Circa 1810. (**k**) SAYREVILLE, New Jersey, U.S.A. Xerxes Price. Impressed. Circa 1800.

MAINE.   **MANN & CO.**   *MANTELL + THOMAS*   Manufactured by Jos Hemphill Philad—
          HANLEY   *PENN YAN*

a   b   c   d

(a) EAST LIVERPOOL, Ohio, U.S.A. Knowles, Taylor and Knowles, Est. 1854. (b) HANLEY, Great Britain. Mann and Company. 19th century. (c) YATES COUNTY, New York, U.S.A. Pen Yan Pottery. Circa 1840. (d) PHILADELPHIA, Pennsylvania, U.S.A. Joseph Hemphill. 1832+.

MARAN

M...fre de M.M...   1754
Guerhard et   MANUFACTURED BY
Lehl à Paris.   OTT & BREWER   **MAP**   **R**   MARKELL, IMMON & CO
                                                     AKRON
                                                       O.

e   f   g   h   i

(e) PARIS, France. Guerhard, potter. Hard paste. 1786-1829.
(f) TRENTON, New Jersey, U.S.A. Ott and Brewer. Circa 1875.
(g) PARIS, France. Morelle, potter. Hard paste. Painted blue. 1725.
(h) MARANS, France. Pierre Roussencq, founder. Fayence. 1740.
(i) AKRON, Ohio, U.S.A. Markell, Immon, and Company. Impressed. Circa 1870.

MARTIN CRAFTS   **MASON & RUSSELL**
NASHUA, N.H.   **CORTLAND**
                   N.Y.   MASON'S CAMBRIAN
                                      ARGIL

j   k   l

(j) NASHUA, New Hampshire, U.S.A. Martin Crafts. Impressed. Circa 1850. (k) CORTLAND, New York, U.S.A. Mason and Russell. Impressed. Circa 1870. (l) FENTON, Great Britain. Mason. Circa 1819-1920.

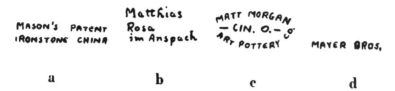

a   b   c   d

(a) FENTON, Great Britain. Fayence. Printed. 1813-1825. (b) ANS-BACH, Germany. Fayence. 1730. (c) CINCINNATI, Ohio, U.S.A. Matt Morgan Art Pottery Company. Circa 1885. (d) HANLEY, Great Britain. Circa 1820.

e   f   g

(e) LANE END, Great Britain. Fayence. Impressed or printed. 1800. (f) STOKE-ON-TRENT, Great Britain. Minton and Boyle. Impressed. 1836-1841. (g) ORLEANS, France. Hard paste. Circa 1760.

h   i   j   k

(h) SAVONA, Italy. M. Forelli. 1740. (i) SOMERVILLE, Massachusetts, U.S.A. Circa 1870. (j) TRENTON, New Jersey, U.S.A. Maddock Pottery Company. Circa 1900. (k) CLERMONT-FERRAND, France. Fayence. 1730.

MELROSE

M.C.WEBSTER   Meigh   MELLORIA   T.   M·C·A 1750.J.R
HARTFORD

a   b   c   d   e

(**a**) HARTFORD, Connecticut, U.S.A. M. C. Webster and Son. Impressed. Circa 1850. (**b**) HANLEY, Great Britain. Pottery. Impressed. 1780. (**c**) TRENTON, New Jersey, U.S.A. Crescent Pottery Company. Est. 1881. (**d**) EAST LIVERPOOL, Ohio, U.S.A. C. C. Thompson Pottery Company. Circa 1880. (**e**) MOUSTIERS, France. Hard paste, soft paste. 18th century.

MIDDLES BRO
POTTERY CO.

f   g   h   i

(**f**) MIDDLESBOROUGH, Great Britain. Earthenware. Impressed. 1845. (**g**) MILAN, Italy. Fayence. 18th century. (**h**) MILAN, Italy. Felice Clerici, potter. 1745. (**i**) LIMOGES, France. After 1891.

M.Imp^{te}
de Sevres   MINER   MINTON.   MINTON. & BOYLE

j.   k   l   m

(**j**) SEVRES, France. Hard paste, soft paste. Painted red. 1804-1809. (**k**) SYMMES CREEK, Ohio, U.S.A. William Miner. Impressed. Circa 1870. (**l**) STOKE-ON-TRENT, Great Britain. Minton. 1868. (**m**) STOKE-ON-TRENT, Great Britain. Minton and Boyle. 1836-1845.

MINTON & CO.   MIRAGAÏA   MN⁵⁹ᵉ   M. MASON
                                Sèvres

a   b   c   d

(a) STOKE-ON-TRENT, Great Britain. Minton. Circa 1870. (b)
MIRAGAYA, Portugal. Fayence. 18th century. (c) SEVRES, France.
Soft paste. Stenciled red. 1803. (d) FENTON, Great Britain. Late
18th century.

M. & N.   Moitte.   Moore & Co.   MORAVIAN
                      Southwick

e   f   g   h

(e) HANLEY, Great Britain. Mayer and Newbold, potters. First
half 19th century. (f) PARIS, France. Clignancourt, factory. Est.
1771. (g) SOUTHWICK, Great Britain. Pottery and hard paste.
1803. (h) DOYLESTOWN, Pennsylvania, U.S.A. Henry C. Mercer.
Circa 1890.

Morley & Ashworth   MORTLOCK   MOX   Mr.   M.Sansont
   Hanley   Wm Cookworthy's
                                        Factory Plymouth
                                        1770

i   j   k   l   m

(i) SHELTON, Great Britain. Staffordshire. Circa 1850. (j) SWIN-
TON, Great Britain. Rockingham Pottery Works. William Brameld,
owner. 1745-1842. (k) ALCORA, Spain. Est. 1750. (l) PLYM-
OUTH, Great Britain. Hard paste. Painted blue. 1770. (m) VAL-
SOUS MEUDON, France. White earthenware. 1802-1818.

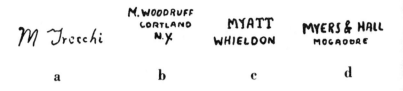

a	b	c	d

(**a**) MILAN, Italy. Fayence. 18th century. (**b**) CORTLAND, New York, U.S.A. Madison Woodruff. Impressed. Circa 1870. (**c**) FENTON, Great Britain. Thomas Whieldon. Impressed. Circa 1775. (**d**) MOGADORE, Ohio, U.S.A. Myers and Hall. Impressed. Circa 1875.

SECTION **N**
See also Sections
M, Lines

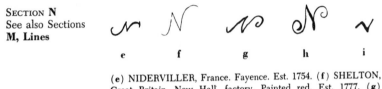

e	f	g	h	i

(**e**) NIDERVILLER, France. Fayence. Est. 1754. (**f**) SHELTON, Great Britain. New Hall, factory. Painted red. Est. 1777. (**g**) DERBY, Great Britain. Incised blue, red. Circa 1770. (**h**) NIDERVILLER, France. Count Custine period. Fayence, porcelain. 1770-1793. (**i**) OLEAN, New York, U.S.A. I. H. Wands. Impressed. Circa 1860.

j	k	l	m	n

(**j**) NEVERS, France. Fayence. Circa 1700. (**k**) NEVERS, France. Fayence. Circa 1700. (**l**) NIDERVILLER, France. Hard paste. 1780-1800. (**m**) LIMBACH, Germany. Porcelain. Est. 1772. (**n**) BRISTOL, Great Britain. Pottery, porcelain. Overglaze blue, gold. 18th century.

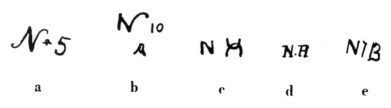

a   b   c   d   e

(**a**) THE HAGUE, Holland. Porcelain. Painted red. Est. 1773.
(**b**) PINXTON, Great Britain. Soft paste. Red. Circa 1800. (**c**)
NIDERVILLER, France. Count Custine period. Fayence, porcelain.
1770-1793. (**d**) WROTHAM, Great Britain. 17th century. (**e**)
ROUEN, France. Jean-Nicolas Bellanger, potter. Fayence. 1788.

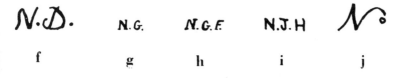

f   g   h   i   j

(**f**) BUEN RETIRO, Spain. Soft paste. 1759-1808. (**g-h**) GIESS-
HUBEL, Germany. Porcelain and earthenware. 1803-1850. (**i**) CIN-
CINNATI, Ohio, U.S.A. Matt Morgan Art Pottery Company. Est.
1883. (**j**) SHELTON, Great Britain. Painted black. Est. 1777.

k   l   m   n

(**k**) URBINO, Italy. Pottery. 16th century. (**l**) THURINGIA, Germany. Ilmenau, factory. Christian Nonne and Roesch, owners. Porcelain. 1786. (**m**) NANTGARW, Wales. Hard paste. Impressed. 1813.
(**n**) NANTGARW, Wales. Hard paste. Painted red. 1811.

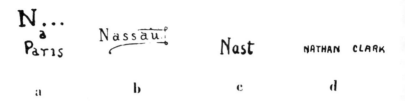

a   b   c   d

(a) PARIS, France. Jean-Nepomucene-Herman Nast, porcelain manufacturer. Painted red. 1754-1817. (b) TRENTON, New Jersey, U.S.A. Mercer Pottery Company. Before 1904. (c) PARIS, France. Jean-Nepomucene-Herman Nast, porcelain manufacturer. Hard paste. Stenciled red. 1785-1817. (d) ATHENS, New York, U.S.A. Nathan Clark. Circa 1830.

NATHAN CLARK LYONS   *Neale*   **Neale & Co.**   Neale & Palmer

e   f   g   h

(e) ATHENS, New York, U.S.A. Nathan Clark. Circa 1830. (f) HANLEY, Great Britain. Fayence. Impressed. 1776. (g) HANLEY, Great Britain. Neale and Company. Staffordshire. 1778. (h) HANLEY, Great Britain. Neale and Palmer. Staffordshire. 1786.

Neale & Wilton   Neaid   NEELD   **Neumark**

i   j   k   l

(i) HANLEY, Great Britain. Staffordshire. Circa 1780. (j-k) HANLEY, Great Britain. Pottery. Impressed. 1780. (l) NEUMARK, Bohemia. Porcelain. Impressed. Circa 1833-1870+.

NEWCASTLE	NEWCOMB COLLEGE	New Hall	N. FURMAN NO.39 PECK SLIP, N.Y.	N & H PRAG
a	b	c	d	e

(a) NEWCASTLE-ON-TYNE, Great Britain. Pottery. Impressed. 1800. (b) NEW ORLEANS, Louisiana, U.S.A. Est. 1896. (c) SHELTON, Great Britain, New Hall factory. Painted red. Circa 1800. (d) CHEESEQUAKE, New Jersey, U.S.A. Noah Furman. Circa 1850. (e) PRAGUE, Bohemia. Lead-glazed earthernware. 1810-1862.

NICHOLS & ALFORD MANUFACTURERS BURLINGTON, VT.	NICHOLS + BOYNTON BURLINGTON, VT.	Niderr.
f	g	h

(f) BURLINGTON, Vermont, U.S.A. Nichols and Alford. Circa 1855. (g) BURLINGTON, Vermont, U.S.A. Nichols and Boynton. Impressed. Circa 1855. (h) NIDERVILLER, France. Fayence. Est. 1754.

NORTON & FENTON BENNINGTON, VT.	NORWICH	NOTTN. 1703
i	j	k

(i) BENNINGTON, Vermont, U.S.A. Norton and Fenton. Stoneware. Impressed. Circa 1845. (j) NORWICH, Connecticut, U.S.A. Charles Lathrop. Impressed. Circa 1790. (k) NOTTINGHAM, Great Britain. Pottery. 1703.

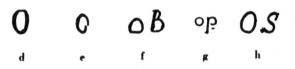

| a | b | c |

(**a-b**) BASSANO, Italy. Soft paste. Circa 1760. (**c**) ALT-ROHLAU, Bohemia. August Nowotny, owner. Pottery, porcelain. 1813-1945+.

SECTION O
See also Sections
**Circle and Sign,
Crown and Circle,
Star and Sun**

$$O \quad O \quad \bigcirc B \quad \text{o}\mathbb{P} \quad OS$$

| d | e | f | g | h |

(**d**) BOW, Great Britain. Porcelain. Circa 1750. (**e**) ST. PETERS-BURG, Russia. Porcelain. Circa 1762. (**f**) MENNECY-VILLEROY, France. Porcelain, fayence. Est. 1734. (**g**) MENNECY-VILLEROY, France. Porcelain, fayence. Painted blue. Circa 1773. (**h**) ANS-BACH, Bavaria. George Oswald, painter, potter. 1692-1733.

| i | j | k | l | m |

(**i**) WHEELING, West Virginia, U.S.A. Ohio Valley China Company. 1887+ (**j**) MOUSTIERS, France. Olerys and Laugier, managers. Hard paste, soft paste. 1739. (**k-l**) TRENTON, New Jersey, U.S.A. Ott and Brewer. Circa 1880. (**m**) BRAMPTON, Great Britain. Brownware. Circa 1825.

OLIVER
A PARIS OPAQVE CHINA

Opaque China
B.B. & I.

Opaque China
B and C

a   b   c   d

(**a**) PARIS, France. Olivier, potter. Fayence. Late 18th century.
(**b**) CAMBRIAN, Wales. Earthenware. Circa 1807. (**c**) SWANSEA,
Great Britain. Baker, Bevans, and Irwin. Circa 1830. (**d**) GREAT
BRITAIN. Bridgwood and Clark. 1857.

OPAQUE CHINA   OPAQUE   O. P. Co.   O.P.Co.   O.P. CO.
JWANSEA   PORCELAIN   CHINA.   IMPERIAL   SYRACUSE
                                                               CHINA

e   f   g   h   i

(**e**) SWANSEA, Wales. Circa 1840. (**f**) GREAT BRITAIN. Old
Hall Works, factory. Earthenware. Circa 1800. (**g-h-i**) SYRACUSE,
New York, U.S.A. Onondaga Pottery Company. Est. 1871.

ORCUT, BELDING & CO.   ORCUTT, GUILFORD & Co.   ORCUTT HUMISTON & CO.
ASHFIELD,   ASHFIELD, MASS.   TROY, N.Y.
MASS

j   k   l

(**j-k**) ASHFIELD, Massachusetts, U.S.A. Orcutt, Belding and Company. Impressed. 1850. (**l**) TROY, New York. U.S.A. Orcutt, Humiston and Company. Impressed. Circa 1855.

ORIENTAL
STONE
J. & G. ALCOCK   Orleans   OWENS FEROZA   OWENS UTOPIAN

a   b   c   d

(**a**) COBRIDGE, Great Britain. J. and G. Alcock. Est. 1843. (**b**) LOIRET, France. Duke of Orleans, patron. Est. 1753. (**c-d**) ZANESVILLE, Ohio, U.S.A. J. B. Owens Pottery Company. Circa 1890.

SECTION **P**
See also Sections
B, Lines

P   P   P   P   P   P

e   f   g   h   i   j

(**e-f**) LIVERPOOL, Great Britain. James and John Pennington, potters and painters. Middle 18th century. (**g-h**) LIVERPOOL, Great Britain. James and John Pennington, potters and painters. Pottery and hard paste. Painted gold or color. 1760. (**i-j**) DERBYSHIRE, Great Britain. Pinxton, factory. Soft paste. Painted. 1796-1801.

P   P   P   P   P   P

k   l   m   n   o   p

(**k-l**) SILESIA, Germany. Count Leopold von Proskau, factory owner. Fayence. 1763-1769. (**m**) NYMPHENBERG, Germany. Porcelain. Impressed or incised. Est. 1755. (**n**) PRAGUE, Germany. Lead-glazed earthenware. 1810-1862. (**o**) PHILADELPHIA, Pennsylvania, U.S.A. Bonnin and Morris. Incised. Circa 1770. (**p**) LIVERPOOL, Great Britain. Seth Pennington, potter. Painted gold or color. Second half 18th century.

P   P   ℘   ℘   P   P

a   b   c   d   e   f

(**a**) LIVERPOOL, Great Britain. Seth Pennington, potter. Painted gold and colors. Second half 18th century. (**b**) HOLLAND. De Porceleyne Schootel (The Porcelain Dish). Johannes Pennis, potter. Fayence. Delft. 1723-1763. (**c**) KIEL, Germany. J. S. Tannich, founder. Fayence. 1763. (**d**) DERBYSHIRE, Great Britain. Pinxton factory. Soft paste. 1796-1813. (**e**) PRAGUE, Germany. Lead-glazed earthenware. 1795-1810. (**f**) DERBYSHIRE, Great Britain. Pinxton factory. Soft paste. 1796-1813 (mark doubtful).

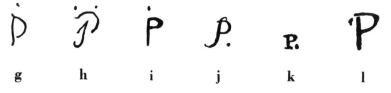

g   h   i   j   k   l

(**g-h-i**) HOLLAND. De Porceleyne Schootel (The Porcelain Dish). Johannes Pennis, potter. Fayence. Delft. 1723-1763. (**j**) APREY, France. Fayence. Est. 1744. (**k**) SAINT CLOUD, France. Fayence, porcelain. Est. 1758. (**l**) HOLLAND. De Metale Pot (The Metal Pot). Fayence. Delft. Circa 1639.

m   n   o   p   q   r

(**m**) HOLLAND. Jacob Pietersz, potter. Fayence. Delft. 1663-1682. (**n**) HOLLAND. De Porceleyne Schootel (The Porcelain Dish). Fayence. Delft. 1759. (**o**) LILLE, France. Phillippe-Auguste Petit, potter. Painted color. 1778. (**p**) HOLLAND. De Porceleyne Byl (The Porcelain Hatchet). Fayence. Delft. 1679. (**q**) CHANTILLY, France. Pigory, owner. Soft paste. Early 19th century. (**r**) CINCINNATI, Ohio, U.S.A. Rookwood Pottery Company. 1886.

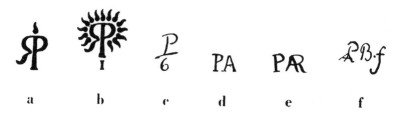

a   b   c   d   e   f

(**a-b**) CINCINNATI, Ohio, U.S.A. Rookwood Pottery Company.
One flame added to mark for each year after 1886. (**c**) SILESIA,
Germany. Count Leopold von Proskau, founder. Fayence. 1783-1793.
(**d**) ROUEN, France. Fayence. Painted color. 16th century. (**e**)
ROUEN, France. Fayence. 1720. (**f**) MOUSTIERS, France. Fay-
ence. Est. 1738.

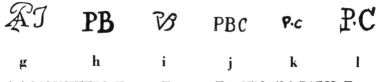

g   h   i   j   k   l

(**g**) MOUSTIERS, France. Fayence. Est. 1738. (**h**) PARIS, France.
Circa 1800. (**i**) HOLLAND. De Fortuyn (The Fortune). Fayence.
Delft. Painted blue. 1691. (**j**) GARD, France. Nimes, factory. Pottery. Impressed. 1830. (**k**) ALCORA, Spain. Fayence, porcelain. Est.
1727. (**l**) NEVERS, France. Fayence. 16th century.

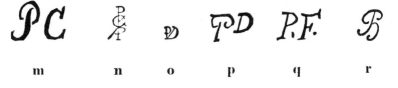

m   n   o   p   q   r

(**m**) ROUEN, France. Paul Caussy, potter. Fayence. From 1707.
(**n**) HOLLAND. Jacobus and Asriaen Pynaker, Albrecht de Keyser,
potters. Fayence. Delft. Painted blue. 1680. (**o**) HOLLAND. De
Porceleyne Fles (The Porcelain Bottle). Pieter van Doorne, potter.
Fayence. Delft. Painted blue. 1764. (**p**) ROUEN, France. Pierre
Dumont, painter. Second half 18th century. (**q**) MOUSTIERS,
France. Hard paste, soft paste. Est. 1738. (**r**) STRASBURG, France.
Paul Hannong, proprietor. Underglaze blue. 1740-1760.

a b c d e f

(**a**) STRASBURG, France. Paul Hannong, proprietor. Underglaze blue. 1740-1760. (**b**) FRANKENTHAL, Germany. Paul Hannong, director. Porcelain. Circa 1755. (**c-d-e**) STRASBURG, France. Paul Hannong, proprietor. Porcelain. Underglaze blue. 1740-1760. (**f**) HOLLAND. Philip Wouvermans, artist. Fayence. Delft. Painted. Circa 1600.

g h i j k l

(**g**) ROUEN, France. Circa 1720. (**h**) HOLLAND. De Drie Porceleyne Fleschen (The Three Porcelain Bottles). Fayence. Delft. 1672. (**i**) HOLLAND. De Drie Vergulde Astonne (The Three Golden Ash Barrels). Gerrit Pietersz Kam, potter. Fayence. Delft. 1674-1700. (**j**) HOLLAND. De Drie Porceleyne Fleschen (The Three Porcelain Bottles). Fayence. Delft. 1672. (**k-l**) PARIS, France. 1786-1793.

m n o p q r

(**m**) PARIS, France. 1786-1793. (**n-o**) DERBYSHIRE, Great Britain. Pinxton factory. Soft paste. Est. 1796. (**p**) ROUEN, France. Pierre Dumont, potter. After 1750. (**q**) HOLLAND. De Romeyn (The Roman). Petrus van Meerum, potter. Fayence. Delft. Painted blue. 1764. (**r**) DERBYSHIRE, Great Britain. Pinxton, factory. Soft paste. Est. 1796.

a   **b**   c   d   e

(a) ROUEN, France. Fayence. Circa 1720. (b) NEVERS, France. Fayence. 1630. (c) CHODAU, Germany. 1850-1872. (d) HOLLAND. De Porceleyne Fles (The Porcelain Bottle). Pieter van Doorne, artist. Fayence. Delft. Painted blue. 1764. (e) HOLLAND. De Fortuyn (The Fortune). P. van der Briel. Fayence. Delft. Painted blue. 1753-1769.

f   **g**   **h**   **i**

(f) HOLLAND. Fayence. Delft. 1725. (g-h) HOLLAND. De Romeyn (The Roman). Petrus van Meerum, potter. Fayence. Delft. Painted blue. 1764. (i) BURTON-ON-TRENT, Great Britain. Ashby Potter's Guild. Pottery. Est. 1909.

j   **k**   **l**   **m**

(j) HOLLAND. De Paauw (The Peacock). Fayence. Delft. 1729-1740. (k-l) SCHELTEN, Bohemia. S. L. Palme, artist. Porcelain. Impressed. Est. Circa 1840. (m) ALBANY, New York, U.S.A. Paul Cushman. Impressed. Circa 1815.

PAUL· CUSHMAN· STOE· WARE
FACTORY· 1809· HALF· A· MILE
WEST OF ALBANY GOAL   ṕaũn   P & B   P. BELL

a   b   c   d

(a) ALBANY, New York, U.S.A. Paul Cushman. Impressed. Circa 1815. (b) HOLLAND. De Paauw (The Peacock). Fayence. Delft. 1729-1740. (c) HANLEY, Great Britain. Powell and Bishop. Impressed. Circa 1875. (d) WINCHESTER, Virginia, U.S.A. Peter Bell. Circa 1800.

P. CROSS   PEACoCK
HARTFORD   POTTERY   PEARL WARE   Pennington

e   f   g   h

(e) HARTFORD, Connecticut, U.S.A. Peter Cross. Circa 1810. (f) FENTON, Great Britain. Foley China Works. 20th century. (g) LANE END, Great Britain. Chetham and Wooley, factory. Staffordshire. 18th and 19th centuries. (h) LIVERPOOL, Great Britain. Seth Pennington, potter. Hard paste, fayence. Impressed. Painted gold. 1760.

PEN YAN   PEORIA   PETER KELLEY   PFALTZGRAFF
           ILLINOIS   POTTERY

i   j   k   l

(i) YATES COUNTY, New York, U.S.A. Pen Yan Pottery. Circa 1840. (j) PEORIA, Illinois, U.S.A. Peoria Pottery Company. Circa 1880. (k) PHILADELPHIA, Pennsylvania, U.S.A. Peter Kelley. Impressed. Circa 1840. (l) YORK, Pennsylvania, U.S.A. Pfaltzgraff Pottery. Impressed. Circa 1875.

Phillip Kline   *Phillips*   PHILLIPS & Co.

       a   b   c

(**a**) CARVERSVILLE, Pennsylvania, U.S.A. Phillip Kline. Circa
1808. (**b**) LONGPORT, Great Britain. G. Phillips, potter. Blue-
printed earthenware. 19th century. (**c**) SUNDERLAND, Great
Britain. John Phillips, potter. Pottery. Printed color. 18th-19th century.

Phillips & C°
Sunderland. 1813   "*Phillips Longport*"   Phoenix Pottery

       d   e   f

(**d**) SUNDERLAND, Great Britain. Pottery. 18th-19th century.
(**e**) LONGPORT, Great Britain. G. Phillips, potter. Blue-printed
earthenware. 19th century. (**f**) PHOENIXVILLE, Pennsylvania,
U.S.A. Phoenix Pottery. 1867-1872.

Porcelaine Mousseline

T&H
Limoges FRANCE

PORCELAINE OPAQUE
FRENCH
T.P.W.

Pinxton. POINTONS

       g   h   i   j

(**g**) DERBYSHIRE, Great Britain. Pinxton factory. Soft paste. 1796.
(**h**) STOKE-ON-TRENT, Great Britain. Pointons. Late 19th century. (**i**) HAVILAND, France. Porcelain. Printed red, green. 1895.
(**j**) TRENTON, New Jersey, U.S.A. Trenton Pottery Works. Late
19th century.

Poupre
a japonng

Pouyat &
Russinger

P. P. Coy. L.
Stone China

a   b   c

(**a**) MOULINS, France. Fayence. 1730. (**b**) PARIS, France. Hard paste. Painted red. 1773. (**c**) PLYMOUTH, Great Britain. Plymouth Pottery Company. 1850.

P P SANDFORD
BARBADOESNECK   **PRAGER**   **Pratt**

PREMIUM STONE CHINA
HOMER LAUGHLIN

d   e   f   g

(**d**) BARBADOES NECK, New Jersey, U.S.A. P. P. Sanford. 18th century. (**e**) PRAGUE, Bohemia. Prager. Porcelain. 1810-1862. (**f**) FENTON, Great Britain. Felix Pratt, potter. Staffordshire. 1780-1820. (**g**) EAST LIVERPOOL, Ohio, U.S.A. Homer Laughlin China Company. Printed. Est. 1874.

P. RICE   *PROSKAU*   **Pull**

h   i   j   k

(**h**) PUTNAM, Ohio, U.S.A. Prosper Rice. Impressed. Circa 1840. (**i**) SILESIA, Germany. Proskau, factory. Impressed. Est. 1763. (**j**) PARIS, France. Fayence. 1855. (**k**) HOLLAND. Piet Vizeer, painter. Fayence. Delft. 1752.

SECTION **R**
See also Sections
B, Lines

a   b   c   d   e   f

(**a**) THURINGIA, Germany. Rudolstadt, factory. Fayence. Est. 1720. (**b**) CHELSEA, Great Britain. Louis-Francois Roubiliac, sculptor. Impressed. Circa 1738. (**c**) MARSEILLES, France. Porcelain. Est. 1766. (**d**) REGENSBURG, Germany. Porcelain decorating shop. Painted blue. 1782. (**e**) THURINGIA, Germany. Gotha, factory. Hard paste. Est. 1757. (**f**) MARSEILLES, France. Joseph Gaspard Robert, potter. Porcelain. Circa 1754.

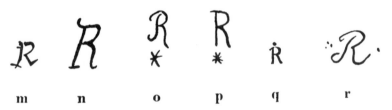

g   h   i   j   k   l

(**g**) THURINGIA, Germany. Gotha, factory. Hard paste. Est. 1757. (**h**) RUCKINGEN, Germany. Fayence. Est. 1720. (**i**) BRISTOL, Great Britain. Porcelain. Circa 1750. (**j**) THURINGIA, Germany. Gotha, factory. Hard paste. Est. 1757. (**k**) RATO, Portugal. Fayence. Painted yellow, violet. 1767. (**l**) BOW, Great Britain. Porcelain. 1750-1760.

m   n   o   p   q   r

(**m**) RENAC, France. Est. 1762. (**n**) ROUEN, France. 16th century. (**o-p**) THURINGIA, Germany. Rauenstein, factory. Porcelain. 1783. (**q**) MARSEILLES, France. Joseph Gaspard Robert, potter. Porcelain. Circa 1754. (**r**) HOLLAND. De Roos (The Rose). Fayence. Delft. Est. 1675.

a   b   c   d   e

(**a**) HOLLAND. De Roos (The Rose). Fayence. Delft. Est. 1675.
(**b**) MILAN, Italy. Fayence, porcelain. 1850. (**c**) HOLLAND. De
Boot (The Boat). Fayence. Delft. Est. 1667. (**d**) BOW, Great Britain. Porcelain. 1750-1760. (**e**) FAENZA, Italy. Fayence. Circa 1775.

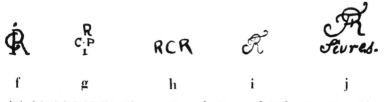

f   g   h   i   j

(**f**) MARSEILLES, France. Joseph Gaspard Robert, potter. Fayence, porcelain. 1754-1793. (**g**) PARIS, France. Christopher Potter,
owner. Hard paste. 1789-1807. (**h**) PHILADELPHIA, Pennsylvania,
U.S.A. Richard Remmey. Impressed. Est. 1859. (**i-j**) SEVRES,
France. Hard paste, soft paste. Painted blue, gold. 1793-1804.

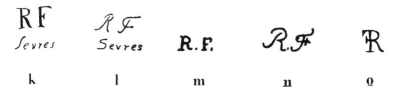

k   l   m   n   o

(**k-l-m-n**) SEVRES, France. Soft paste, hard paste. Painted blue,
gold. 1793-1804. (**o**) MARSEILLES, France. Joseph Gaspard Robert, potter. Fayence, porcelain. 1754-1793.

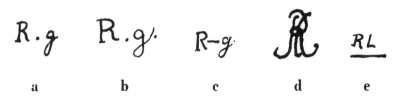

a   b   c   d   e

(**a-b-c**) REGENSBURG, Germany. Porcelain-decorating shop. 1793; or THURINGIA, Germany. Gotha, factory. William Rotberg, founder. Hard paste. Underglaze blue or impressed. These three marks are attributed to both factories. (**d**) MEISSEN, Germany. Hard paste. Underglaze blue. Circa 1730. (**e**) THURINGIA, Germany. Bernburg, factory. Fayence. Est. 1725.

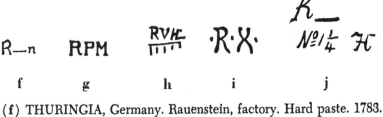

f   g   h   i   j

(**f**) THURINGIA, Germany. Rauenstein, factory. Hard paste. 1783. (**g**) HEGEWALD, Bohemia. Porcelain. 1850. (**h**) COLOGNE, Germany. Stoneware. Painted blue. 1600. (**i**) MARSEILLES, France. Joseph Gaspard Robert, potter. Fayence, porcelain. 1754-1793. (**j**) RORSTRAND, Sweden. Fayence. Circa 1760.

RAINFORTH & CO.

RALPH B. BEECH
Patented Jan. 3, 1851
KENSINGTON, PA

k   l   m

(**k**) LEEDS, Great Britain. Rainforth, potter. Late 18th-early 19th century. (**l**) EAST LIVERPOOL, Ohio, U.S.A. United States Pottery Company. 1898-1932. (**m**) PHILADELPHIA, Pennsylvania, U.S.A. Ralph Beech. Impressed. Est. 1845.

RALPH SIMPSON **R·A·L·P·H· T·A·Y·L·O·R**

a   b

(a) GREAT BRITAIN. Ralph Simpson, potter. Slipware. 1707.
(b) GREAT BRITAIN. Ralph Taylor, potter. Slipware. 1697.

RALPH TOFT   RALPH • TURNOR   RA WOOD BURSLEM   R.B.& S.

c   d   e   f

(c) WROTHAM, Great Britain. Ralph Toft, potter. Slipware. 1677.
(d) GREAT BRITAIN. Ralph Turner, potter. Slipware. 1681.
(e) BURSLEM, Great Britain. Ralph Wood, potter. Salt-glazed
stoneware. 1749-1770. (f) LEEDS, Great Britain. Circa 1875.

R.COCHRAN & CO.   R G Remmey   R. DANIEL   R. Drach
    GLASGOW

g   h   i   j

(g) GLASGOW, Scotland. R. Cochran and Company. Circa 1860.
(h) PHILADELPHIA, Pennsylvania, U.S.A. Richard Remmey. Impressed. Est. 1859. (i) COBRIDGE, Great Britain. Ralph Daniel,
potter. 1750. (j) BEDMINSTER, Pennsylvania, U.S.A. Rudolf
Drach. Circa 1790.

Real IRONSTONE CHINA	REED.	REGINA C P. CO.	REGINA H. & G.	Reid & Co.
a	b	c	d	e

(a) SHELTON, Great Britain. Job Ridgway, potter. Stone-china, porcelain. 1802. (b) MEXBOROUGH, Great Britain. John Reed, potter. Late 18th century. (c) EVANSVILLE, Indiana, U.S.A. Crown Pottery Company. Est. 1891. (d) LONGTON, Great Britain. Holland and Green. 1853-1882. (e) LIVERPOOL, Great Britain. William Reid, potter. Porcelain. Impressed, 1755-1759.

Re i niir	RENA	Rendsburg Duue	RFB PORCELANNA E SMC
f	g	h	i

(f) HOLLAND. De Romeyn (The Roman). Fayence. Delft. 1697. (g) EVANSVILLE, Indiana, U.S.A. Crown Pottery Company. Est. 1891. (h) RENDSBURG, Germany. Fayence, lead-glazed earthenware. 1764-1818. (i) BUEN RETIRO, Spain. Soft paste. 1759-1808.

R Hancock fecit	RICHARD MARE	RICHEY & HAMILTON PALATINE, W. VA.
j	k	l

(j) WORCESTER, Great Britain. Hard paste. 1756-1774. (k) GREAT BRITAIN. Richard Mare, potter. Slipware. 1697. (l) PALATINE, West Virginia, U.S.A. Richey and Hamilton. Blue. Circa 1875.

RIDGWAYS RIDGWAY & SONS RIEDINGER + CARIE POUGHKEEPSIE RILEY

a b c d

(**a-b**) SHELTON, Great Britain. Job Ridgway, potter. 1794-1802.
(**c**) POUGHKEEPSIE, New York, U.S.A. Riedinger and Caire (Rudinger). Impressed. Circa 1875. (**d**) BURSLEM, Great Britain. J.
and R. Riley, potters. Earthenware. Early 19th century.

R. & J. Baddeley   R. M. W. & Co.   Robertson & Sons CHELSEA KERAMIC ART WORKS C.K.A.W.   ROCKET

e f g h

(**e**) SHELTON, Great Britain. Ralph and John Baddeley, proprietors. Salt-glazed stoneware. Impressed. 1750. (**f**) SHELTON, Great
Britain. William Ridgway, Morley, Wear, potters. Staffordshire.
Circa 1840. (**g**) CHELSEA, Massachusetts, U.S.A. James Robertson
and Son. Impressed. Circa 1880. (**h**) EAST LIVERPOOL, Ohio,
U.S.A. William Brunt Pottery Company. 1877-1911.

Rockingham   ROCKINGHAM   ROGERS JOHN   ROOKWOOD 1882

i j k l

(**i**) SWINTON, Great Britain. Rockingham, factory. Bramels and
Company. Late 18th-early 19th century. (**j**) SWINTON, Great Britain. Rockingham, factory. Bramels and Company. 1840. (**k**) NEW
YORK, New York, U.S.A. John Rogers. Terracotta. Circa 1875. (**l**)
CINCINNATI, Ohio, U.S.A. Rookwood, factory. Impressed. 1882+.

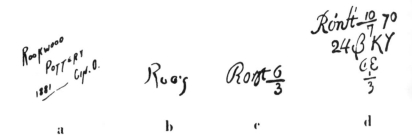

a   b   c   d

(**a**) CINCINNATI, Ohio, U.S.A. Rookwood Pottery Company. Impressed. 1881. (**b**) HOLLAND. De Roos (The Rose). A. Cosijn, artist. Fayence. Delft. 1675. (**c-d**) RORSTRAND, Sweden. Fayence. Est. 1725.

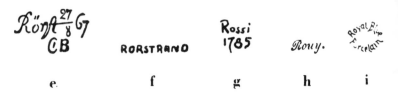

e.   f   g   h   i

(**e**) RORSTRAND, Sweden. Fayence. Est. 1725. (**f**) RORSTRAND, Sweden. Fayence, cream-colored ware. Circa 1790-circa 1800. (**g**) COIMBRA, Portugal. Fayence. 18th-early 19th century. (**h**) ROUY, France. Fayence. Est. 1790. (**i**) TRENTON, New Jersey, U.S.A. Burgess and Campbell. Est. 1879.

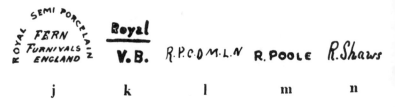

j   k   l   m   n

(**j**) COBRIDGE, Great Britain. Circa 1890. (**k**) EAST LIVERPOOL, Ohio, U.S.A. Vodrey Brothers. Circa 1875. (**l**) CINCINNATI, Ohio, U.S.A. Rookwood Pottery Factory. Est. 1886. (**m**) BURSLEM, Great Britain. Fayence. Late 18th and early 19th centuries. (**n**) BURSLEM, Great Britain. Staffordshire. Impressed. 1735.

Rubelles
A.D.T. *Ruskin* *Ruskin Pottery* **R.W. MARTIN & BROS.**

a   b   c   d

(a) RUBELLES, France. Fayence. 1856. (b) WEST SMETHWICK,
Great Britain. Pottery. 20th century. (c) WEST SMETHWICK, Great
Britain. Pottery. 1904+. (d) GREAT BRITAIN. R. W. Martin and
Brothers. Stoneware. 1900.

Ⲙ S   S   s   S   S   S   SECTION S
                                                See also Section
   e   f   g   h   i   j   **Lines**

(e) SAINT PETERSBURG, Russia. Hard paste. Painted blue. 1744.
(f-g-h-i-j) CAUGHLEY, Great Britain. Hard paste. Painted blue.
Est. 1750.

S   S   s   S   ·S   S.

k   l   m   n   o   p

(k) ROUEN, France. Fayence. Circa 1760. (l) PARIS, France. Rue
de la Roquette, factory. Souroux, potter. 1773. (m) SCHLAGGEN-
WALD, Bohemia. Hard paste. Painted. 1793-1866. (n) NYMPH-
ENBURG, Germany. Porcelain. Impressed or incised. Est. 1747.
(o) SINCENY, France. Fayence. Est. 1733. (p) SCHLAGGEN-
WALD, Bohemia. Hard paste. 1793-1866.

a   b   c   d   e   f

(a-b) SCHLAGGENWALD, Bohemia. Porcelain. 1793-1866. (c) SCHREZHEIM, Germany. Fayence. Est. 1752-1862. (d) SINCENY, France. Fayence. Painted. Est. 1733. (e) ST. CLOUD, France. Fayence, porcelain. Est. 1678-1766. (f) EISENACH, Germany. Est. 1858.

g   h   i   j   k

(g) NORD, France. St. Amand les Eaux, factory. Fayence. Est. 1718. (h) ROUEN, France. Fayence. 1760. (i) STRASBURG, Virginia, U.S.A. Samuel Bell. Impressed. Circa 1850. (j-k) SCHLESWIG, Germany. Fayence. Est. 1755.

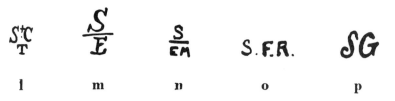

l   m   n   o   p

(l) ST. CLOUD, France. Henri-Charles Trou, potter. Pottery and soft paste. Painted. Circa 1700. (m) SCHLESWIG, Germany. Lucke and Schmattau, founders. Fayence. 1755-1814. (n) SCHLESWIG, Germany. Fayence. 1755-1814. (o) PIRKENHAMMER, Germany. Fischer and Reichenbach. Hard paste. Impressed. 1815-1845. (p) ROUEN, France. Fayence. 1760.

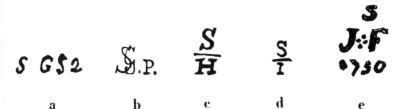

a   b   c   d   e

(a) ROUEN, France. Fayence. 1760. (b) CASTELLI, Italy. 17th
and 18th centuries. (c-d) SCHLESWIG. Germany. Lucke and
Schmattau, founders. Fayence. 1755-1814. (e) BRISTOL, Great
Britain. Joseph Flower, painter. Delft. 1739-1751.

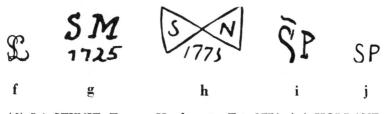

f   g   h   i   j

(f) LA SEYNIE, France. Hard paste. Est. 1774. (g) HOLLAND
T'Hart (The Stag). Fayence. Delft. 1707. (h) BUEN RETIRO,
Spain. Porcelain. 1759-1808. (i) ROUEN, France. Fayence. 1760.
(j) SCEAUX, France. Fayence, porcelain. 1748-1794.

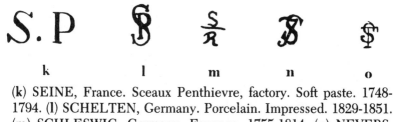

k   l   m   n   o

(k) SEINE, France. Sceaux Penthievre, factory. Soft paste. 1748-
1794. (l) SCHELTEN, Germany. Porcelain. Impressed. 1829-1851.
(m) SCHLESWIG, Germany. Fayence. 1755-1814. (n) NEVERS,
France. Jacques Seigne, painter. Fayence. Painted. 1700. (o)
SCHAFFHAUSEN, Germany. Tobias Stimmer. Pottery., Painted.
16th century.

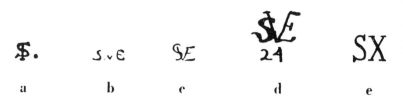

a   b   c   d   e

(a) GERMANY. 17th century. (b-c-d) HOLLAND. De Griekse A (The Greek A). S. v. Eenhoorn, potter. Fayence. Delft. 1674. (e) SEINE, France. Sceaux Penthievre, factory. Jacques Chapelle, potter. Soft paste. 1749-1763.

f   g   h   i   j

(f-g-h) SEINE, France. Sceaux Penthievre, factory. Jacques Chapelle, potter. Soft paste. 1749-1763. (i) CAUGHLEY, Great Britain. Porcelain. 1750-1814. (j) SEINE, France. Sceaux, factory. Richard Glot, potter. Fayence, soft paste. 1772-1794.

S.A. & CO.	Sadler	Sadler & Green	Saint-Omer
k	l	m	n

(k) BURSLEM, Great Britain. Smith, Ambrose and Company. Staffordshire. Circa 1800. (l) LIVERPOOL, Great Britain. John Sadler, engraver. Pottery and hard paste. Printed. 1756-1770. (m) LIVERPOOL, Great Britain. John Sadler, engraver. Hard paste. Printed. 1756-1770. (n) SAINT OMER, France. Fayence. 1750-1780.

Salamander Works Woodbridge N.J

SALOPIAN

SALT

a

b

c

(**a**) WOODBRIDGE, New York, U.S.A. Salamander Works. Impressed. Circa 1875. (**b**) CAUGHLEY, Great Britain. Porcelain. Impressed. 1750-1814. (**c**) HANLEY, Great Britain. Ralph Salt, potter. Earthenware. 1820.

Samuel Troxel Potter 1825

SAPPHO
J. M. & S. CO

d

e

f

(**d**) MONTGOMERY COUNTY, Pennsylvania, U.S.A. Troxel Pottery. 1825. (**e**) SARREGUEMINES, France. Fayence. Est. 1770-19th century. (**f**) TRENTON, New Jersey, U.S.A. John Moses and Sons. Circa 1875.

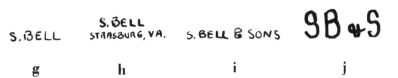

S.BELL

S.BELL
STRASBURG, VA.

S. BELL B SONS

SB&S

g

h

i

j

(**g**) STRASBURG, Virginia, U.S.A. Samuel Bell. Impressed. 1843-1852. (**h**) STRASBURG, Virginia, U.S.A. Samuel and Solomon Bell. Impressed. 1852-1882. (**i**) STRASBURG, Virginia, U.S.A. S. Bell and Sons. Impressed. 1882-1908. (**j**) SWINTON, Great Britain. Don Pottery, factory. Creamware. 1834.

Schiedam
A: klos   *Schleswig*   26
Sceaux   S & Co

a   b   c   d

(a) SEINE, France. Sceaux Penthievre, factory. Soft paste. Painted
blue. 1748-1794. (b) SCHIEDAM, Holland. Fayence. 1775-1790.
(c) SCHLESWIG, Germany. Fayence. 1755-1814. (d) ISLE-
WORTH, Great Britain. Staffordshire-like ware. 1760-19th century.

SCOTT
Scott   Scott Brothers & Co.   PB   SCROMAN
                                             A MOABIT.

e   f   g   h

(e-f) SUNDERLAND, Great Britain. Anthony Scott and family,
potters. 18th century. (g) PORTBELLO, Scotland. Cream-colored
ware. Est. 1770. (h) MOABIT, Germany. Porcelain. Blue. Est. 1835.

                      S.E. HEIGHSHOE   SEMI-VITREOUS
                        SOMERSET   ARDMORE
                          O   MERCER CHINA

i   j   k   l

(i-j) SEBRING, Ohio, U.S.A. Sebring Pottery Company. Est. 1887.
(k) SOMERSET, Ohio, U.S.A. Heighshoe, owner. Impressed. Circa
1850. (l) TRENTON, New Jersey, U.S.A. Mercer Pottery Company.
Circa 1870.

a   b   c   d

(a) STEUBENVILLE, Ohio, U.S.A. Steubenville Pottery Company. Circa 1904. (b) PITTSBURGH, Pennsylvania, U.S.A. Star Encaustic Tile Company. Est. 1882. (c) HARTFORD, Connecticut, U.S.A. Seth Goodwin. Circa 1810. (d) SEVRES, France. Soft paste, hard paste. 1793-1800.

e   f   g   h   i

(e) SEVRES, France. Soft paste, hard paste. Black for hard paste, blue for soft paste. 1941. (f) SEVRES, France. Painted black on hard paste, blue on soft paste. 1928-1940. (g-h) SEVRES, France. Soft paste, hard paste. Painted. 1792-1800. (i) EAST LIVERPOOL, Ohio, U.S.A. Sevres China Company. 1900-1908.

Sewell & Donkin   SEWELL   ST. ANTHONY's

j   k

(j) NEWCASTLE-ON-TYNE, Great Britain. Sewell and Donkin, potters. Pottery. Early 19th century. (k) NEWCASTLE-ON-TYNE, Great Britain. Sewell, potter. Impressed. Early 19th century.

Seymour & Steadman
   Ravenna, O.   S&G.   S&G   SGIB

      a   b   c   d

(a) RAVENNA, Ohio, U.S.A. Seymour and Steadman. Impressed.
Circa 1850. (b) GERMANY. Schiller and Gerbing. After 1829-circa
1885. (c) ISLEWORTH, Great Britain. Joseph Shore, owner. 1760.
(d) VENICE, Italy. 1750.

                                            SHEPLEY & SMITH
                                            WEST TROY
S.&G ISLEWORTH   S.GREENWOOD   SHAW   N.Y.

      e   f   g   h

(e) ISLEWORTH, Great Britain. Shore and Goulding, owners. Staffordshire-like ware. Est. 1760. (f) FENTON, Great Britain. Staffordshire. Circa 1780. (g) LIVERPOOL, Great Britain. Thomas Shaw,
potter. Pottery. 1716. (h) WEST TROY, New York, U.S.A. Shepley
and Smith. Impressed. Circa 1880.

S. HOLLINS   Shore & Co.   SHORTHOSE   Shorthose & Co.

      i   j   k   l

(i) SHELTON, Great Britain. Samuel Hollins, potter. Stoneware.
Impressed. Last quarter 18th century. (j) ISLEWORTH, Great
Britain. Joseph Shore, owner. Staffordshire-like ware. 1760-19th century. (k) HANLEY, Great Britain. J. Shorthose, potter. Staffordshire. 1785-1823. (l) HANLEY, Great Britain. J. Shorthose, potter.
Black basaltes and porcelain. Impressed, printed blue. Late 18th-
19th century.

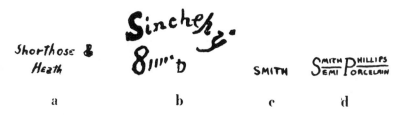

Shorthose & Heath   **b**   SMITH   SMITH PHILLIPS SEMI PORCELAIN

a   b   c   d

(a) HANLEY, Great Britain. Shorthose and Heath, potters. Black basaltes and porcelain. Late 18th-19th century. (b) SINCENY, France. Pottery. Painted. 1733. (c) WOMELSDORF, Pennsylvania, U.S.A. Impressed. Circa 1880. (d) EAST LIVERPOOL, Ohio, U.S.A. Smith-Phillips China Company. Late 19th century.

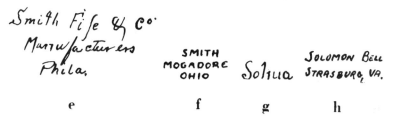

Smith Fise & Co. Manufacturers Phila,   SMITH MOGADORE OHIO   Soliua   SOLOMON BELL STRASBURG, VA.

e   f   g   h

(e) PHILADELPHIA, Pennsylvania, U.S.A. Smith, Fise and Company. Circa 1810. (f) MOGADORE, Ohio, U.S.A. J. C. Smith. Impressed. Circa 1860. (g) ALCORA, Spain. Miguel Soliva, painter. Porcelain, fayence. 1727-1750. (h) STRASBURG, Virginia, U.S.A. Samuel and Solomon Bell. Impressed. Circa 1875.

SOMERSET
POTTERY WORKS   S. PAUL   SP. CO =   SPODE.

i   j   k   l

(i) SOMERSET, Massachusetts. U.S.A. Somerset Pottery Works. Impressed. Circa 1875. (j) SAINT PAUL, France. Fayence. 18th-19th century. (k) KAOLIN, South Carolina, U.S.A. Southern Porcelain Company. Circa 1860. (l) STOKE-ON-TRENT, Great Britain. Porcelain. Impressed, painted red, blue, black, gold. 1770.

$\int pode$

SPODE

SPODE & COPELAND

a   b   c

(a-b-c) STOKE-ON-TRENT, Great Britain. Spode, factory. Impressed or printed red, blue, black, gold. 1770-1797.

SPODE
COPELANDS CHINA
ENGLAND

SPODE
Felspar Porcelain

Spode's
Imperial

d   e   f

(d) STOKE-ON-TRENT, Great Britain. Spode, factory. Bone-porcelain. 1940-1956. (e)• STOKE-ON-TRENT, Great Britain. Spode, factory. Printed. 1825. (f) STOKE-ON-TRENT, Great Britain. W. T. Copeland and Sons. Bone-porcelain. 1823.

SPODE, SON
& COPELAND

S.PURDY

S. PURDY
ATWATER

S. PURDY
PORTAGE CO.
O

g   h   i   j

(g) STOKE-ON-TRENT, Great Britain. Copeland and Spode, factory. Impressed, printed blue. 1797-1816. (h-i-j) ATWATER, Ohio, U.S.A. Solomon Purdy. Impressed. Circa 1820.

S. QUIGLEY

FRANKLIN FACTORY
CINCINNATI
O.

S. PURDY
ZOAR

S. RISLEY
NORWICH

Stanford

a   b   c   d

(a) ZOAR, Ohio, U.S.A. Zoar Pottery. Impressed. Circa 1845.
(b) CINCINNATI, Ohio, U.S.A. S. Quigley. Circa 1835 (doubtful mark). (c) NORWICH, Connecticut, U.S.A. Sidney Risley. Impressed. Circa 1835. (d) LIVERPOOL, Ohio, U.S.A. Knowles, Taylor, and Knowles. Est. 1854.

STAR POTTERY   Steel   Steen   STEVENSON

e   f   g   h

(e) STRASBURG, Virginia, U.S.A. J. S. Eberley. Impressed. 1880-1905. (f) BURSLEM, Great Britain. Daniel Steel, potter. Blue jasper stoneware. Impressed. 1766-1824. (g) HOLLAND. Jan Steen. Fayence. Delft. Painted blue. 1650. (h) COBRIDGE, Great Britain. Ralph Stevenson, potter. Earthenware. 1815.

Stockholm
AF..
BS.

Stockton

STONE CHINA
MERCER POTTERY CO.

STONE CHINA.
WARRANTED.

i   j   k   l

(i) RORSTRAND, Sweden. Fayence. 1725-1758. (j) SUNDERLAND, Great Britain. After 1800. (k) TRENTON, New Jersey, U.S.A. Mercer Pottery Company. Est. 1869. (l) BALTIMORE, Maryland, U.S.A. D. F. Haynes and Company. 1887-1890.

Storyhulm 22/8. 1751
D̶B̶

.S. T. P.

SWAN HILL
POTTERY

a   b   c

(**a**) RORSTRAND, Sweden. Fayence. 1725-1758. (**b**) MONTGOM-
ERY COUNTY, Pennsylvania, U.S.A. Samuel Troxel. Circa 1830.
(**c**) SOUTH AMBOY, New Jersey, U.S.A. James Carr. Impressed.
1852.

SWI꒾NSEA   *Swansea*   SWANSEA
NANGRAW   SYDNEY

d   e   f   g

(**d-e**) SWANSEA, Wales. Hard paste. Stenciled red or impressed.
1814-1824. (**f**) NANTGARW, Wales. Swansea factory. Impressed.
1814. (**g**) EAST LIVERPOOL, Ohio, U.S.A. C. C. Thompson Pottery Company. Est. 1888.

SECTION **T**
See also Sections
Anchor, Arrow,
Lines

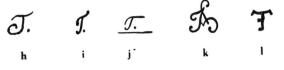

h   i   j˙   k   l

(**h**) TETTAU, Germany. Porcelain. 1794-1940. (**i**) TANNOWA,
Germany. Fayence, porcelain. 1813-1880. (**j**) KIEL, Germany. Johann Tannich, founder. Fayence. 1763-1768. (**k**) FRANKENTHAL,
Germany. Joseph Asam Hannong, owner. Porcelain. 1759-1762.
(**l**) BOW, Great Britain. Thomas Frye, manager. Porcelain. 1744-
1759.

a b c d e

(**a-b**) BOW, Great Britain. Thomas Frye, manager. Porcelain. 1744-1759. (**c-d**) HOLLAND. Antoni Ter Humpelin. Fayence. Delft. Painted blue. 1650. (**e**) PARIS, France. Theodore Deck. Fayence. 1859-circa 1891.

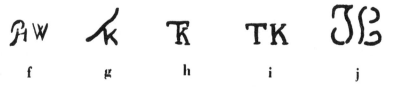

f g h i j

(**f**) HOLLAND. Philip Wouvermans. Fayence. Delft. Painted blue. 1600. (**g-h-i**) KLOSTERLE, Germany. Porcelain, lead-glazed earthenware. 1793. (**j**) PREMIERES, France. Lavalle, potter. 1783.

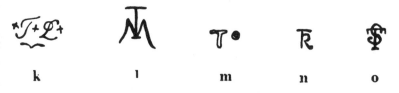

k l m n o

(**k**) MOUSTIERS, France. Joseph Olery, painter. Fayence. 1721. (**l**) NAPLES, Italy. Late 19th century. (**m**) BRISTOL, Great Britain. Tebo, modeler. Porcelain. 1770-1775. (**n**) NEVERS, France. Tite Ristori. Pottery. Painted. 1850. (**o**) SCHAFFHAUSEN, Germany. Tobias Stimmer. Pottery. Painted. 1560.

$\mathfrak{B}.$ $\mathcal{JV}$ T.W.J.L.   Tannawa

a   b   c   d

(a) NEVERS, France. Fayence. 18th century. (b) LIONVILLE, Pennsylvania, U.S.A. T. Vickers. 1805. (c) SOUTH AMBOY, New Jersey, U.S.A. Warne and Letts. 1806. (d) TANNOWA, Bohemia. Fayence, porcelain. 1840-1872.

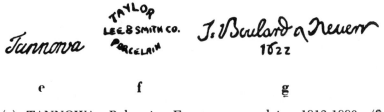

e   f   g

(e) TANNOWA, Bohemia. Fayence, porcelain. 1813-1880. (f) EAST LIVERPOOL, Ohio, U.S.A. Taylor, Smith, and Taylor Company. 1900-1901. (g) NEVERS, France. Fayence. 1622.

T. CRAFTS & SON
    WHATELY
      MASS.   Tetschen   TEXAS   T. FELL & CO.

h   i   j   k

(h) WHATELEY, Massachusetts, U.S.A. Crafts, Thomas and Elbridge. Impressed. Circa 1830. (i) BODENBACH, Germany. 1829. (j) EAST LIVERPOOL, Ohio, U.S.A. Cartwright Brothers. 1890. (k) NEWCASTLE, Great Britain. Thomas Fell, potter. 1817.

T FERESCH   T.FLETCHER & CO.   T. G. BOONE + SONS POTTERS
                                          NAVY ST BROOKLYN

a   b   c

(a) KLUM, Germany. Porcelain. Circa 1800. (b) SHELTON, Great
Britain. Fletcher, owner. Staffordshire. 18th century. (c) BROOK-
LYN, New York, U.S.A. T. G. Boone. Circa 1845.

T. GREEN   T. HAIG   T. HARLEY   t'hart
                                Lane End

d   e   f   g

(d) FENTON, Great Britain. Staffordshire. 1830-1849. (e) PHILA-
DELPHIA, Pennsylvania, U.S.A. Thomas Haig. 1850. (f) LANE
END, Great Britain. Staffordshire. Impressed. 1809. (g) HOL-
LAND. T'Hart (The Stag). Fayence. Delft. Painted blue. 1764.

The Admiral   THE EDWARD NORTON CO,   T. Hess T
                 BENNINGTON, VT.

h   i   j

(h) EAST LIVERPOOL, Ohio, U.S.A. United States Pottery Company. Est. 1846. (i) BENNINGTON, Vermont, U.S.A. Edward Norton and Company. Impressed. 1886-1894. (j) HOLLAND. Fayence.
Delft. 1730.

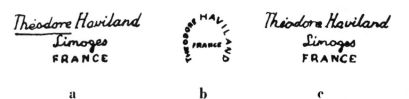

a   b   c

(a) HAVILAND, France. Painted red, green. 1914. (b) HAVI-
LAND, France. Whiteware. Printed green. 1920-1936. (c) HAVI-
LAND, France. Decorated ware. Printed red. 1920.

Theodore Haviland
Limoges
FRANCE

THEODORE HAVILAND
NEW YORK

Theodore Haviland
New York

MADE IN AMERICA

d   e   f

(d) HAVILAND, France. Decorated ware. Printed red. 1925+. (e)
NEW YORK, New York, U.S.A. Haviland, company. Printed green,
black. 1936. (f) NEW YORK, New York, U.S.A. Haviland, company.
Printed dark red, black. After 1937.

THE OLIVER
CHINA CO.
SEBRING, O.

TRENTON POTTERIES CO
HOTEL CHINA CO

THE
WHEELING
POTTERY
CO.

THE WHEELING
STONE CHINA
POTTERY CO.

g   h   i   j

(g) SEBRING, Ohio, U.S.A. Oliver China Company. Est. 1899.
(h) TRENTON, New Jersey, U.S.A. Trenton Potteries Company.
Est. 1865. (i-j) WHEELING, West Virginia, U.S.A. Wheeling Pottery Company. Est. 1879.

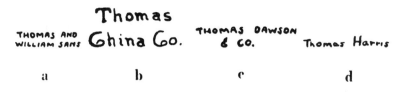

a b c d

(a) GREAT BRITAIN. Thomas and William Sans, potters. Slipware. 1707. (b) EAST LIVERPOOL, Ohio, U.S.A. C. C. Thompson Pottery Company. Est. 1888. (c) SUNDERLAND, Great Britain. Thomas Dawson, potter. Circa 1850. (d) CUYAHOGA FALLS, Ohio, U.S.A. Thomas Harris. Impressed. Est. 1863.

THOMAS TOFT   THOMAS SHARPE   Thos Furnival & Sons Cobridge Staffore   T&J HOLLINS

e f g h

(e) BURSLEM, Great Britain. Thomas Toft, potter. Slipware. 1670. (f) GREAT BRITAIN. Thomas Sharpe, potter. Circa 1830. (g) COBRIDGE, Great Britain. Thomas Furnival. After 1850. (h) HANLEY, Great Britain. Hollins, potter. Stoneware. Impressed. Circa 1820.

T., J. & J. MAYER   T. Johnson   T. Mayer   T. O. GOODWIN HARTFORD

i j k l

(i) HANLEY, Great Britain. Thomas, John, Joseph Mayer, potters. After 1836. (j) GREAT BRITAIN. T. Johnson, potter. Slipware. 1694. (k) STOKE-ON-TRENT, Great Britain. Fayence. Impressed. 1820. (l) HARTFORD, Connecticut, U.S.A. Thomas Goodwin. Circa 1850.

Tomlinson & Co.   **TOULOUSE**   T. P. Co.   T. READ
                                          CHINA

a   b   c   d

(a) FERRYBRIDGE, Great Britain. W. Tomlinson, potter. 18th-
19th century. (b) TOULOUSE, France. Fayence. Early 19th century. (c) TRENTON, New Jersey, U.S.A. Trenton Pottery Company. Circa 1870. (d) NEWPORT, Ohio, U.S.A. Thomas Read.
Impressed. Circa 1860.

T. READ   TRENTON CHINA CO.   TRENTON POTTERIES Co.
TUSCARAWAS CO.   TRENTON, N. J.   TRENTON, NEW JERSEY
                                              USA

e   f   g

(e) NEWPORT, Ohio, U.S.A. Thomas Read. Impressed. 1850-1865.
(f) TRENTON, New Jersey, U.S.A. Trenton China Company.
1860-1890. (g) TRENTON, New Jersey, U.S.A. Trenton Potteries
Company. Circa 1900.

TRENT TILE
TRENTON, N.J   BAILEY   BAILEY
U.S.A.   & M. & S CO. & M & S CO.   T. SHARPE   T. SNEYD

h   i   j   k   l

(h) TRENTON, New Jersey, U.S.A. Trenton Tile Company. 1885.
(i-j) TRENTON, New Jersey, U.S.A. John Moses and Sons. Circa
1875. (k) GREAT BRITAIN. Thomas Sharpe, potter. 1821-1838.
(l) HANLEY, Great Britain. T. Sneyd, potter. Staffordshire. Impressed. 1800.

a	b	c	d	e
Tucker & Hulme China Manufacturers Philadelphia 1825	Tucker & Hulme Philadelphia 1828	TURADA WELLER	**TURNER**	TURNER

(**a**) PHILADELPHIA, Pennsylvania, U.S.A. Tucker and Hulme. Est. 1825. (**b**) PHILADELPHIA, Pennsylvania, U.S.A. Tucker and Hulme. 1828+. (**c**) ZANESVILLE, Ohio, U.S.A. S. A. Weller. Late 19th century. (**d**) CAUGHLEY, Great Britain. Porcelain. 1750. (**e**) CAUGHLEY, Great Britain. Hard paste, fayence. Impressed. 1772.

f	g	h
Tuyn	T.WETHERILL	TWIGG

(**f**) HOLLAND. De Porceleyne Schootel (The Porcelain Dish). Fayence. Delft. 1764. (**g**) LAMBETH, Great Britain. Delft. 19th century. (**h**) SWINTON, Great Britain. Pottery. 1750.

i	j	k	
U&C	U DALWITZ	UPTON BELL WAYNESBORO, PA.	SECTION **U** See also Sections **V, W, Lines, Shield**

(**i**) SARREGUEMINES, France. Fayence, porcelain. Est. 1770. (**j**) DALLWITZ, Germany. Est. 1804. (**k**) WAYNESBORO, Pennsylvania, U.S.A. Upton Bell. Impressed. Circa 1895.

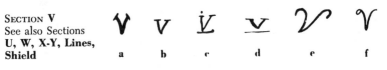

a   b   c   d   e   f

(a) VENICE, Italy. Nathaniel Hewelcke, potter. Porcelain. Incised.
1757-1763. (b) VIANNA DO CASTELLO, Portugal. Fayence. Est.
1774. (c) HOLLAND. De Drie Klokken (The Three Bells). Fayence. Delft. 1675. (d) VIANNA DO CASTELLO, Portugal. Fayence. Est. 1774. (e) VARAGES, France. Fayence. 18th century.
(f) LIONVILLE, Pennsylvania, U.S.A. T. and J. Vickers. 1806.

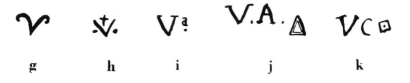

g   h   i   j   k

(g) VARAGES, France. Fayence. 18th century. (h) VINOVO,
Italy. Porcelain. Underglaze blue or incised. Est. 1776. (i) VENICE,
Italy. Francesco and Giuseppe Vezzi, porcelain makers. Porcelain.
Painted blue. 1719-1740. (j) VISTA ALEGRE, Portugal. Hard
paste. Est. 1824. (k) ALCORA, Spain. Porcelain, fayence. Est. 1750.

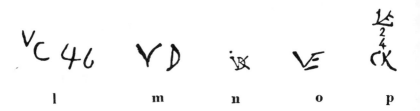

l   m   n   o   p

(l) STRASBURG, France. Valentin Gusi, modeler. Porcelain. Circa
1750. (m) ROUEN, France. Jacques Dubois, potter. 1783. (n-o)
HOLLAND. Jan van der Kloot. Fayence. Delft. Painted blue. 1764.
(p) HOLLAND. De Metale Pot (The Metal Pot). Fayence. Delft.
1691.

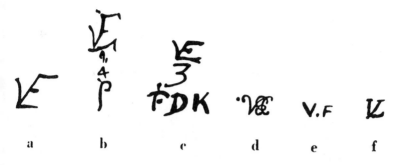

a   b   c   d   e   f

(a) HOLLAND. De Metale Pot (The Metal Pot). Fayence. Delft. 1691. (b-c) HOLLAND. De Dubbelde Schenkkan (The Double Jug). Fayence. Delft. 1689. (d) NIDERVILLER, France. Baron Jean-Louis Beyerle, owner. Fayence. 1754-1770. (e) VINOVO, Italy. Porcelain. Est. 1776. (f) HOLLAND. De Drie Klokken (The Three Bells). Fayence. Delft. 1675.

g   h   i   j   k

(g-h) MARSEILLES, France. Veuve Perrin, potter. Fayence. Painted black. 1790. (i) FAENZA, Italy. Calamelli Virgiliotto, potter and painter. Fayence. 1570. (j) FRANKENTHAL, Germany. Hard paste. Est. 1755-1799. (k) METTLACH, Germany. Fayence. 1789-1836.

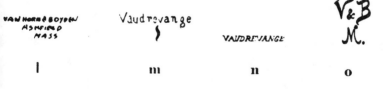

l   m   n   o

(l) ASHFIELD, Massachusetts, U.S.A. Van Horn and Boyden. Impressed. Circa 1855. (m-n-o) METTLACH, Germany. Fayence, glazed earthenware. Est. 1809.

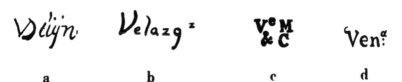

a   b   c   d

(a) HOLLAND. De Porceleyne Schootel (The Porcelain Dish).
Fayence. Delft. 1764. (b) BUEN RETIRO, Spain. Hard paste. 1759-
1808. (c) PARIS, France. Rue Thiroux, factory. Hard paste. 1775.
(d) VENICE, Italy. Hard paste. Painted red, blue. 1700.

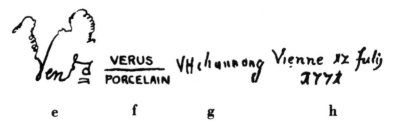

e   f   g   h

(e) VENICE, Italy. Hard paste. Painted blue. 1719. (f) SEBRING,
Ohio, U.S.A. Oliver China Company. 1899-circa 1908 (g) STRAS-
BURG, France. Hard paste. 1729-1771. (h) VIENNA, Austria. Hard
paste. 1770.

i   j   k   l

(i) TRENTON, New Jersey, U.S.A. Glasgow Pottery Company.
Circa 1895. (j) METTLACH, Germany. Villeroy and Boch, potters.
Fayence. 1842. (k) EAST LIVERPOOL, Ohio, U.S.A. Knowles, Taylor, and Knowles. Est. 1854. (l) COBRIDGE, Great Britain. Staffordshire. Impressed. 1773.

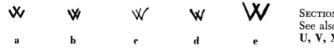

a   b   c   d   e

SECTION **W**
See also Sections
U, V, X-Y, Lines

(**a**) BERLIN, Germany. Wegeley, founder. Hard paste. Painted blue. 1751. (**b**) THURINGIA, Germany. Wallendorf, factory. Porcelain. Est. 1764. (**c**) PLYMOUTH, Great Britain. Hard paste. Painted blue. 1768. (**d**) BORDEAUX, France. Porcelain. Painted gold, underglaze blue. 1781. (**e**) WEESP, Holland. Porcelain. Est. 1759.

f   g   h   i   j

(**f**) PLYMOUTH, Great Britain. Hard paste. Painted red, blue, gold. 1768. (**g**) BUDWEIS, Germany. Porcelain. Circa 1820. (**h**) BERLIN, Germany. Wegeley, founder. Hard paste. Painted blue. 1751. (**i**) BUDWEIS, Germany. Porcelain. Circa 1820. (**j**) STOKE-ON-TRENT, Great Britain. Thomas Wolfe, potter. Impressed. 18th-19th century.

k   l   m   n   o

(**k-l**) WORCESTER, Great Britain. Hard paste. Est. 1751. (**m**) WARSAW, Poland. Wolff, potter. 1783. (**n**) WORCESTER, Great Britain. Hard paste. Est. 1751. (**o**) WALLENDORF, Germany. Painted blue. Est. 1764.

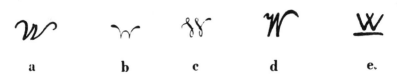

a   b   c   d   e.

(**a**) ROUEN, France. Fayence. 1720. (**b-c**) WORCESTER, Great Britain. Hard paste. Est. 1751. (**d**) PHILADELPHIA, Pennsylvania, U.S.A. Joseph Hemphill. Circa 1835. (**e**) BERLIN, Germany. Wegeley, founder. Porcelain. 1751.

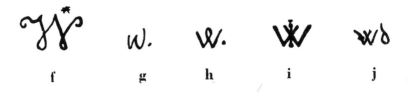

f   g   h   i   j

(**f-g-h**) WALLENDORF, Germany. Porcelain. Painted blue. Est. 1764. (**i**) HOLLAND. De Oude Moriaan's Hooft (The Old Moor's Head). Fayence. Delft. 1661. (**j**) WIESBADEN, Germany. Fayence. Est. 1770.

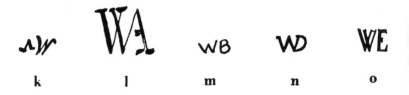

k   l   m   n   o

(**k**) ROUEN, France. Michel Vallet, potter. Fayence. 1757 (**l**) APT, France. Fayence. Est. 1728. (**m**) COBRIDGE, Great Britain. W. Brownfield, potter. 1836. (**n**) HOLLAND. De Drie Klokken (The Three Bells). Fayence. Delft. 1764. (**o**) BERLIN, Germany. Wegeley, founder. Porcelain. 1751.

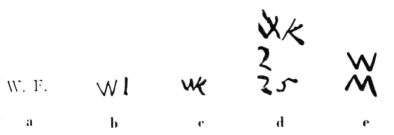

W. F.

a   b   c   d   e

(**a**) BRISTOL, Great Britain. Pottery. 1853. (**b**) CHELSEA, Great Britain. Porcelain. 1745-1784. (**c**) HOLLAND. De Drie Porceleyne Fleschen (The Three Porcelain Bottles). Fayence. Delft. 1697. (**d**) HOLLAND. Fayence. Delft. 1663. (**e**) WORCESTER, Great Britain. Porcelain. Est. 1751.

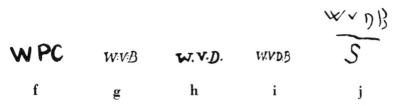

f   g   h   i   j

(**f**) WORCESTER, Great Britain. Hard paste. Est. 1751. (**g**) HOLLAND. De Twee Wildemans (The Two Savages). Fayence. Delft. 1750. (**h**) HOLLAND. De Boot (The Boat). Fayence. Delft. 1707. (**i**) HOLLAND. De Fortuyn (The Fortune). Fayence. Delft. 1764. (**j**) HOLLAND. De Fortuyn (The Fortune). Fayence. Delft. 1759.

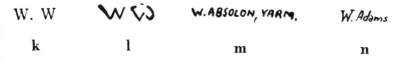

k   l   m   n

(**k**) GREAT BRITAIN. Slipware. 1749. (**l**) HOLLAND. De Boot (The Boat). Fayence. Delft. 1707. (**m**) YARMOUTH, Great Britain. Absolon, enameler. Circa 1800. (**n**) TUNSTALL, Great Britain. William Adams. Pottery. Impressed. 1805.

W.ADAMS & Co.   W. ADAMS & SONS   W. ADAMS & SONS
                                                STOKE.UPON.TRENT

      a   **b**   **c**

(**a**) TUNSTALL, Great Britain. William Adams, potter. Pottery.
Impressed. 1787. (**b**) STOKE-ON-TRENT, Great Britain. W.
Adams, potter. Circa 1825. (**c**) STOKE-ON-TRENT, Great Britain.
W. Adams, potter. Pottery. Impressed. Circa 1850.

WAGONER BROS
  VANPORT
    PA.   W.A.GRAY & SONS   WAIT & RICKETTS
                                                 SPRINGFIELD, O.

    d   **e**   **f**

(**d**) VANPORT, Pennsylvania, U.S.A. Wagoner Brothers. Impressed. Circa 1865. (**e**) PORTBELLO, Scotland. Est. 1770 (**f**)
SPRINGFIELD, Ohio, U.S.A. Wait and Ricketts. Impressed. Circa
1870.

WALDORF   WALTER ORCUTT & CO.   WARNE'
MERCER CHINA   ASHFIELD, MASS.   Walton   S.AMBOY
                                                             N.JERSEY

  g   **h**   **i**   **j**

(**g**) TRENTON, New Jersey, U.S.A. Mercer Pottery Company. Est.
1868. (**h**) ASHFIELD, Massachusetts, U.S.A. Walter Orcutt and
Company. Impressed. Circa 1850. (**i**) BURSLEM, Great Britain.
John Walton, potter. Earthernware. 18th-19th century. (**j**) SOUTH
AMBOY, New Jersey, U.S.A. Thomas Warne. Circa 1800.

WARNE & LETTS
S. AMBOY
N. JERSY

WARWICK
-SEMI-
PORCELAIN

WASHINGTON
KTOK
CHINA

W. & B.

a   b   c   d

(a) SOUTH AMBOY, New Jersey, U.S.A. Warne and Letts. Circa
1805. (b) WHEELING, West Virginia, U.S.A. Warwick China
Company. Est. 1887. (c) EAST LIVERPOOL, Ohio, U.S.A.
Knowles, Taylor, and Knowles. Est. 1854. (d) WEDGWOOD,
Great Britain. Wedgwood and Bentley. Earthernware. 1769-1780.

WB&S

W. BULLOCK
ROSEVILLE, O.

W. BURTON
CODNOR PARK

W. DIXON

e   f   g   h

(e) COBRIDGE, Great Britain. W. Brownfield, potter. 1836. (f)
ROSEVILLE, Ohio, U.S.A. W. Bullock. Impressed. Circa 1875.
(g) GREAT BRITAIN. W. Burton. 1821-30. (h) SUNDERLAND,
Great Britain. W. Dixon, potter. 18th-19th century.

WEBSTER & SEYMOUR
HARTFORD

Wedgwood

WEDGWOOD

Wedgwood &
Bentley

i   j   k   l

(i) HARTFORD, Connecticut, U.S.A. Webster and Seymour. Impressed. 1857-1873. (j) ETRURIA, Great Britain. Wedgwood, factory. Pottery. Impressed. 1771. (k) ETRURIA, Great Britain.
Wedgwood, factory. Pottery, porcelain. Impressed on pottery, 1771;
printed red, blue, gold on porcelain, 1769-present. (l) ETRURIA,
Great Britain. Wedgwood, factory. Wedgwood and Bentley, owners.
Pottery. Incised. 1769-1780.

Wedgwood & Co.
Ferrybridge

WEDGWOOD & CO

WEDGWOOD
ENGLAND

a

b

c

(a-b) FERRYBRIDGE, Great Britain. Ralph Wedgwood, owner. Stoneware, cream-colored ware. Impressed. 1796-1800. **(c)** ETRURIA, Great Britain. Wedgwood, factory. Pottery. After 1891.

Wedgwood
Eturia
England

Wedgwood & Sons

WEDGWOOD

d

e

f

(d) ETRURIA, Great Britain. Wedgwood, factory. Pottery. After 1891. **(e)** ETRURIA, Great Britain. Wedgwood, factory. Pottery. 1790. **(f)** ETRURIA, Great Britain. Wedgwood, factory. Pottery. Impressed. After 1780.

WEEKS, COOK,
& WEEKS

W.E.P.CO.
CHINA

WEST END
POTTERY CO.

WHITE & WOOD

g

h

i

j

(g) AKRON, Ohio, U.S.A. Weeks, Cook, and Weeks. Circa 1882. **(h)** EAST LIVERPOOL, Ohio, U.S.A. West End Pottery Company. Circa 1893-1910. **(i)** EAST LIVERPOOL, Ohio, U.S.A. West End Pottery Company. Est. 1893. **(j)** BINGHAMTON, New York, U.S.A. White and Wood. Impressed. 1850.

W.H. Lehew & Co.
Strasburg, VA   **WIEN**   **WIENER**   WILLIAM AND GEORGE TAYLOR

   a   b   c   d

(a) STRASBURG, Virginia, U.S.A. Lehew and Company. Impressed. Est. 1885. (b) BUDWEIS, Germany. Porcelain. 1818. (c) BUDWEIS, Germany. Porcelain. 1846+. (d) GREAT BRITAIN. William and George Taylor. Slipware. 1707.

Williams & Reppert
Greensboro
PA.

William Ellis Tucker
China Manufacturer
Philadelphia
1725

WILLIAM • SANS

   e   f   g

(e) GREENSBORO, Pennsylvania, U.S.A. Williams and Peppert. Impressed, blue. Circa 1875. (f) PHILADELPHIA, Pennsylvania, U.S.A. W. E. Tucker. Overglaze. Circa 1828. (g) BURSLEM, Great Britain. Staffordshire. Impressed. 1670.

William • Jalov   WINCANTON   WOLFE & HAMILTON STOKE

   h   i   j

(h) GREAT BRITAIN. Slipware. Circa 1675. (i) BRISTOL, Great Britain. Wincanton, factory. Earthernware. Est. 17th century. (j) STOKE-ON-TRENT, Great Britain. Wolfe and Hamilton, potters. Painted red. 18th-19th century.

WOOD & CALDWELL

WM E WARNER
WEST TROY
N.Y.

W.P.P.Co.
S.-MI-PORCELAIN

W.GOULDING
June 20.th 1770

a   b   c   d

(a) BURSLEM, Great Britain. Staffordshire. Impressed. 1790.
(b) WEST TROY, New York, U.S.A. William Warner. Circa 1850.
(c) WELLSVILLE, Ohio, U.S.A. Pioneer Pottery Company. 1896-1900. (d) ISLEWORTH, Great Britain. Richard and William Goulding, potters. Slipware. 1760.

W.MARTEEN

Wolfe & Hamilton
STOKE

WOMELSDORF

WOOD
POTTER
DAYTON
O.

e   f   g   h

(e) PENNSYLVANIA, U.S.A. W. Marteen. Circa 1875. . (f) STOKE-ON-TRENT, Great Britain. Wolfe and Hamilton, potters. 18th-19th century. (g) WOMELSDORF, Pennsylvania, U.S.A. Willoughby Smith. Impressed. 1864-1905. (h) DAYTON, Ohio, U.S.A. Wood. Impressed. Circa 1870.

Woronzou and Co.   W.RICH   W.SMITH

W.S. & Cos
Wedgewood

i   j   k   l

(i) LIANELLY, Wales. Earthenware. Circa 1870. (j) GREAT BRITAIN. W. Rich, potter. Slipware. 1700. (k) WOMELSDORF, Pennsylvania, U.S.A. Willoughby Smith. Impressed. 1864-1905. (l) STOCKTON-ON-TEES, Great Britain. William Smith and Company. Cream-colored ware. 1826-1848.

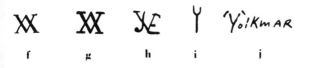

a   b   c   d   e

(a) ROSEVILLE, Ohio, U.S.A. W. S. Mayers, Painted blue. Circa 1870. (b) HANLEY, Great Britain. Circa 1820. (c) HOLLAND. Willem van der Velde, artist. Fayence. Delft. Painted color. 1660. (d) DALLWITZ, Bohemia. W. W. Lorenz. Cream-colored earthenware. 1832-1850. (e) EAST LIVERPOOL, Ohio, U.S.A. Knowles, Taylor and Knowles. Est. 1854.

XX   XX   XE   Y   'Volkmar

f   g   h   i   j

Section X-Y
See also Sections
V, W, Lines

(f-g) VAUX, France. Hard paste. 1769; or BORDEAUX, France. Porcelain. 1781-87. (h) HOLLAND. De Griekse A (The Greek A). Fayence. Delft. 1674. (i) THURINGIA, Germany. Rudolstadt, factory. Hard paste. Painted color. 1758. (j) BEDFORD, New York, U.S.A. Leon Volkmar. 1930.

Z   Z   ZR   Z:DEX   ZOAR

k   l   m   n   o

Section Z
See also Section
Lines

(k-l-m) ZURICH, Switzerland. Pottery, hard paste. Painted blue. After 1763. (n) HOLLAND. De Drie Astonne (The Three Ash Barrels). Fayence. Delft. 1720. (o) ZOAR, Ohio, U.S.A. Zoar Pottery. Impressed. Circa 1850.

SECTION **ANCHOR**
See also Sections
Arrow, Lines

a   b   c   d   e   f

(a) LEEDS, Great Britain. Cream-colored ware. Painted. Est. 1760.
(b) HOLLAND. De Ster (The Star). Fayence. Delft. 1705. (c-d)
SCEAUX, France. Pottery, soft paste. Painted blue. 1748. (e-f)
CHELSEA, Great Britain. Soft paste. Painted gold, red, brown,
purple. 1745-1784.

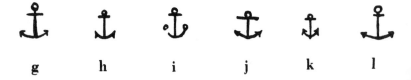

g   h   i   j   k   l

(g) WORCESTER, Great Britain. Painted red. Est. 1751. (h-i)
CHELSEA, Great Britain. Soft paste. Painted red or gold. 1745-
1784. (j) SCEAUX, France. Pottery, soft paste. Painted blue. 1784.
(k-l) CHELSEA, Great Britain. Porcelain. 1745-1784.

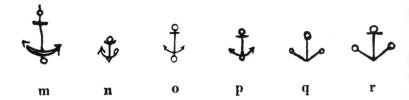

m   n   o   p   q   r

(m) CHELSEA, Great Britain. Porcelain. 1754-1784. (n) SCEAUX,
France. Fayence, porcelain. After 1775. (o) Mettlach, Ger-
many. Glazed earthenware. Circa 1836-circa 1850. (p) POPPELS-
DORF, Germany. Fayence. Impressed. Est. 1755. (q-r) CHELSEA,
Great Britain. Soft paste. Painted gold, red. 1745-1784.

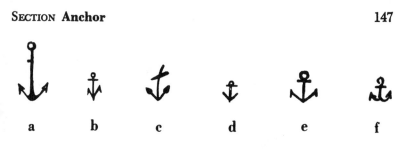

a   b   c   d   e   f

(**a**) SAVONA, Italy. Fayence. 17th-18th century. (**b-c**) CHELSEA, Great Britain. Porcelain. Underglaze blue, gold. 1750-1769. (**d**) DERBY, Great Britain. Porcelain. 1770-1780. (**e**) CHELSEA, Great Britain. Porcelain. Underglaze blue, gold. 1750-1769. (**f**) BUEN RETIRO, Spain. Soft paste. 1759-1808.

g   h   i   j   k   l

(**g**) VENICE, Italy. Hard paste. Painted red. 1765. (**h**) BOW, Great Britain. Hard paste. Painted red, blue. Est. 1744. (**i**) CHELSEA, Great Britain. Porcelain. Underglaze blue, gold. 1750-1769. (**j**) CINCINNATI, Ohio, U.S.A. Rookwood Pottery Company. Before 1883. (**k-l**) CHELSEA, Great Britain. Soft paste. Painted gold, red. 1745.

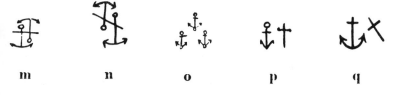

m   n   o   p   q

(**m-n**) CHELSEA, Great Britain. Soft paste. Painted gold, red. 1745-1784. (**o**) COLOGNE, Germany. Eugen Cremer, potter. Pottery. Painted blue. 1800. (**p-q**) BOW, Great Britain. Soft paste. Painted red, brown. 1760-1780.

a b c d e

(a) CHELSEA, Great Britain. Soft paste. Painted gold, red. 1745-1784. (b) BOW, Great Britain. Soft paste. Painted red, blue, brown. 1760-1780. (c) CHELSEA, Great Britain. Soft paste. 1745-1784. (d-e) BOW, Great Britain. Soft paste. Painted red, brown. 1760-1780.

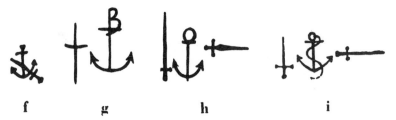

f g h i

(f-g-h-i) BOW, Great Britain. Soft paste. Painted red, blue, brown. 1760-1780.

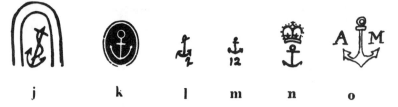

j k l m n o

(j) BOW, Great Britain. Porcelain. 1745-1770. (k-l-m) CHELSEA, Great Britain. Soft paste. Underglaze blue, red, blue, purple. 1749-1756. (n) DERBY, Great Britain. Soft paste. Painted gold, lilac, red. 1777. (o) ARMAND MARSEILLE, Germany. Circa 1910-1919.

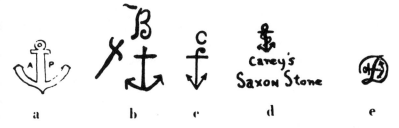

a   b   c   d   e

(**a**) TRENTON, New Jersey, U.S.A. Anchor Pottery Company. Printed. Circa 1895. (**b**) BOW, Great Britain. Porcelain. 1745-1770. (**c**) SHROPSHIRE, Great Britain. Coalport or Coalbrookdale factory. Porcelain. Painted blue. Est. 1799. (**d**) FENTON, Great Britain. Impressed. 1845. (**e**) DERBY-CHELSEA, Great Britain. Soft paste. Painted gold or red. 1770.

f   g   h   i   j

(**f**) DERBY-CHELSEA, Great Britain. Porcelain. Painted blue, lilac, gold. 1770. (**g**) LONGPORT, Great Britain. John Davenport, potter. Earthenware, porcelain. 1793-1882. (**h**) LONGPORT, Great Britain. John Davenport, potter. Earthenware, porcelain. Impressed. 1793-1882. (**i**) DERBY, Great Britain. Porcelain. 1745. (**j**) NEWCASTLE, Great Britain. Thomas Fell, potter. Impressed. 18th-19th century.

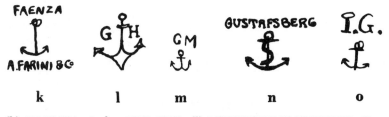

k   l   m   n   o

(**k**) FAENZA, Italy. 1850-1878. (**l**) NEUHOLDENSLEBEN, Germany. Hubbe Brothers. Circa 1882-1898. (**m**) VENICE, Italy. Giovanni Marcone. Soft paste. Painted gold, color. 1700. (**n**) GUSTAFSBERG, Sweden. Fayence. 1839-1860. (**o**) VENICE, Italy. Porcelain. Painted red. 1765-1811.

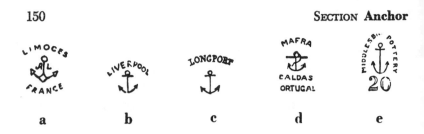

a   b   c   d   e

(a) LIMOGES, France. Porcelain. 1855+. (b) LIVERPOOL, Great Britain. Cream-colored earthenware. 1796-1833. (c) LONGPORT, Great Britain. John Davenport, potter. Earthenware, porcelain. Impressed. 1793-1882. (d) CALDAS, Portugal. Mafra, maker. Pottery. Impressed. 1800. (e) MIDDLESBOROUGH, Great Britain. Pottery. Printed or impressed. 1800.

f   g   h   i   j

(f) CHELSEA, Great Britain. Porcelain. Underglaze blue, purple, blue. 1752-1756. (g) BOW, Great Britain. Porcelain. 1745-1770. (h) LONGTON, Great Britain. 1885. (i) SEINE, France. Sceaux, factory. Porcelain, fayence. 1748-1794. (j) SEINE, France. Sceaux, factory. Porcelain, fayence. 1775.

k   l   m   n   o

(k-l) WORCESTER, Great Britain. Richard Holdship, decorator. Hard paste. Painted color. 1756-1774. (m) COBRIDGE, Great Britain. After 1891. (n) TRENTON, New Jersey, U.S.A. Thomas Maddock and Sons. Est. 1882. (o) BUEN RETIRO, Spain. Soft paste. 1759-1808.

SECTION **ANIMAL
AND FISH**
See also Sections
**Circle and Sign,
Crown and Shield,
Shield, Square**

a b c d

(**a**) DEDHAM, Massachusetts, U.S.A. Dedham Pottery Company.
1897. (**b**) FURSTENBERG, Germany. Porcelain. Est. 1747. (**c**)
HESSE CASSEL, Germany. Hard paste. Painted blue. 1763. (**d**)
OIRON, France. 16th century.

e f g h i

(**e-f**) AMSTERDAM, Holland. Hard paste. Painted blue 1772. (**g**)
FRANKENTHAL, Bavaria. Hard paste. Painted blue. 1754. (**h**)
SYRACUSE, New York, U.S.A. Onondaga Pottery Company. Est.
1871. (**i**) TRENTON, New Jersey, U.S.A. Fell and Thropp Company. 19th century.

ROBLIN

ROBLIN

Baguley
Rockingham Works.

*Rockingham Works
Bramield*

j k l m

(**j-k**) SAN FRANCISCO, California, U.S.A. Irelan Linna. Est. 1899.
(**l-m**) SWINTON, Great Britain. Rockingham, factory. Hard paste.
Painted red. 1824.

18 EB 50
FOLEY BONE CHINA
MADE IN ENGLAND

E. BRAIN & CO., LTD.

THE C.C.T.P. CO.

TRADE   MARK

SEMI-GRANITE.

HC

a   b   c   d

(**a**) STOKE-ON-TRENT, Great Britain. Foley China, E. Brain and Company. Porcelain. 20th century. (**b**) EAST LIVERPOOL, Ohio, U.S.A. Taylor, Smith and Taylor Company. Est. 1899. (**c**) EAST LIVERPOOL, Ohio, U.S.A. C. C. Thompson Pottery Company. Est. 1888. (**d**) HESSE CASSEL, Germany. Hard paste. Underglaze blue. 1763.

IRON STONE CHINA
K.T&K.

BUFFALO POTTERY
1907

e   f

(**e**) EAST LIVERPOOL, Ohio, U.S.A. Knowles, Taylor, and Knowles. Est. 1854. (**f**) BUFFALO, New York, U.S.A. Buffalo Pottery Company. Circa 1905.

ADAMS
ENGLAND

BARKER
POTTERY

BELLEEK

TRADE   MARK
WEDGWOOD & CO.

g   h   i   j

(**g**) TUNSTALL, Great Britain. Printed. After 1891. (**h**) SWINTON, Great Britain. Don Pottery. Printed, impressed. 19th century. (**i**) IRELAND. Belleek, factory. Painted color. Circa 1863-1891. (**j**) BURSLEM, Great Britain. Ralph Wedgwood, owner. Cream-colored ware. 1862-1890.

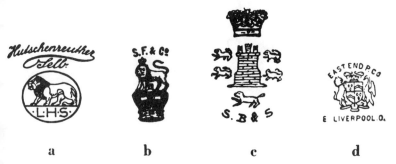

a　　　　　b　　　　　c　　　　　d

(a) GERMANY, Lorenz Hutschenreuther. Hard paste. Est. 1864.
(b) STOKE-ON-TRENT, Great Britain. S. Fielding and Company.
19th century. (c) LONGTON, Great Britain. 19th century. (d)
EAST LIVERPOOL, Ohio, U.S.A. East End Pottery Company. 19th
century.

e　　　　　f　　　　　g　　　　　h

(e) BEAVER FALLS, Pennsylvania, U.S.A. Est. 1881. (f)
PHOENIXVILLE, Pennsylvania, U.S.A. Est. 1894. (g) LIVER-
POOL, Ohio, U.S.A. John Goodwin. Est. 1844. (h) STEUBEN-
VILLE, Ohio, U.S.A. Steubenville Pottery Company. Est. 1879.

i　　　　　j　　　　　k　　　　　l

(i-j-k) EAST LIVERPOOL, Ohio, U.S.A. Vodrey Brothers. Circa
1875. (l) WORCESTER, Great Britain. Hard paste. 1820-1840.

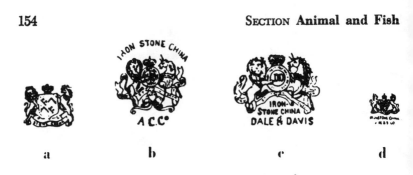

a   b   c   d

(a) WELLSVILLE, Ohio, U.S.A. Pioneer Pottery Company. Circa 1890. (b) TRENTON, New Jersey, U.S.A. American Crockery Company. 1890. (c) TRENTON, New Jersey, U.S.A. Prospect Hill Pottery Company. Circa 1880 + . (d) TRENTON, New Jersey, U.S.A. Glasgow Pottery Company. Circa 1895.

e   f   g   h

(e) TRENTON, New Jersey, U.S.A. Glasgow Pottery Company. Circa 1880. (f) JERSEY CITY, New Jersey, U.S.A. Rouse and Turner. Est. 1875. (g) PEORIA, Illinois, U.S.A. Peoria Pottery Company. Circa 1888-1890. (h) TRENTON, New Jersey, U.S.A. Empire Pottery Company. 1863-circa 1884.

i   j   k   l

(i) EVANSVILLE, Indiana, U.S.A. Crown Pottery Company. ca. 1891. (j) NEW YORK, New York, U.S.A. New York City Pottery Company. 1871. (k) TRENTON, New Jersey, U.S.A. East Trenton Pottery Company. Circa 1888-1905 + . (l) EAST LIVERPOOL, Ohio, U.S.A. East End Pottery Company. 1894-1901, 1903-1907.

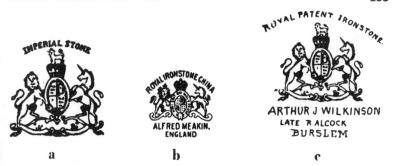

a   b   c

(a) SHELTON, Great Britain. After 1850. (b) TUNSTALL, Great Britain. Est. 1897+. (c) BURSLEM, Great Britain. 1885-1964+.

d   e   f   g

(d) TRENTON, New Jersey, U.S.A. Glasgow Pottery Company. Circa 1895. (e) TRENTON, New Jersey, U.S.A. Ott and Brewer. Circa 1863+. (f) WHEELING, West Virginia, U.S.A. Wheeling Pottery Company. 1880-1886. (g) STEUBENVILLE, Ohio, U.S.A. Steubenville Pottery Company. Circa 1900+.

h   i   j   k

(h) BURSLEM, Great Britain. T. and R. Boote. Circa 1900. (i) EAST LIVERPOOL, Ohio, U.S.A. William Brunt Pottery Company. Circa 1894. (j) TORONTO, Ohio, U.S.A. American China Company. 1894-1910. (k) CINCINNATI, Ohio, U.S.A. Brockman Pottery Company. (1888-1912).

a   b   c   d

(a) ELIZABETH, New Jersey, U.S.A. L. B. Beerbower (Beer-bauer) Company. Impressed. After 1880. (b) TRENTON, New Jersey, U.S.A. Glasgow Pottery Company. 1875. (c) TRENTON, New Jersey, U.S.A. Ott and Brewer. Circa 1875. (d) TRENTON. New Jersey, Prospect Hill Pottery Company. 1879 +.

e   f   g   h

(e) TRENTON, New Jersey, U.S.A. Prospect Hill Pottery Company. 1876 +. (f) TRENTON, New Jersey, U.S.A. Willetts Manufacturing Company. 1879-1884. (g-h) PEORIA, Illinois, U.S.A. Peoria Pottery Company. Circa 1888-1890.

i   j   k   l

(i) TRENTON, New Jersey, U.S.A. Fell and Thropp Company. Circa 1900 (j) TRENTON, New Jersey, U.S.A. East Trenton Pottery Company. Est. 1888. (k) TRENTON, New Jersey, U.S.A. Cook Pottery Company. Circa 1893-circa 1926. (l) LILLE, France. Hard Paste. Stenciled and painted red. 1784.

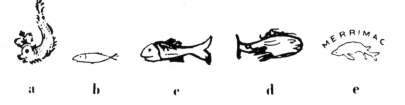

a b c d e

(a) LILLE, France. Hard paste. Stenciled and painted red. 1784.
(b-c) NYON, Switzerland. Hard paste. Underglaze blue. 1780.
(d) SAVONA, Italy. Pescetto, potter. Fayence. 17th-18th century.
(e) NEWBURYPORT, Massachusetts, U.S.A. Merrimac Ceramic
Company. 1902-1908.

f g

(f) NYON, Switzerland. Hard paste. Underglaze blue. 1780. (g)
SEVILLE, Spain. Glazed pottery. 19th century.

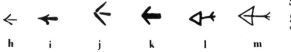

h i j k l m

SECTION **ARROW**

See also Sections
T, Anchor, Lines

(h) LEEDS, Great Britain. Pottery. Impressed. Est. 1774. (i)
CAUGHLEY, Great Britain. Hard paste. Painted blue. 1754. (j)
BRISTOL, Great Britain. Pottery, porcelain. Painted blue, gold.
18th century. (k) GERMANY. Painted blue. 19th century (l)
BOW, Great Britain. Porcelain. 1750. (m) DERBY, Great Britain.
Porcelain. Circa 1830.

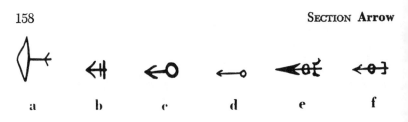

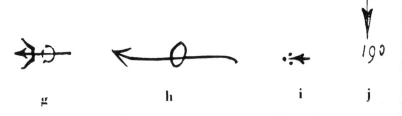

(**a**) DERBY, Great Britain. Porcelain. 1745-1848. (**b-c**) BOW, Great Britain. Porcelain. Est. 1750. (**d**) PLYMOUTH, Great Britain. Hard paste. Painted blue. 1768-1770. (**e-f**) BOW, Great Britain. Porcelain. Est. 1750.

(**g-h**) BOW, Great Britain. Soft paste. Painted blue. Est. 1750. (**i**) STOKE-ON-TRENT, Great Britain. Minton, factory. Hard paste. Painted gold, color. 1851. (**j**) LOWESTOFT, Great Britain. Robert Allen, painter. Porcelain. 1757-1780.

(**k**) YARMOUTH, Great Britain. W. Absolon, enameler. Porcelain, earthenware. Impressed. 19th century. (**l**) LEEDS, Great Britain. Pottery. Impressed. Est. 1774. (**m-n**) PARIS, France. Rue de la Roquette, factory. Hard paste. Painted blue. 1774. (**o**) PARIS, France. La Courtille, factory. Hard paste. Underglaze blue, incised. 1771.

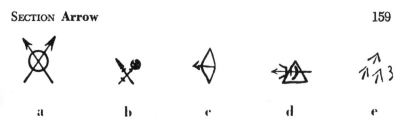

a   b   c   d   e

(**a**) BOW, Great Britain. Soft paste. Painted blue. Est. 1750. (**b**) NYMPHENBURG, Germany. Impressed or incised. 18th century. (**c-d**) BOW, Great Britain. Soft paste. Painted blue. Est. 1750. (**e**) HOLLAND. Fayence. Delft. Painted blue. 1764.

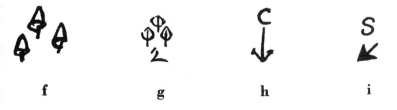

f   g   h   i

(**f-g**) HOLLAND. De Drie Klokken (The Three Bells). Fayence. Delft. Est. 1671. (**h-i**) CAUGHLEY, Great Britain. Porcelain. Est. 1750.

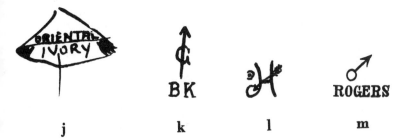

j   k   l   m

(**j**) HANLEY, Great Britain. Impressed or printed. Circa 1870. (**k**) GIESSHUBEL, Germany. Porcelain, earthenware. Est. 1803. (**l**) EAST LIVERPOOL, Ohio, U.S.A. Harker Pottery Company. Printed. 1890. (**m**) DALE HALL, Great Britain. John and James Rogers, potters. Staffordshire. 1786-1842.

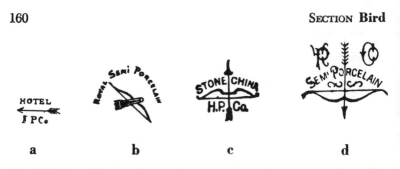

a   b   c   d

(a) PEORIA, Illinois, U.S.A. Peoria Pottery Company. 1889-1890.
(b) SHELTON, Great Britain. Job Ridgways, potter. Porcelain, stone
china. 1794-1802. (c) EAST LIVERPOOL, Ohio, U.S.A. Harker Pottery Company. Printed. 1890-circa 1900. (d) EAST LIVERPOOL,
Ohio, U.S.A. Harker Pottery Company. Printed. 1890.

Section **BIRD**
See also Sections
**Circle and Sign,
Crown and Circle,
Crown and Shield,
Shield, Square**

e   f   g   h   i   j

(e) GREENPOINT, New York, U.S.A. Union Porcelain Works.
1878. (f) BROOKLYN, New York, U.S.A. Union Porcelain Works.
Est. 1874. (g) WHEELING, West Virginia, U.S.A. Wheeling Pottery Company. Est. 1879. (h-i-j) ANSBACH, Bavaria. Hard paste.
Painted blue. Est. 1706.

k   l   m   n   o

(k) ANSBACH, Bavaria. Hard paste. Est. 1706. (l) ST. PETERS-
BURG, Russia. Porcelain. Circa 1743. (m) CHARLOTTENBERG,
Germany. Porcelain. 1760. (n) ROYAL BERLIN, Germany. Est.
1751. (o) THE HAGUE, Holland. Fayence. 1775.

(a) THE HAGUE, Holland, Fayence. Painted blue. 1775. (b) THE HAGUE, Holland. Fayence. 1775. (c) THE HAGUE, Holland. Fayence. Painted blue. 1775. (d) LIVERPOOL, Great Britain. Herculaneum. Circa 1833. (e) FENTON, Great Britain. Hulme and Christie. 19th century.

(f) LIVERPOOL, Great Britain. Herculaneum. Circa 1833. (g) AMSTERDAM, Holland. Possibly at Arnheim. J. V. Kerckofi, artist. 1755-1770. (h) AMSTERDAM, Holland. Fayence. Circa 1780. (i) FLORENCE, Italy. Cantagalli. Fayence. Late 19th century. (j) BURSLEM, Great Britain. Charles Ford. 19th century.

(k) SOUTH AMBOY, New Jersey, U.S.A. Swan Hill Pottery. Hanks and Fish. 1849. (l) TUNSTALL, Great Britain. James Beech. Circa 1845. (m) TUNSTALL, Great Britain. Boulton, Machin, and Tennant. 1889-1899. (n) LIMOGES, France. 1842-1898.

a   b   c   d   e

(a) EAST LIVERPOOL, Ohio, U.S.A. Union Potteries Company. 1894-1905. (b) BOSTON, Massachusetts, U.S.A. New England Pottery Company. 1854-1914. (c) CROOKSVILLE, Ohio, U.S.A. Crooksville China Company. Late 19th century. (d) EAST LIVERPOOL, Ohio, U.S.A. Homer Laughlin China Company. 1877-present. (e) CORONA, New York, U.S.A. American Art Ceramic Company. 1901-circa 1909.

f   g   h   i

(f) EAST LIVERPOOL, Ohio, U.S.A. Potters Cooperative Company. Circa 1896. (g) TRENTON, New Jersey, U.S.A. Glasgow Pottery Company. John Moses and Sons. 1878+. (h) SEVRES, France. 1852. (i) SEVRES, France. Hard paste. Painted red. Circa 1810.

j   k   l   m   n

(j) LIVERPOOL, Ohio, U.S.A. John E. Goodwin. Printed. Stoneware. 1844-1853. (k) NEW YORK, New York, U.S.A. East Morrisania China Works. Circa 1893. (l) NEW MILFORD, Connecticut, U.S.A. New Milford Pottery Company. 1892-1903. (m) EAST LIVERPOOL, Ohio, U.S.A. Knowles, Taylor, and Knowles. Circa 1880-circa 1890. (n) STOKE-ON-TRENT, Great Britain. W. H. Goss. 1862-1903.

a   b   c   d

(a) EAST LIVERPOOL, Ohio, U.S.A. Vodrey Brothers. 1857-1885.
(b) TRENTON, New Jersey, U.S.A. American Crockery Company.
Circa 1890. (c) STOKE-ON-TRENT, Great Britain. T. Mayer. Circa
1829. (d) CINCINNATI, Ohio, U.S.A. Rookwood Potteries. 1880-
1882.

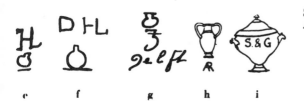

SECTION **BOWL
AND URN**

e   f   g   h   i

(e-f) HOLLAND. De Porcelyn Fles (The Porcelain Bottle). Fayence. Delft. 1770. (g) HOLLAND. Thoovt and Labouchere. Fayence. Delft. 1895. (h) ALT-ROHLAU, Germany. Pottery, porcelain. Est. 1813. (i) GERMANY. Schemlzer and Gericke. Circa
1886-circa 1931.

j   k   l   m

(j) LIMOGES, France. Porcelain. Circa 1875. (k-l) WEDG-
WOOD, Great Britain. Porcelain. Printed black, color. After 1878.
(m) BEAVER FALLS, Pennsylvania, U.S.A. Mayer Pottery Company. Before 1864.

a   b   c   d

(**a**) BRISTOL, Great Britain. Hard paste. Printed blue. 1800. (**b**) JERSEY CITY, New Jersey, U.S.A. American Pottery Manufacturing Company. 1833-1840. (**c**) SHELTON, Great Britain. Job Ridgways, potter. 1794. (**d**) GREAT BRITAIN. Podmore, Walker, and Company. Circa 1755.

SECTION **CIRCLE AND SIGN**
See also Sections
O, Crown and Circle, Shield

e   f   g   h   i

(**e**) FAENZA, Italy. Fayence. 16th century. (**f**) COPENHAGEN, Denmark. Fayence. Iron porcelain. 1929. (**g**) STOKE-ON-TRENT, Great Britain. Spode, factory. Impressed. 1784. (**h**) FAENZA, Italy. Fayence. 16th century. (**i**) HOCHST, Germany. Hard paste. Painted blue, red, gold. 1750-1765.

j   k   l   m   n

(**j**) TYLERSPORT, Pennsylvania, U.S.A. Michael School (Scholl). Impressed. Circa 1830. (**k-l**) FAENZA, Italy. Fayence. 16th century. (**m-n**) VALENCIA, Spain. Fayence. 16th century.

a   b   c   d   e

(**a-b**) WORCESTER, Great Britain. Hard paste. Underglaze blue. Est. 1751. (**c-d-e**) FAENZA, Italy. Fayence. 16th century.

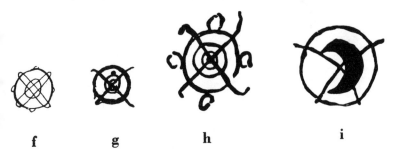

f   g   h   i

(**f-g-h-i**) FAENZA, Italy. Fayence. 16th century.

j   k   l   m   n

(**j**) BOW, Great Britain. Soft paste. Est. 1750. (**k**) HOCHST, Germany. Porcelain, fayence. Painted gold, color. Est. 1746. (**l**) WORCESTER, Great Britain. Kerr and Binns. Porcelain. 1852-1862. (**m**) SEGOVIA, Spain. 19th century. (**n**) SARREGUEMINES, France. Fayence, porcelain. Est. 1770.

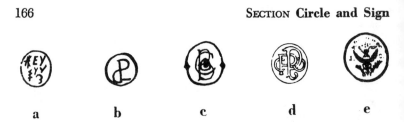

a   **b**   **c**   **d**   **e**

(a) HOLLAND, De Romeyn (The Roman). Fayence, Delft. 1675.
(b) WOODBRIDGE, New Jersey, U.S.A. C. L. and H. A. Poillon.
1901-1928. (c) TRENTON, New Jersey, U.S.A. Ott and Brewer.
Circa 1875. (d) PEORIA, Illinois, U.S.A. Peoria Pottery Company.
Circa 1885. (e) NEW YORK CITY, New York, U.S.A. Carr and Morrison. Circa 1875.

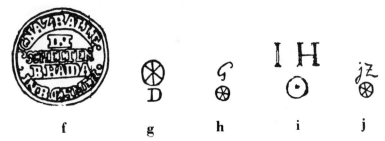

f   **g**   **h**   **i**   **j**

(f) GERMANY. Porcelain. Circa 1855. (g-h) HOCHST, Germany.
Fayence, hard paste. Painted blue, red, gold. 1750-1765. (i) SHELTON, Great Britain. Joshua Heath, potter. Circa 1760. (j)
HOCHST, Germany. Fayence, hard paste. Painted blue, red, gold.
1750.

k   **l**   **m**   **n**   **o**

(k) HOLLAND, De Fortuyn (The Fortune). Fayence. Delft.
Painted blue. 1691. (l) CHELSEA, Massachusetts, U.S.A. Low Art
Tile Company. Est. 1888. (m) WHEELING, West Virginia, U.S.A.
Wheeling Pottery Company. Est. 1879. (n) HOLLAND. Fayence.
Delft. Painted blue. 1680. (o) JERSEY CITY, New Jersey, U.S.A.
Jersey City Pottery Company. Est. 1840.

a   b   c   d   e

(**a**) JERSEY CITY, New Jersey, U.S.A. American Pottery Company. Est. 1840. (**b-c**) TRENTON, New Jersey, U.S.A. Anchor Pottery Company. Printed. After 1894. (**d**) KITTANNING, Pennsylvania, U.S.A. Wick China Company. 19th century. (**e**) BALTIMORE, Maryland, U.S.A. Haynes, Bennett, and Company. After 1890.

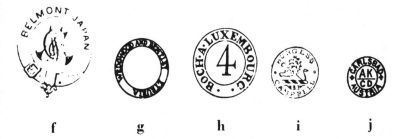

f   g   h   i   j

(**f**) MINTON, England. Hard paste. After 1868. (**g**) ETRURIA, Great Britain. Wedgwood and Bentley, factory. 1769-1780. (**h**) LUXEMBOURG, Belgium. Fayence. Est. 1767. (**i**) TRENTON, New Jersey, U.S.A. Burgess and Campbell. Impressed. Est. 1879. (**j**) GIESSHUBEL, Germany. Porcelain, fayence. Circa 1850.

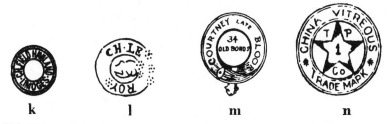

k   l   m   n

(**k**) LIMOGES, France. Charles Field Haviland Company. 1882. (**l**) CHOISY-LE-ROY, France. Hard Paste. Est. 1785. (**m**) DERBY, Great Britain. Porcelain. Est. 1745-1848. (**n**) TRENTON, New Jersey, U.S.A. Trenton Potteries Company. Est. 1865.

a   b   c   d   e

(**a**) SEVRES, France. Overglaze red. Year of decoration. 1872-1899.
(**b**) MONTPELLIER, France. Pottery. Impressed. 1800. (**c**)
SEVRES, France. Red. Year of gilding. 1872-1899. (**d**) TRENTON,
New Jersey, U.S.A. Cook Pottery Company. 1894-1900. (**e**) BALTI-
MORE, Maryland, U.S.A. D. F. Haynes and Company. Est. 1879.

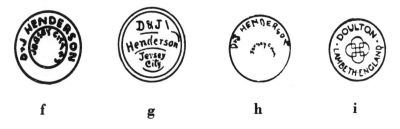

f   g   h   i

(**f**) WOODBRIDGE, New Jersey, U.S.A. Salamander Works. Im-
pressed. 1825-1900. (**g-h**) JERSEY CITY, New Jersey, U.S.A. Jersey
City Pottery Company. 1829-1833. (**i**) LAMBETH, Great Britain.
Doulton Company. After 1891.

j   k   l   m

(**j**) TRENTON, New Jersey, U.S.A. Cook Pottery Company. Circa
1900. (**k**) PHOENIXVILLE, Pennsylvania, U.S.A. Griffen, Smith,
and Hill. Impressed. Circa 1880. (**l**) BURSLEM, Great Britain.
Enoch Wood and Sons. 1790. (**m**) ILMENAU, Germany. Porcelain. 19th century.

a b c d

(a) PARIS, France. Jules-Joseph-Henri Brianchon & Gillet. Porcelain. 1864+. (b) GERMANY. Benedikt Brothers. 1884. (c) BURSLEM, Great Britain. E. F. Bodley and Company. Earthernware. After 1860. (d) TRENTON, New Jersey, U.S.A. Glasgow Pottery Company. Circa 1875.

e f g h i

(e) LIVERPOOL, Ohio, U.S.A. John Goodwin. Stoneware. Printed. Est. 1844. (f) GOTHA, Germany. Porcelain. Est. 1757. (g) ALTROHLAU, Germany. Cream-colored earthenware. Est. 1813. (h) TRENTON, New Jersey, U.S.A. Glasgow Pottery Company. 1863-1890. (i) KEENE, New Hampshire, U.S.A. Hampshire Pottery Company. Est. 1871.

j k l m n

(j) EAST LIVERPOOL, Ohio, U.S.A. Harker Pottery Company. Circa 1840. (k) HAVILAND, France. Porcelain. Green, brown, tan. 1880-1889. (l-m) HAVILAND, France. Whiteware. Painted green, reddish brown. 1879-1883. (n) JERSEY CITY, New Jersey, U.S.A. D. J. Henderson. Impressed. Circa 1830.

a   b   c   d

(a) LETTIN, Germany. Est. 1858. (b) EAST LIVERPOOL, Ohio,
U.S.A. Homer Laughlin China Company. Printed. Est. 1873. (c)
HANLEY, Great Britain. Humphrey Palmer. Staffordshire. Circa
1760. (d) WHEELING, West Virginia, U.S.A. Wheeling Pottery
Company. Est. 1879.

e   f   g   h   i

(e) WELLSVILLE, Ohio, U.S.A. Wellsville China Company. Est.
1879. (f) HANLEY, Great Britain. I. Neale. 1786. (g) PHOENIX-
VILLE, Pennsylvania, U.S.A. Beerbower and Griffen. Est. 1877.
(h) BALTIMORE, Maryland, U.S.A. Edwin Bennett. (Mark often
seen without circle.) 1856-1890. (i) POUGHKEEPSIE, New York,
U.S.A. Jacob Caire. Impressed. Circa 1850.

j   k   l   m   n

(j) WOOSTER, Ohio, U.S.A. Joseph Routson. Late 19th century.
(k) BUEN RETIRO, Spain. Hard paste. 1805. (l) BERLIN, Germany.
Soft paste. Painted blue. 1849-1870. (m) LAMBETH, Great Britain.
Doulton. Pottery. Circa 1873-circa 1914. (n) SEVRES, France.
Painted red. Circa 1890.

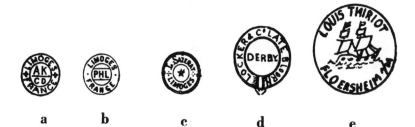

| a | b | c | d | e |

(**a-b-c**) LIMOGES, France. Hard paste. 1842-1898. (**d**) DERBY, Great Britain. William Locker, owner. Porcelain. 1848. (**e**) FLOR-SHEIM, Germany. Fayence. Est. 1773.

| f | g | h | i | j |

(**f**) SEVRES, France. Decorator's mark. Painted red. After 1940. (**g**) BALTIMORE, Maryland, U.S.A. D. F. Haynes and Company. Est. 1879. (**h**) STOKE-ON-TRENT, Great Britain. Minton, factory. 1870. (**i**) MONTPELLIER, France. Fayence. 1834. (**j**) SEVRES, France. Soft paste, hard paste. 1890.

| k | l | m | n | o |

(**k**) NEW CASTLE, Pennsylvania, U.S.A. New Castle Pottery Company. 19th century. (**l**) SHELTON, Great Britain. Fayence. Printed color. 1820. (**m**) ORLEANS, France. Hard paste. Circa 1800. (**n**) EAST LIVERPOOL, Ohio, U.S.A. Vodrey Brothers. Circa 1875. (**o**) DOCCIA, Italy. 18th-19th century.

a   b   c   d   e

(a) WELLSVILLE, Ohio, U.S.A. Wellsville China Company. Est. 1879. (b) TRENTON. New Jersey, U.S.A. Glasgow Pottery Company. Circa 1875. (c) TRENTON, New Jersey, U.S.A. American Art China Works. Est. 1891. (d) CINCINNATI, Ohio, U.S.A. Cincinnati Art Pottery Company. Est. 1879. (e) SEVRES, France. Hard paste. Painted red. 1850.

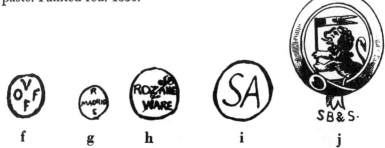

f   g   h   i   j

(f) URBINO, Italy. Pottery. 16th century. (g) BUEN RETIRO, Spain. Hard paste. Circa 1805. (h) ZANESVILLE, Ohio, U.S.A. Roseville Pottery Company. 19th century. (i) ST. AMAND LES EAUX, France. Soft paste. 1800. (j) SWINTON, Great Britain. Don Pottery. Impressed or printed blue. 19th century.

k   l   m   n   o

(k) GERMANY. Hornberg. Fayence. Late 19th century. (l) MOABIT, Germany. 1835. (m-n) SEVRES, France. Hard paste. Printed gold, blue, color. 1830-1848. (o) NEW CASTLE, Pennsylvania, U.S.A. Shenango China Company. 19th century.

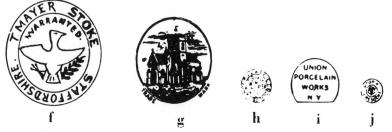

a   b   c   d   e

(a) EAST LIVERPOOL. Ohio, U.S.A. Smith-Phillips China· Company. Late 19th century. (b) LONGPORT, Great Britain. Stubbs and Kent. Circa 1805. (c) GERMANY. Fayence. 19th century. (d) Syracuse, New York, U.S.A. Onandaga Pottery Company. Est. 1871. (e) TILLOWITZ, Germany. Fayence, earthenware. Est. 1804.

f   g   h   i   j

(f) STOKE-ON-TRENT, Great Britain. T. Mayer, Circa 1830. (g) CHURCH GRESLEY, Great Britain. Porcelain. After 1875. (h) BEAVER FALLS, Pennsylvania, U.S.A. Mayer Pottery Company. Est. 1881. (i) BROOKLYN, New York, U.S.A. Union Porcelain Works. Est. 1875. (j) TRENTON, New Jersey, U.S.A. Crescent Pottery Company. Est. 1881.

k   l   m   n   o

(k) TILTONVILLE, Ohio, U.S.A. Vance Faience Company. Impressed. After 1880. (l) COLORADO SPRINGS, Colorado, U.S.A. Van Briggle Pottery Company. Est. 1901. (m) BALTIMORE, Maryland, U.S.A. Edwin Bennett. Circa 1875. (n) ETRURIA, Great Britain. Wedgwood and Bentley. Pottery and hard paste. Impressed. 1769-1780. (o) PEORIA, Illinois. Peoria Pottery Company. 1873-1894.

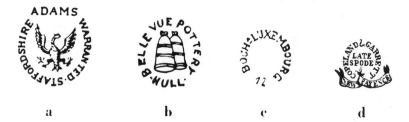

a   b   c   d

(**a**) TUNSTALL, Great Britain. Blue printed ware. 1804-1840. (**b**) HULL, Great Britain. Bellevue Pottery Company. 1825. (**c**) METT-LACH, Germany. Villeroy and Boch. 19th-20th century. (**d**) STOKE-ON-TRENT, Great Britain. W. T. Copeland and Sons. Hard paste, fayence. 1833-1847.

e   f   g   h

(**e-f**) STOKE-ON-TRENT, Great Britain. Copeland and Garrett. 1833-1847. (**g**) GERMANY. F. A. Mehlem, factory. Est. 1836. (**h**) TRENTON, New Jersey, U.S.A. Glasgow Pottery Company. Circa 1875.

i   j   k   l   m

(**i**) LIVERPOOL, Ohio, U.S.A. Knowles, Taylor, and Knowles. After 1870. (**j**) LIMOGES, France. J. Pouyat, potter. Earthenware. 1842. (**k**) METTLACH, Germany. Fayence. Glazed earthenware. Est. 1809. (**l**) MOUSTIERS, France. Fayence. Stenciled. 1780. (**m**) WELLSVILLE, Ohio, U.S.A. Wellsville China Company. Est. 1879.

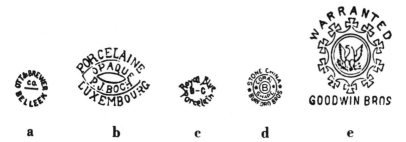

a   b   c   d   e

(a) TRENTON, New Jersey, U.S.A. Ott and Brewer. 1867-1892.
(b) METTLACH, Germany. Villeroy and Boch. 19th-20th century.
(c) TRENTON, New Jersey, U.S.A. Burgess and Campbell. Est.
1879. (d) EAST LIVERPOOL, Ohio, U.S.A. Burford Brothers Pottery Company. 1875-1900. (e) LIVERPOOL, Ohio, U.S.A. John Goodwin. Printed. Est. 1844.

f   g   h   i   j

(f-g-h-i-j) FORD CITY, Pennsylvania, U.S.A. Ford City Company,
Earthenware. Late 19th century.

k   l   m   n   o

(k) TRENTON, New Jersey, U.S.A. Burroughs and Mountford.
Circa 1880. (l) TRENTON, New Jersey, U.S.A. Glasgow Pottery
Company. Circa 1875. (m) BEAVER FALLS, Pennsylvania, U.S.A.
Mayer Pottery Company. Est. 1881. (n-o) TRENTON, New Jersey,
U.S.A. Burgess and Campbell. Est. 1879.

a   b   c   d   e

(a-b) TRENTON, New Jersey, U.S.A. Burgess and Campbell. Est. 1879. (c) EAST LIVERPOOL, Ohio, U.S.A. Knowles, Taylor, and Knowles. Circa 1870. (d) TRENTON, New Jersey, U.S.A. Glasgow Pottery Company. Circa 1875. (e) BEAVER FALLS, Pennsylvania, U.S.A. Mayer Pottery Company. Est. 1881.

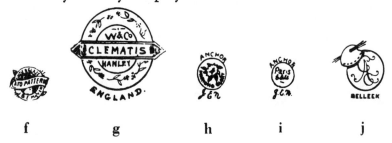

f   g   h   i   j

(f) BEAVER FALLS, Pennsylvania, U.S.A. Mayer Pottery Company. Est. 1881. (g) HANLEY, Great Britain. Late 19th century. (h-i) TRENTON, New Jersey, U.S.A. Anchor Pottery Company. Printed. 1894. (j)TRENTON, New Jersey, U.S.A. Ceramic Art Company. Lenox. Hard paste. Painted violet, 1894-1896; green or gold, 1897-1898; black, 1898-1906.

k   l   m   n

(k) EAST LIVERPOOL, Ohio, U.S.A. Homer Laughlin China Company. Printed. Est. 1872. (l-m) ESTE, Italy. Porcelain. 18th-19th century. (n) STOKE-ON-TRENT, Great Britain. E. Brain and Company Ltd. Foley China. 20th century.

a   b   c   d

(a) TRENTON, New Jersey, U.S.A. Greenwood Pottery. Printed. 1886+. (b) GERMANY. Hutschenreuther. Hard paste. 1906. (c) TRENTON, New Jersey, U.S.A. Maddock Pottery Company. After 1893. (d) STOKE-ON-TRENT, Great Britain, Grimwade Brothers. After 1891.

e   f   g   h   i

(e) ELIZABETH, New Jersey, U.S.A. L. B. Beerbower (Beerbauer) and Company. Impressed. After 1879. (f) EAST LIVERPOOL, Ohio, U.S.A. Knowles, Taylor, and Knowles. After 1870. (g) TRENTON, New Jersey, U.S.A. Crescent Pottery Company. Est. 1881. (h) STOCKTON, California, U.S.A. Stockton Art Pottery Company. 1895-1902. (i) JERSEY CITY, New Jersey, U.S.A. American Pottery Company. Impressed, printed. 1833-1845.

j   k   l   m

(j) ANDENNE, Belgium. Bernard Lammens, owner, 1820. (k-l) SEVRES, France. Hard paste. Printed color. Pieces made for royalty. Circa 1834. (m) GERMANY. Schmidt Brothers. Est. 1847.

a   b   c   d

(**a**) EAST LIVERPOOL, Ohio, U.S.A. C. C. Thompson Pottery Company. Est. 1888. (**b**) TRENTON, New Jersey, U.S.A. Ott and Brewer (Otter and Brewer) Circa 1875. (**c**) RHEINSBERG, Germany. Fayence. Est. 1762. (**d**) TRENTON, New Jersey, U.S.A. Mercer Pottery Company. White earthenware. Est. 1868.

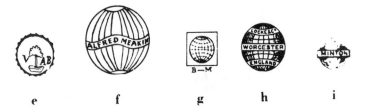

e   f   g   h   i

(**e**) COLOGNE, Germany. Pottery. 17th century. (**f**) TUNSTALL, Great Britain. Alfred Meakin. Est. 1881. (**g**) TRENTON, New Jersey, U.S.A. Burroughs and Mountford. Circa 1880. (**h**) WORCESTER, Great Britain. Edward Locke and Company. After 1891. (**i**) STOKE-ON-TRENT, Great Britain. Minton, factory. Hard paste. After 1868.

j   k   l   m   n

(**j**) BALTIMORE, Maryland, U.S.A. Edwin Bennett. Circa 1875. (**k**) LONGTON, Great Britain. J. Holdcraft. 1890-1939. (**l**) EAST LIVERPOOL, Ohio, U.S.A. Brunt, Bloor, and Martin. After 1875. (**m**) EAST LIVERPOOL, Ohio, U.S.A. Globe Pottery Company. Est. 1888. (**n**) TRENTON, New Jersey, U.S.A. Ott and Brewer. Circa 1875.

a b c d

(a) TRENTON, New Jersey, U.S.A. Mercer Pottery Company. Est. 1868. (b-c) BALTIMORE, Maryland, U.S.A. Circa 1875. (d) CHITTENANGO, New York, U.S.A. Chittenango Pottery Company. Est. 1897.

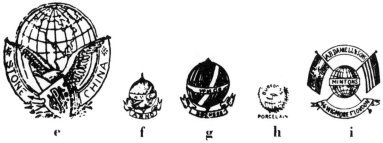

e f g h i

(e) WHEELING, West Virginia, U.S.A. Wheeling Pottery Company. 1879-circa 1910. (f-g) TRENTON, New Jersey, U.S.A. Willetts Manufacturing Company. Circa 1860. (h) EAST LIVERPOOL, Ohio, U.S.A. Burford Brothers Pottery Company. Circa 1885. (i) STOKE-ON-TRENT, Great Britain. Minton factory. After 1870.

j k l m

(j) LONGTON, Great Britain. Moore Brothers. Late 19th century. (k) STOKE-ON-TRENT, Great Britain. Minton, factory.19th-20th century. (l) TRENTON, New Jersey, U.S.A. Crescent Pottery Company. Est. 1881. (m) LONGTON, Great Britain. 20th century.

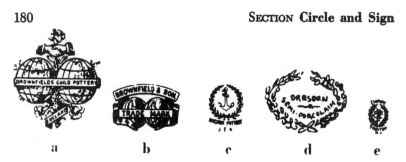

a   b   c   d   e

(a-b) COBRIDGE, Great Britain. Brownfield Company. After 1891.
(c) TRENTON, New Jersey, U.S.A. Anchor Pottery Company.
Printed. After 1891. (d) EAST LIVERPOOL, Ohio, U.S.A. Brunt,
Bloor, and Martin. 1875. (e) TRENTON, New Jersey, U.S.A. Empire Pottery Company. Circa 1892.

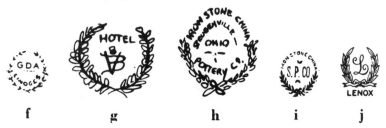

f   g   h   i   j

(f) LIMOGES, France. Charles Field Haviland. 1900-1941. (g)
EAST LIVERPOOL, Ohio, U.S.A. Vodrey Brothers, Circa 1875.
(h-i) STEUBENVILLE, Ohio, U.S.A. Steubenville Pottery Company. Circa 1904. (j) TRENTON, New Jersey, U.S.A. Lenox China
Company. Hard paste. 1906-1952.

k   l   m   n

(k) TRENTON, New Jersey, U.S.A. Lenox China Company. Hard
paste. Decorated ware. Printed violet, 1894-1896; green or gold,
1897-1906. (l) WELLSVILLE, Ohio, U.S.A. Circa 1880. (m)
TRENTON, New Jersey. U.S.A. Glasgow Pottery Company. 1880+.
(n) STOKE-ON-TRENT, Great Britain. W. T. Copeland and Sons.
Spode. 1847-1891.

a   b   c   d   e

(a) WHEELING, West Virginia, U.S.A. Wheeling Pottery Company. Est. 1879. (b-c) TRENTON, New Jersey, U.S.A. Ceramic Art Company. Lenox. After 1891. (d) EAST LIVERPOOL, Ohio, U.S.A. Union Potteries Company. 1894-1905. (e) TRENTON, New Jersey, U.S.A. Keystone Pottery Company. 19th century.

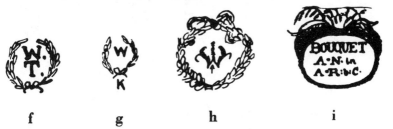

f   g   h   i

(f-g) TEINITZ, Germany. Impressed or stamped. 1801-1839. (h) WHEELING, West Virginia, U.S.A. Wheeling Pottery Company. Est. 1879. (i) ALT-ROHLAU, Germany, 1813.

j   k

(j) SHELTON, Great Britain. Job Ridgway, potter. Stone china. 1802. (k) LANE DELPH, Great Britain. Staffordshire. Circa 1800.

a   b   c

(**a**) STOKE-ON-TRENT, Great Britain. Copeland and Garrett. Spode. 1833-1847. (**b**) STOKE-ON-TRENT, Great Britain. Minton factory. Hard paste. Printed 1800. (**c**) SHARTLESVILLE, Pennsylvania, U.S.A. J. S. Henne. Impressed. 1800.

d   e   f

(**d-e**) SCHLAGGENWALD, Germany. 1793-1866. (**f**) METT-LACH, Germany. Villeroy and Boch. 1842.

g   h   i   j

(**g**) TRENTON, New Jersey, U.S.A. Millington, Astbury, and Poulson. 1859-1870. (**h**) CREIL, France. Fayence. 1794-1895. (**i**) BENNINGTON, Vermont, U.S.A. United States Pottery. Impressed. Circa 1855. (**j**) COPENHAGEN, Denmark. Fayence. Stamped. 1863.

a   b   c   d

(a) JERSEY CITY, New Jersey, U.S.A. American Pottery Manufacturing Company. Underglaze, printed. Circa 1835. (b) HOLLAND. Arij de Milde, artist. Redware. 1680-1708. (c) BURTON-ON-TRENT, Great Britain. Ashby Potter's Guild. Pottery. Est. 1909. (d) GERMANY. Gebr. Bauscher. Restaurant china. 1881-1927.

e   f   g   h   i

(e) ANDENNE, Belgium. B. Lammens, owner. Fayence. Impressed. 1820. (f) DERBY, Great Britain. Porcelain. 1811-1848. (g) SWINTON, Great Britain. Bramels and Company. Rockingham Works. 1840. (h) CINCINNATI, Ohio, U.S.A. Cincinnati Art Pottery Company. Est. 1879. (i) GERMANY. Fischern. Porcelain. 1848.

j   k   l   m

(j) EAST LIVERPOOL, Ohio, U.S.A. Cartwright Brothers. 1890. (k) CHOISY-LE-ROY, France. Hard paste. 1804. (l) BALTIMORE, Maryland, U.S.A. F. Haynes and Company. 1880. (m) STOKE-ON-TRENT, Great Britain. Spode, factory. 20th century.

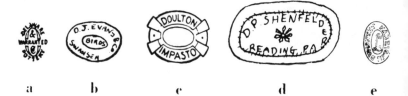

a   b   c   d   e

(**a**) TRENTON, New Jersey, U.S.A. Delaware Pottery Company.
Est. 1884. (**b**) SWANSEA, Great Britain. Circa 1865. (**c**) LAM-
BETH, Great Britain. Doulton, factory.1840. (**d**) READING, Penn-
sylvania, U.S.A. Daniel Shenfelder. Impressed. Est. 1869. (**e**) MON-
TET, France. Pottery. Impressed. 1800.

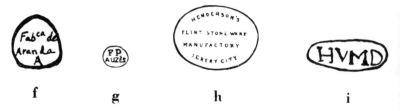

f   g   h   i

(**f**) ALCORA, Spain. Porcelain. Painted red, gold, black. 1727-1749.
(**g**) UZES, France. Pottery. Impressed. 1800. (**h**) JERSEY CITY,
New Jersey, U.S.A. D. and J. Henderson. Impressed. 1829-1833.
(**i**) HOLLAND. H. v. Middledyk. Fayence. Delft. 1764.

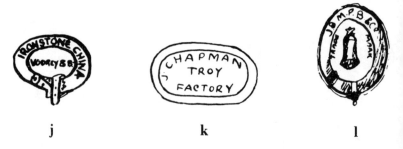

j   k   l

(**j**) EAST LIVERPOOL, Ohio, U.S.A. Vodrey Brothers. Circa 1875.
(**k**) TROY, New York, U.S.A. J. Chapman. 1815. (**l**) SCOTLAND.
J. and M. P. Bell. After 1842.

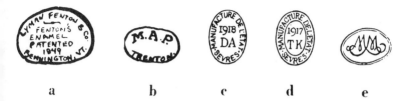

| a | b | c | d | e |

(**a**) BENNINGTON, Vermont, U.S.A. Lyman Fenton Company. 1849. (**b**) TRENTON, New Jersey, U.S.A. Millington, Astbury, and Poulson. 1859-1870. (**c-d**) SEVRES, France. Painted black, hard paste; painted blue on soft paste. 1917-1920. (**e**) VAL-SOUS-MEUDON, France. Mittenhoff and Mouron, owners. White earthenware. 1806.

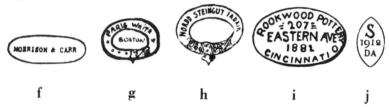

| f | g | h | i | j |

(**f**) NEW YORK, New York, U.S.A. Morrison and Carr. Circa 1870. (**g**) BOSTON, Massachusetts. New England Pottery Company. 1888. (**h**) GERMANY. Nordd Steingut Fabrik. Est. 1870. (**i**) CINCINNATI, Ohio, U.S.A. Rookwood Pottery Company. Est. 1876. (**j**) SEVRES, France. Painted black on hard paste; blue on soft paste. 1912-1917, 1921-1927.

| k | l | m | n | o |

(**k**) SEVRES, France. Issued without decoration. 1871. (**l**) WOODBRIDGE, New York, U.S.A. Salamander Works. Impressed. 1848. (**m**) BALTIMORE, Maryland, U.S.A. F. Haynes and Company. Est. 1882. (**n**) BOHEMIA. Schelten. Porcelain. 1855. (**o**) TRENTON, New Jersey, U.S.A. Thomas Maddock's Sons Company. 1902.

a b c d e f

(**a**) LEEDS, Great Britain. Thomas Nicholson and Company. After 1854. (**b**) TRENTON, New Jersey, U.S.A. Delaware Pottery Company. Est. 1884. (**c**) BENNINGTON, Vermont, U.S.A. United States Pottery Company. 1852-1858. (**d-e**) BEAVER FALLS, Pennsylvania, U.S.A. Mayer Pottery Company. Est. 1881. (**f**) ALT-ROHLAU, Germany. 1813.

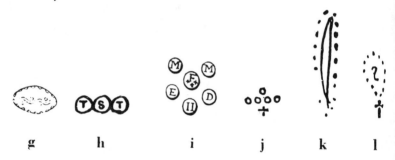

g h i j k l

(**g**) COLOGNE, Germany. Pottery. Painted blue.. 17th century. (**h**) EAST LIVERPOOL, Ohio, U.S.A. Taylor, Smith, and Taylor Company. Est. 1899. (**i**) FLORENCE, Italy. Soft paste. Painted color. 16th century. (**j**) LIMBACH, Germany. Hard paste. Painted 1761. (**k**) TURKEY. 17th or 18th century. (**l**) BOURG-LA-REINE, France. Hard paste. Painted 1773.

SECTION **COPIES OF ORIENTAL MARKS**
See also Section **Lines**

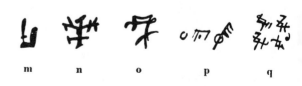

m n o p q

(**m**) ELBOGEN, Bohemia. Hard paste. Impressed. 1810. (**n**) CAUGHLEY, Great Britain. 1772-1799. (**o**) CAUGHLEY, Great Britain. 1772-1799. (**p**) OFFENBACH, Germany. Lay, artist. Fayence. 1739. (**q**) WORCESTER, Great Britain. Before 1783.

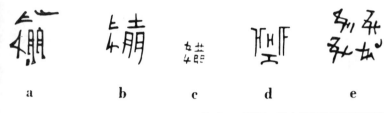

a b c d e

(a) WORCESTER, Great Britain. Before 1783. (b) WORCESTER, Great Britain. 1751-1783. (c) WORCESTER, Great Britain. Painted red, blue. Circa 1780. (d) WORCESTER, Great Britain. 1751-1781. (e) WORCESTER, Great Britain. Dr. Wall. 1751-1783.

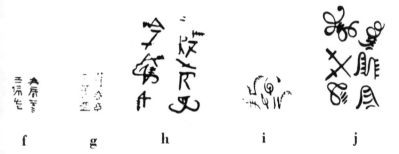

f g h i j

(f) HOLLAND. Fayence. Delft. Painted blue. Circa 1800. (g) HOLLAND. Fayence. Delft. Painted blue. Circa 1800. (h) HOLLAND. De Romeyn (The Roman). Fayence. Delft. 1671. (i) WORCESTER, Great Britain. 1751-1783. (j) WORCESTER, Great Britain. Dr. Wall. Porcelain. 1751-1783.

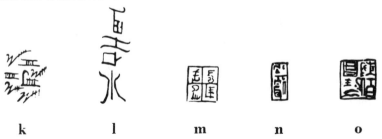

k l m n o

(k) WORCESTER, Great Britain. Painted blue. 1751. (l) BURSLEM. Great Britain. John and David Elers. 1688-1710. (m) MEISSEN, Germany. Hard paste, Bottger ware. Painted blue. Circa 1700. (n-o) MEISSEN, Germany. Bottger red ware. Circa 1700.

a   b   c   d

(**a-b**) MEISSEN, Germany. Bottger red ware: Circa 1700. (**c**)
COALBROOKDALE, Great Britain. Hard paste. 1796-1861. (**d**)
PARIS, France. Samson, the imitator. Mark on imitation Lowestoft.
Circa 1875.

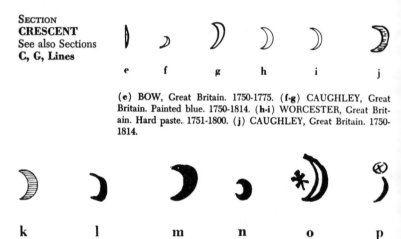

SECTION
CRESCENT
See also Sections
C, G, Lines

e   f   g   h   i   j

(**e**) BOW, Great Britain. 1750-1775. (**f-g**) CAUGHLEY, Great
Britain. Painted blue. 1750-1814. (**h-i**) WORCESTER, Great Britain. Hard paste. 1751-1800. (**j**) CAUGHLEY, Great Britain. 1750-
1814.

k   l   m   n   o   p

(**k**) WORCESTER, Great Britain. Hard paste. 1751-1800. (**l**) BOW,
Great Britain. Porcelain. 1750-1775. (**m**) CAUGHLEY, Great Britain. 1750-1814. (**n**) WORCESTER, Great Britain. Painted color.
1751-1800. (**o**) PINXTON, Great Britain. Soft paste. 1796-1801.
(**p**) NYMPHENBERG, Germany. Porcelain. Impressed or incised.
18th century.

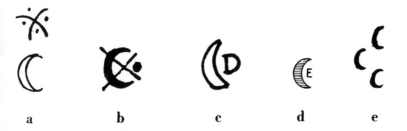

a   b   c   d   e

(a) TURKEY. Porcelain. Circa 1850. (b) FAENZA, Italy. Fayence. 16th century. (c) CAUGHLEY, Great Britain. 1750-1814. (d) WORCESTER, Great Britain. Blueware. 1751-1800. (e) MUNDEN, Germany. Fayence. 18th century.

f   g   h   i   j   k

(f-g-h) MARIEBERG, Sweden. Pottery and soft paste. Painted color. 1750. (i) WORCESTER, Great Britain. Flight. Hard paste. Painted blue. 1783-1792. (j) CAUGHLEY, Great Britain. Hard paste. Painted blue. 1750. (k) EAST LIVERPOOL, Ohio, U.S.A. William Brunt Pottery Company. 1850-1895.

l   m   n   o   p

(l-m) TRENTON, New Jersey, U.S.A. Ott (Otter) and Brewer. Circa 1882. (n-o) STOKE-ON-TRENT, Great Britain. 19th-20th century. (p) BEAVER FALLS, Pennsylvania, U.S.A. Mayer Pottery Company. Est. 1881.

Section **CROWN**
See also Sections
Crown and Circle,
Crown and Shield

a   b   c   d   e

(a) NOTTINGHAM, Great Britain. Lovatt and Lovatt. 19th-20th century. (b) EDGERTON, Wisconsin, U.S.A. Pauline Pottery Company. Impressed. 1888. (c-d) DERBY, Great Britain. 1755-1770. (e) EDGERTON, Wisconsin, U.S.A. Pauline Pottery Company. Impressed. Est. 1883.

f   g   h   i   j

(f) TURIN, Italy. Fayence. 16th-17th century. (g) EVANSVILLE, Indiana, U.S.A. Crown Pottery Company. Est. 1891. (h) LONG-TON, Great Britain. R. H. Plant and Company. 19th century. (i) BUEN RETIRO, Spain. Soft paste. 1759-1808. (j) LUDWIGS-BURG, Germany. Hard paste. Painted blue. 1758-1793.

k   l   m   n   o   p

(k) LUDWIGSBURG, Germany. Hard paste. Painted blue. 1758-1793; or BUEN RETIRO, Spain. Soft paste and pottery. Painted color. 1760. (l) NIDERVILLER, France. Fayence, porcelain. Painted blue. Est. 1754. (m) SAINT PETERSBURG, Russia. Fayence, porcelain. Painted color. 1796-1801. (n) DERBY, Great Britain. Soft paste. Painted gold. 1770-1810. (o) CHELSEA, Great Britain. Underglaze blue. 1745-1784. (p) SAINT PETERSBURG, Russia. Hard paste. Painted color. 1801.

a   b   c   d   e

(**a**) SAINT PETERSBURG, Russia. Hard paste. Painted blue or color. 1855-1881. (**b**) PARIS, France. Hard paste. Painted red. 1778. (**c**) SAINT PETERSBURG, Russia. 1855-1881. (**d**) SAINT PETERSBURG, Russia. One dot added for each year after 1870. (This is really four marks.) 1871-1881. (**e**) NAPLES, Italy. 18th century.

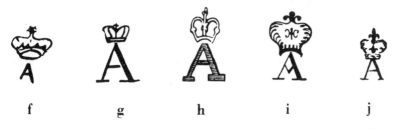

f   g   h   i   j

(**f**) SAVONA, Italy. 17th-18th century. (**g-h-i**) PARIS, France. Rue Thiroux, factory. 1775-1869. (**j**) PARIS, France. Hard paste. Painted red. 18th century.

k   l   m   n   o

(**k**) VENICE, Italy. 1753. (**l**) MEISSEN, Germany. Bottger red ware. 18th century. (**m**) BRUSSELS, Belgium. Hard paste. Painted color. 1800. (**n**) DERBY, Great Britain. Bloor. 1811-1848. (**o**) NAPLES, Italy. 18th century.

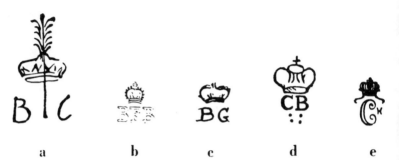

a   b   c   d   e

(**a**) NAPLES, Italy. 17th century. (**b**) WORCESTER, Great Britain. Hard paste. 1813-1840. (**c**) NAPLES, Italy. 17th century. (**d**) FRIEDBURG, Germany. Fayence. 1768. (**e**) SEVRES, France. 1830-1848.

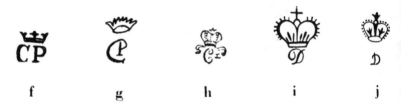

f   g   h   i   j

(**f**) PARIS, France. Hard paste. Painted blue. 1769. (**g**) BRUSSELS, Belgium. 19th century. (**h**) SEVRES, France. Hard paste. Painted blue. 1829. (**i-j**) DERBY, Great Britain. Porcelain. Painted red, violet. 1780.

k   l   m   n   o

(**k**) CLIGNANCOURT, France. Est. 1771. (**l**) MEISSEN, Germany. After 1880. (**m**) DERBY, Great Britain. Bloor. 1811-1848. (**n**) HILDESHEIM, Germany. Hard paste. Painted blue. 1760. (**o**) FULDA, Germany. Hard paste. Painted blue. 1763-1780.

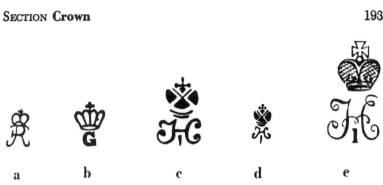

a   b   c   d   e

(a) GINORI, Italy. Capo-di-Monte, factory. Soft paste. Painted color. 1780. (b) LEEDS, Great Britain. Earthenware. Est. 1760. (c-d) SAINT PETERSBURG, Russia. Porcelain. Painted color. Est. 1744. (e) SAINT PETERSBURG, Russia. Porcelain. Painted color. 1825-1855.

f   g   h   i   j

(f) GERMANY. Hesse Darmstadt. Hard paste. Painted blue. 1756. (g-h-i-j) VINCENNES, France. Hard paste. 1765.

k   l   m   n   o

(k) VINCENNES, France. Hard paste. 1765. (l-m) CLIGNAN-COURT, France. Painted red. Est. 1771. (n) BUEN RETIRO, Spain. Soft paste. 1759-1808. (o) NAPLES, Italy. 17th century.

194

a   b   c   d   e

(**a-b**) BUEN RETIRO, Spain. Hard paste, soft paste. 1759-1808.
(**c-d-e**) GINORI, Italy. Capo-di-Monte, factory. Soft paste. Painted
red, blue, or impressed. 18th century.

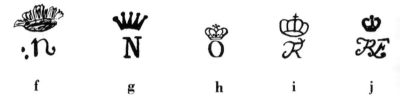

f   g   h   i   j

(**f-g**) GINORI, Italy. Capo-di-Monte, factory. Circa 1820. (**h**) OR-
LEANS, France. Pottery. Painted color. 1753. (**i**) LUDWIGSBURG,
Germany. Porcelain, fayence. 1756-1824. (**j**) GINORI, Italy. Painted
red, color. Circa 1773.

k   l   m   n   o

(**k**) GINORI, Italy. Capo-di-Monte, factory. Painted red, color.
Circa 1773. (**l**) SEVRES, France. Hard paste, soft paste. Painted
color. 1854. (**m**) MEISSEN, Germany. Sachsiche Porzellen Manufactur. Hard paste. Painted blue. 1750. (**n**) SAVONA, Italy. 17th-
18th century. (**o**) SEVRES, France. 1830-1848.

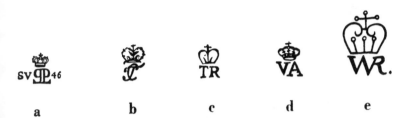

a   b   c   d   e

(a) SEVRES, France. Hard paste. Impressed or printed color. 1845.
(b) FRANKENTHAL, Germany. Hard paste. Painted blue. 1761.
(c) LUDWIGSBURG, Germany. Hard paste. Painted blue. 1806.
(d) VISTA ALEGRE, Portugal. Porcelain. 1830-present. (e) LUD-
WIGSBURG, Germany. Painted gold. 1816.

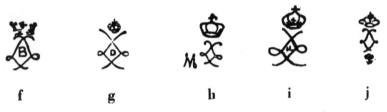

f   g   h   i   j

(f) CLIGNANCOURT, France. Hard paste. Est. 1771. (g) DERBY,
Great Britain. Hard paste. Painted red or violet. 1798. (h-i-j) SEV-
RES, France. Hard paste. 1700.

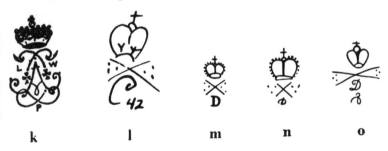

k   l   m   n   o

(k) POPPELSDORF, Germany. Fayence, porcelain. 1825. (l)
DERBY. Great Britain. Painted red, gold. 1811-1848. (m-n-o)
DERBY, Great Britain. 1784-1848.

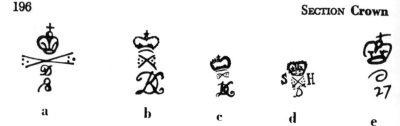

a   b   c   d   e

(**a**) DERBY, Great Britain. William Duesbury. Porcelain. 1784-1810.
(**b-c**) DERBY, Great Britain. Duesbury and Kean. Porcelain. 1795.
(**d**) DERBY, Great Britain. Stevenson and Hancock. Hard paste.
Painted color. 1850-1870. (**e**) DERBY, Great Britain. Painted red,
gold. 1815-1830.

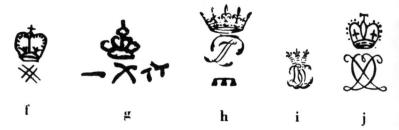

f   g   h   i   j

(**f**) DERBY, Great Britain. Circa 1800. (**g**) SEVRES, France. Hard
paste. 1814-1848. (**h**) VINCENNES, France. Hard paste. 1765.
(**i**) CLIGNANCOURT, France. Painted red. Est. 1771. (**j**) DERBY,
Great Britain. Royal Crown Derby factory. Porcelain. 1876-1953.

k   l   m   n   o

(**k**) COPENHAGEN, Denmark. Royal Copenhagen factory. Underglaze blue. 1905. (**l**) COPENHAGEN, Denmark. Royal Copenhagen. 1929. (**m**) COPENHAGEN, Denmark. Royal Copenhagen,
factory. Underglaze green, wavy lines blue. 1894-1900. (**n**) COPEN-
HAGEN, Denmark. Royal Copenhagen factory. Underglaze green,
wavy lines blue. 1923. (**o**) BELLEEK, Ireland. Est. 1863.

Powell & Bishop

a   b   c   d   e

(**a**) FENTON, Great Britain. Crown Staffordshire Porcelain Company. 1870. (**b**) LONGTON, Great Britain. R. H. Plant and Company. Late 19th century. (**c**) HANLEY, Great Britain. Powell and Bishop. Impressed or printed. 1865-1878. (**d-e**) MARIEBERG, Sweden. Pottery and soft paste. Painted color. 1750.

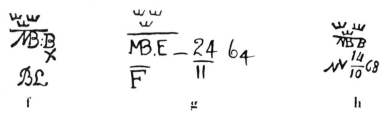

f   g   h

(**f**) MARIEBERG, Sweden. Pottery and soft paste. 1766. (**g**) MARIEBERG, Sweden. Pottery and soft paste. November 24, 1764. (**h**) MARIEBERG, Sweden. Pottery and soft paste. October 14, 1768.

BELLEEK

i   j   k   l   m

(**i**) LONGTON, Great Britain. William Adderley and Company. After 1870. (**j**) BURSLEM, Great Britain. A. J. Wilkinson. Late 19th century. (**k**) LONGTON, Great Britain. Charles Allerton. After 1891. (**l**) TRENTON, New Jersey, U.S.A. Ott (Otter) and Brewer. 1876. (**m**) TRENTON, New Jersey, U.S.A. Burroughs and Mountford. 1879-1882.

a   b   c   d   e

(**a-b**) DERBY, Great Britain. Robert Bloor. 1811-1848. (**c**) SHEL-
TON, Great Britain. After 1891. (**d**) EVANSVILLE, Indiana, U.S.A.
Crown Pottery Company. Est. 1891. (**e**) FENTON, Great Britain.
Crown Staffordshire Porcelain Company. 1900.

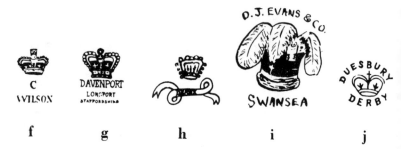

f   g   h   i   j

(**f**) HANLEY, Great Britain. Robert Wilson, owner. 1786. (**g**)
LONGPORT, Great Britain. Davenport. Circa 1810. (**h**) DERBY,
Great Britain. Robert Bloor. Printed red. 1811-1848. (**i**) SWANSEA,
Great Britain. D. J. Evans and Company. 1859-1870. (**j**) DERBY,
Great Britain. 1760.

k   l   m   n   o

(**k-l-m**) DERBY, Great Britain. William Duesbury. 1760. (**n**) BAL-
TIMORE, Maryland, U.S.A. Edwin Bennett. 1856-1890. (**o**) COAL-
PORT, Great Britain. After 1891.

a b c d

(a) WORCESTER, Great Britain. Royal Service for the Duke of Clarence. Circa 1793. (b) WORCESTER, Great Britain. Hard paste. Painted color. 1793-1807. (c) GINORI, Italy. 18th century. (d) LIVERPOOL, Great Britain. Herculaneum. Impressed or printed. 1840.

e f g h

(e) GIESSHUBEL, Germany. Hamburger and Company. 19th century. (f) COBRIDGE, Great Britain. James Clews, potter. 1819-1829. (g) LIMOGES, France. Circa 1880. (h) GERMANY. Mid-19th century.

i j k l

(i) LUNEVILLE, France. Keller and Guerin, owner. Fayence. Circa 1880. (j) FENTON, Great Britain. Ashworth. 1813-1851. (k) HANLEY, Great Britain. George Ashworth. After 1859. (l) STOKE-ON-TRENT, Great Britain. Minton, factory. Circa 1870.

a   b   c   d   e

(a) TRENTON, New Jersey, U.S.A. Ott (Otter) and Brewer. 1886.
(b) SPAIN. 19th century. (c) EVANSVILLE, Indiana, U.S.A.
Crown Pottery Company. Est. 1891. (d) TRENTON, New Jersey,
U.S.A. Ott (Otter) and Brewer. 1886. (e) GREAT BRITAIN. Circa
1900+.

f   g   h   i   j

(f) DERBY, Great Britain, Royal Crown Derby. Porcelain. 1890-
1953. (g) STOKE-ON-TRENT, Great Britain. Cauldon Potteries
Limited. 1891-1953. (h) DERBY, Great Britain. Royal Crown
Derby. Porcelain. 1890-1940. (i) BURSLEM, Great Britain. Wood,
potter. Circa 1900+. (j) TUNSTALL, Great Britain, T. G. and F.
Booth. After 1891.

k   l   m   n   o

(k) EAST LIVERPOOL, Ohio, U.S.A. George Murphy Pottery
Company. 19th century. (l) EAST LIVERPOOL, Ohio, U.S.A.
Vodrey Brothers. Circa 1875. (m) SEBRING, Ohio, U.S.A. Sebring
Pottery Company. Est. 1887. (n) FENTON, Great Britain. Crown
Staffordshire Porcelain Company. Circa 1890. (o) TUNSTALL,
Great Britain. Alfred Meakin. After 1891.

a   **b**   **c**   **d**

(a) BURSLEM, Great Britain. John Maddock and Sons. After 1891. (b) LONGTON, Great Britain. John Turner. Est. 1872. (c) DERBY, Great Britain. William Duesbury. Porcelain. 1803. (d) HANLEY, Great Britain. Robert or David Wilson. 18th-19th century.

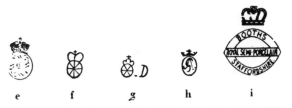

SECTION CROWN AND CIRCLE See also Sections **Crown, Crown and Shield**

e   **f**   **g**   **h**   **i**

(e) WORCESTER, Great Britain. Hard paste. After 1862. (f) HOCHST, Germany. Hard paste. Painted gold, color. 1765. (g) DAMM, Germany. White and cream-colored earthenware. Painted blue. 1827. (h) PARIS, France. Dihl and Guerhard. Hard paste. Painted red. 1780. (i) TUNSTALL, Great Britain. T. G. and F. Booth. Late 19th century.

j   **k**   **l**   **m**

(j) SHELTON, Great Britain. T. C. Brown, Westhead, Moore, and Company. 1858. (k) SHELTON, Great Britain. T. C. Brown, Westhead, Moore, and Company. After 1859. (l) STOKE-ON-TRENT, Great Britain. Wiltshaw and Robinson. Late 19th century. (m) STOKE-ON-TRENT, Great Britain. Spode, factory. Bone porcelain. 1833-1847.

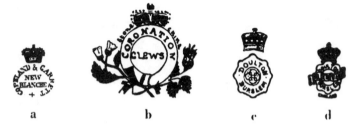

a   b   c   d

(a) STOKE-ON-TRENT, Great Britain. W. T. Copeland and Sons. Spode factory. Bone porcelain. 1833-1847. (b) COBRIDGE, Great Britain. 1814. (c) LAMBETH, Great Britain. Doulton, factory. Est. 1872. (d) LAMBETH, Great Britain. Doulton, factory. 1891.

e   f   g   h

(e) BURSLEM, Great Britain. E. Bourne and J. E. Leigh. Earthenware. 19th century. (f) GREAT BRITAIN. Bates, Elliot, and Company. Est. 1790. (g) GRUNSTADT. Germany. White earthenware. Est. 1801. (h) METTLACH, Germany. Fayence. Est. 1809.

i   j   k   l   m

(i) METTLACH, Germany. Fayence. Est. 1809. (j) HANLEY, Great Britain. J. G. Meakin. After 1891. (k) BURSLEM, Great Britain. John Maddock and Sons. Earthenware. Circa 1945+. (l) SHELTON, Great Britain. Job Ridgways, potter. Stone china, porcelain. Est. 1902. (m) EAST LIVERPOOL, Ohio, U.S.A. Knowles, Taylor, and Knowles. Est. 1854.

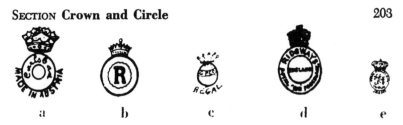

a   b   c   d   e

(**a**) BOHEMIA. Fischern. 1848. (**b**) GREENPOINT, New York, U.S.A. Faience Manufacturing Company. Printed. 1880-1892. (**c**) EAST LIVERPOOL, Ohio, U.S.A. Globe Pottery Company. Est. 1888. (**d**) SHELTON, Great Britain. Job Ridgways. After 1891. (**e**) TRENTON, New Jersey, U.S.A. Glasgow Pottery Company. Circa 1875.

f   g   h   i

(**f**) DERBY, Great Britain. Stevenson, Sharp and Company After 1860. (**g**) TRENTON, New Jersey, U.S.A. Thomas Maddock and Sons. Est. 1882. (**h-i**) SHELTON, Great Britain. Job Ridgways, potter. After 1802.

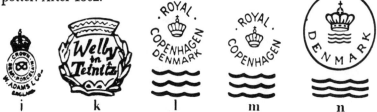

j   k   l   m   n

(j) TUNSTALL, Great Britain. Printed. Circa 1879-circa 1900. (k) TEINITZ, Bohemia. Lead glazed earthenware. Est. 1801. (l) CO-PENHAGEN, Denmark. Royal Copenhagen, factory. Porcelain. Underglaze green, wavy lines blue. 1922-present. (m) COPENHAGEN, Denmark. Royal Copenhagen, factory. Porcelain. Underglaze green, wavy lines blue. 1897-1922. (n) COPENHA-GEN, Denmark. Royal Copenhagen, factory. Porcelain. Overglaze green or red. 1890.

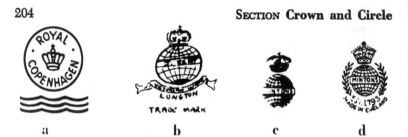

a   b   c   d

(a) COPENHAGEN, Denmark. Royal Copenhagen, factory.Printed blue. 1889. (b) LONGTON, Great Britain. James Kent. 20th century. (c) STOKE-ON-TRENT, Great Britain. Minton, factory. 1888-1911. (d) STOKE-ON-TRENT, Great Britain. Minton, factory. 1911-1953.

e   f   g   h

(e) GREAT BRITAIN. Johnson Brothers. Est. 1883. (f) PARIS, France. Rue de Bondy, factory. Hard paste. Est. 1780. (g) GIESS-HUBEL, Bohemia. Porcelain. After 1891. (h) STOKE-ON-TRENT, Great Britain. W. T. Copeland and Sons. Spode, factory. 1833-1847.

i   j   k   l   m

(i) SEVRES, France. Hard paste. Painted blue. 1829. (j) DERBY, Great Britain. William Duesbury. Circa 1760. (k) COBRIDGE, Great Britain. Andrew Stevenson, potter. 1810-1818. (l) DERBY, Great Britain. Hard paste. Printed color. 1811-1848. (m) WORCES-TER, Great Britain. Robert Chamberlain and Son. Porcelain. 1850.

a   b   c   d   e

(**a**) EAST LIVERPOOL, Ohio, U.S.A. East End Pottery Company. 19th century. (**b**) BALTIMORE, Maryland, U.S.A. D. F. Haynes and Company. Est. 1879. (**c**) LIVERPOOL, Great Britain. Herculaneum. Impressed or printed. 1800-1841. (**d**) STOKE-ON-TRENT, Great Britain. Minton, factory. After 1868. (**e**) TRENTON, New Jersey, U.S.A. Burgess and Campbell. Est. 1879.

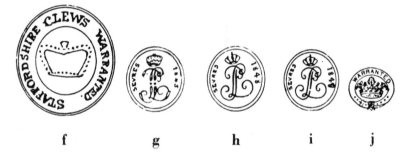

f   g   h   i   j

(**f**) COBRIDGE, Great Britain. James Clews, potter. Blue printed earthenware. 1819-1829. (**g**) SEVRES, France. Hard paste, soft paste. 1845. (**h**) SEVRES, France. Hard paste, soft paste. 1848. (**i**) SEVRES, France. Hard paste. Printed blue. 1848. (**j**) BALTIMORE, Maryland, U.S.A. D. F. Haynes and Company. Est. 1879.

k   l   m   n

(**k**) BALTIMORE, Maryland, U.S.A. Bennett Pottery Company. Est. 1840. (**l**) SAINT PETERSBURG, Russia. 1855-1881. (**m**) SEVRES, France. Hard paste for Catherine II of Russia. 1778. (**n**) WORCESTER, Great Britain. Hard paste. Printed. 1800.

a   b   c   d

(a) STOKE-ON-TRENT, Great Britain. W. T. Copeland and Sons.
Spode, factory. 1850-1867. (b) FENTON, Great Britain. Crown Staffordshire Porcelain Company. 1890. (c) MINTON, Great Britain.
Circa 1951-present. (d) BALTIMORE, Maryland, U.S.A. Edwin Bennett. 1856-1890.

SECTION **CROWN
AND SHIELD**
See also Sections
**Crown, Crown
and Circle**

e   f   g   h   i

(e) GERMANY. Painted blue. 19th century. (f) EISENBERG,
Germany. Earthenware. 1882-1904. (g) HEREND, Hungary. Mo-
ritz Fischer, founder. Blue overglaze. 19th-20th century. (h-i) SAR-
REGUEMINES, France. Fayence, porcelain 19th century.

j   k   l   m   n

(j) BOHEMIA. Porcelain. 1880. (k) GERMANY. Impressed. 1880.
(l) LUXEMBOURG, Belgium. 18th century. (m) THURINGIA,
Germany. Rudolstadt, factory. Impressed or stamped. 19th century.
(n) SARREGUEMINES, France. Fayence, porcelain. 19th century.

a   b   c   d   e

(**a**) MORAVIA, Germany. Frain, factory. Earthenware. 1799-1882.
(**b**) RUDOLSTADT, Germany. Impressed or stamped. 19th century. (**c**) VALOGNES, France. Hard paste. Est. 1793. (**d**) LONGTON, Great Britain. Hilditch and Son. 1795-1830. (**e**) GERMANY. Est. 1840.

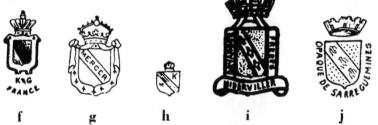

f   g   h   i   j

(**f**) LUNEVILLE, France. Keller and Guerin. Fayence. After 1891.
(**g**) TRENTON, New Jersey, U.S.A. Mercer Pottery Company. Est. 1868. (**h**) GERMANY. Fayence. Est. 1882. (**i**) NIDERVILLER, France. Fayence, porcelain. Circa 1830. (**j**) SARREGUEMINES, France. Fayence, porcelain. 19th century.

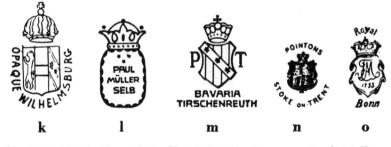

k   l   m   n   o

(**k**) GERMANY. Est. 1835. (**l**) BAYERN, Germany. Paul Muller. Hard paste. 1890-1917. (**m**) TIRSCHENREUTH, Germany. 1903-1981 +. (**n**) STOKE-ON-TRENT, Great Britain. Pointons. 19th century. (**o**) BONN, Germany. F. A. Mehlem, factory. Est. 1836.

| a | b | c | d |

(a) BURSLEM, Great Britain. T. and R. Boote. Earthenware. 1890-1906. (b) STOKE-ON-TRENT, Great Britain. S. Fielding and Company. After 1891. (c) ELBOGEN, Germany. Springer and Company. Earthenware, porcelain. Est. 1815. (d) LONGTON, Great Britain. Foley China Factory. After 1891.

| e | f | g | h |

(e) KLOSTERLE, Germany. Porcelain, lead-glazed earthenware. Est. 1793. (f) HANLEY, Great Britain. After 1891. (g) BURSLEM, Great Britain. Wilkinson. After 1891. (h) ZELL, Germany. Fayence. Circa 1880-1909.

SECTION **FLEUR DE LIS**
See also Section
Lines

| i | j | k | l | m | n |

(i-j) BUEN RETIRO, Spain. Soft paste. 1759-1808. (k-l) NAPLES, Italy. Capo-di-Monte factory. Soft paste. Painted blue. 1736 (moved to Buen Retiro, Spain, 1759). (m-n) MARSEILLES, France. Fayence. Printed color. 1777.

a   b   c   d   e   f

(**a**) MARSEILLES, France. Fayence. Printed color. 1777. (**b-c**) STOKE-ON-TRENT, Great Britain. Minton, factory. Painted green. After 1850. (**d**) ROUEN, France. Fayence. Painted color. 16th century. (**e-f**) MARSEILLES, France. Fayence. Printed color. 1777.

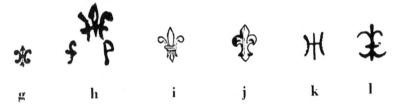

g   h   i   j   k   l

(**g**) BOW, Great Britain. Soft paste. Painted blue. 1730. (**h**) ROUEN, France. Fayence. 17th century. (**i**) SAINT CLOUD, France. Soft paste. Impressed. 1680-1766. (**j**) GINORI, Italy. Painted blue. After 1820. (**k-l**) BUEN RETIRO, Spain. Soft paste. 1759-1808.

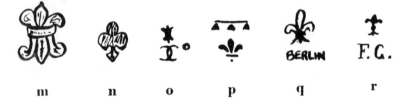

m   n   o   p   q   r

(**m**) BUEN RETIRO, Spain. Soft paste. 1759-1808. (**n**) GINORI, Italy. Painted blue. After 1820. (**o**) BUEN RETIRO, Spain. Soft paste. 1759-1808. (**p**) ORLEANS, France. 1753-1812. (**q**) EAST LIVERPOOL, Ohio. U.S.A. Sevres China Company. Est. 1900. (**r**) BUEN RETIRO, Spain. Soft paste. 1759-1808.

a   b   c   d

(a) EAST LIVERPOOL, Ohio, U.S.A. Sevres China Company. Est. 1900. (b) LOWESBY, Great Britain. Earthenware. Impressed. Est. 1835. (c) LOWESBY, Great Britain. ca. 1835-1840. (d) EAST LIVERPOOL, Ohio, U.S.A. Sevres China Company. Est. 1900.

e   f   g   h

(e) BUEN RETIRO, Spain. Soft paste. 1759-1808. (f) SEVRES, France. Hard paste. Painted blue. 1830. (g) EAST LIVERPOOL, Ohio, U.S.A. Sevres China Company. 1900-1908. (h) DETROIT, Michigan, U.S.A. 1903-present.

SECTION **FLOWER AND TREE**
See also Sections
**Circle and Sign,
Shield, Square**

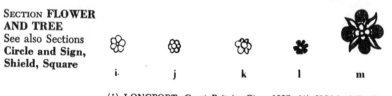

i.   j   k   l   m

(i) LONGPORT, Great Britain. Circa 1825. (j) HOLLAND. De Roos (The Rose). Fayence. Delft. 1764. (k) TYLERSPORT, Pennsylvania, U.S.A. Circa 1830. (l) EAST LIVERPOOL, Ohio, U.S.A. Circa 1840. (m) TYLERSPORT, Pennsylvania, U.S.A. Michael School (Scholl). Impressed. Circa 1830.

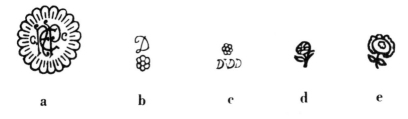

a   b   c   d   e

(**a**) BOSTON, Massachusetts, U.S.A. New England Pottery Company. Est. 1875. (**b-c**) HOLLAND. De Roos (The Rose). Fayence. Delft. Painted blue. 1764. (**d**) CAUGHLEY, Great Britain. Rose and Company. Hard paste. Painted color. 1799. (**e**) COALPORT, Great Britain. 19th century.

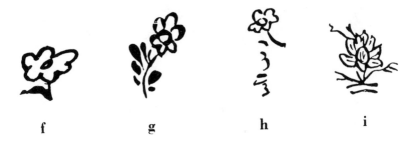

f   g   h   i

(**f-g-h-i**) HOLLAND. De Roos (The Rose). Fayence. Delft. 1675.

j   k   l   m   n

(**j**) HOHENSTEIN, Germany. After 1822. (**k**) FULHAM, Great Britain. 1888. (**l**) BOSTON, Massachusetts, U.S.A. Grueby Faience Company. Est. 1897. (**m**) IMENAU, Germany. Fayence, porcelain. Est. 1777. (**n**) THURINGIA, Germany. Limbach, factory. Porcelain. Est. 1772.

a   **b**   **c**   **d**   **e**

(**a**) THURINGIA, Germany. Volkstedt, factory. Porcelain. Est.
1760. (**b-c**) GROSBREITENBACH, Germany. Hard paste. Painted
color. 1770. (**d**) CHELSEA, Massachusetts, U.S.A. Chelsea Keramic
Art Works. Circa 1890. (**e**) TRENTON, New Jersey, U.S.A. Cook
Pottery Company. Circa 1900.

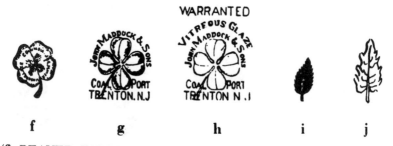

f   **g**   **h**   **i**   **j**

(**f**) BEAVER FALLS, Pennsylvania, U.S.A. Mayer Pottery Com-
pany. Est. 1881. (**g**) TRENTON, New Jersey, U.S.A. John Maddock
and Sons. Circa 1904+. (**h**) TRENTON, New Jersey, U.S.A. John
Maddock and Sons. 1894-1929. (**i**) BERLIN, Germany. Hard paste.
Painted blue, green, gold. Often on damaged pieces. 1800. (**j**) HOL-
LAND. Fayence. Delft. 18th century.

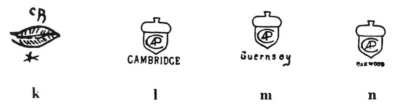

k   **l**   **m**   **n**

(**k**) HOLLAND. De Ster (The Star). Fayence. Delft. 1720. (**l-m-n**)
CAMBRIDGE, Ohio, U.S.A. Cambridge Art Pottery Company. 19th
century.

a   b   c   d   e

SECTION **LINES**
See also Sections
**E, F, H, I, K, L,
M, N, S, T, V, W,
X-Y, Anchor,
Arrow, Copies of
Oriental Marks**

(a) ALTHALDENSLEBEN, Germany. Hard Paste. Impressed. Blue. Circa 1800. (b) SAINT PETERSBURG, Russia. Hard paste. Painted blue. Est. 1744. (c) COPENHAGEN, Denmark. Royal Copenhagen, factory. 1830-1845. (d) LUDWIGSBURG, Germany. Hard paste. Painted red or blue. 1758. (e) COPENHAGEN, Denmark. Royal Copenhagen, factory. 1775-1820, 1850-1870.

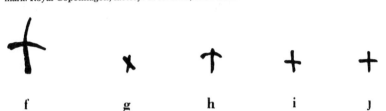

f   g   h   i   J

(**f**) VARAGES, France. Fayence. 1770. (**g**) GINORI, Italy. Capo-di-monte, factory. Blue. 1743-1821. (**h**) LEEDS, Great Britain. Painted color. 1770. (**i-j**) BRISTOL, Great Britain. Porcelain. Painted color. Circa 1770.

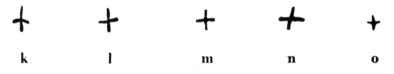

k   l   m   n   o

(**k-l**) VARAGES, France. Fayence. Painted black or red. 1730. (**m**) FULDA, Germany. Fayence. Underglaze blue. 1765-1780. (**n**) GOULT, France. Fayence. 1740. (**o**) VINOVO, Italy. Porcelain. Painted black. 1776-1820.

a   b   c   d   e

(a) FULDA, Germany. Fayence, hard paste. Painted blue. 1765.
(b) BRISTOL, Great Britain. Porcelain. 1750. (c) CHELSEA,
Great Britain. Porcelain. 1745-1784. (d) VARAGES. France. Fayence. Painted black, blue, red. 1730. (e) TURIN, Italy. Porcelain.
Est. 1737.

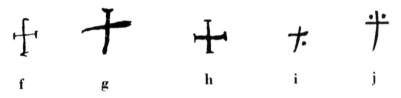

f   g   h   i   j

(f) NYMPHENBURG, Germany. Porcelain. Impressed, incised.
Est. 1755. (g) FAENZA, Italy. Fayence. 16th century. (h) BUEN
RETIRO, Spain. Soft paste. 1759-1808. (i-j) BOW, Great Britain.
Porcelain. 1750.

k   l   m   n   o

(k-l) LONGTON, Great Britain. William Littler, potter. Porcelain,
stoneware. 1750-1760. (m) URBINO, Italy. Fayence. 16th century.
(n) BOW, Great Britain. Porcelain. 1750. (o) WEESP, Holland.
Porcelain. Est. 1759.

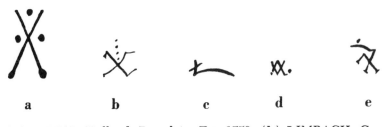

a   b   c   d   e

(a) WEESP, Holland. Porcelain. Est. 1759. (b) LIMBACH, Germany. Porcelain. Painted red, black, purple. 1772-1778. (c) PLYMOUTH, Great Britain. Hard paste. Painted blue, red, gold. 1768. (d) BORDEAUX, France. Fayence, porcelain. Painted gold, blue. Est. 1781. (e) LIMBACH, Germany. Porcelain. Painted red, black, purple. 1772-1788.

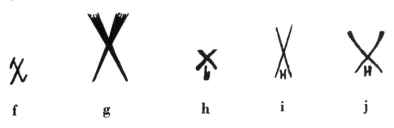

f   g   h   i   j

(f) BOW, Great Britain. Porcelain. 1750. (g) PARIS, France. De La Courtille, factory. Hard paste. 1773. (h) BRISTOL, Great Britain. Porcelain. Est. 1750. (i) GERMANY. 1863. (j) MEISSEN, Germany. Circa 1724.

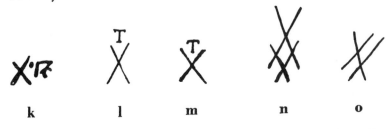

k   l   m   n   o

(k) BRISTOL, Great Britain. Porcelain. Est. 1750. (l-m) MEISSEN, Germany. Carl Thieme. 19th century. (n) MEISSEN, Germany. Herold, manager. Hard paste. Painted blue. 1720. (o) SITZENDORF, Germany. Imitation Meissen porcelain. Est. 1850.

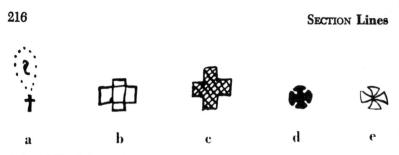

a   b   c   d   e

(a) BOURG-LA-REINE, France. Hard paste. 1773. (b) MOUS-
TIERS, France. Fayence. 1721. (c) NYMPHENBURG, Germany.
Porcelain. Impressed or incised. Est. 1755. (d) CASEMENE,
France. Fayence. Impressed. 1800. (e) COPENHAGEN, Denmark.
Est. 1772.

f   g   h   i   j

(f) COPENHAGEN, Denmark. Hard paste. Painted color. 1772
(mark uncertain). (g-h) ROUEN, France. Fayence. Circa 1740.
(i-j) TRENTON, New Jersey, U.S.A. Burgess and Campbell. Est.
1879.

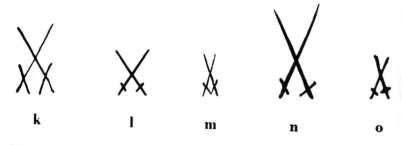

k   l   m   n   o

(k) MEISSEN, Germany. Hard paste. 1818-1924. (l) WORCES-
TER, Great Britain. Hard paste. Circa 1780. (m-n) MEISSEN, Ger-
many. Hard paste. Painted blue. 1919-present. (o) BRISTOL, Great
Britain. Porcelain. 1816-1835.

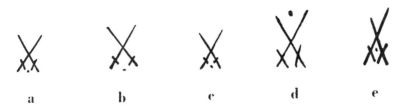

a b c d e

(**a**) DERBY, Great Britain. Porcelain. 1745-1848. (**b**) WORCES-TER, Great Britain. Dr. Wall. Porcelain. 1751-1783. (**c**) MEISSEN, Germany. Hard paste. Painted blue. 1725-1763. (**d**) MEISSEN, Germany. Hard paste. Painted blue. After 1924. (**e**) BRISTOL, Great Britain. Pottery, porcelain. 1750.

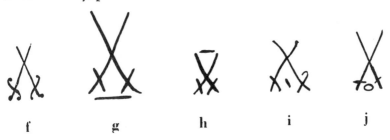

f g h i j

(**f**) MEISSEN, Germany. Hard paste. 1724. (**g-h**) MEISSEN, Germany. Hard paste. Defective porcelain. Painted blue and scratched. 1760. (**i-j**) MEISSEN, Germany. Hard paste. 1763-1774.

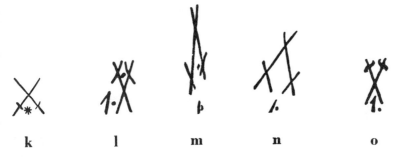

k l m n o

(**k**) MEISSEN, Germany. Marcolini period. Hard paste. 1774-1814. (**l-m-n-o**) BRISTOL, Great Britain. Porcelain. Painted blue, gold. 1770-1781.

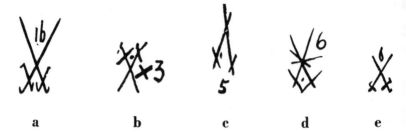

| a | b | c | d | e |

(**a**) WORCESTER. Great Britain. Dr. Wall. Porcelain. 1751-1783.
(**b-c-d**) BRISTOL, Great Britain. Porcelain. Painted blue, gold.
1770-1781. (**e**) WORCESTER, Great Britain. Dr. Wall. Porcelain.
1751-1783.

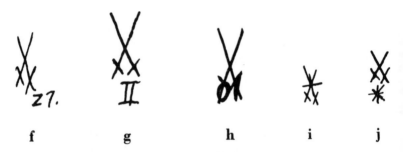

| f | g | h | i | j |

(**f-g**). MEISSEN, Germany. Hard paste. 1818. (**h-i**) BRISTOL,
Great Britain. Pottery, porcelain. Painted blue, gold. 1770-1781.
(**j**) WALLENDORF, Germany. Porcelain. 1776.

| k | l | m | n | o |

(**k-l**) MEISSEN, Germany. Bruhl, manager. Hard paste. Painted
blue. 1750. (**m**) MEISSEN, Germany. Herold, manager. Hard paste.
Painted blue. 1739. (**n**) DORNHEIM. Germany. 19th century.
(**o**) MEISSEN, Germany. Hard paste. Painted blue. 1814-1818.

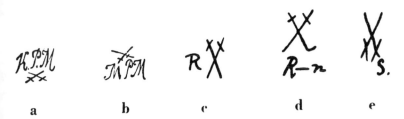

a   b   c   d   e

(a) MEISSEN, Germany. Konigliche Porzellen Manufactur. Hard paste. Painted blue. 1723. (b) MEISSEN, Germany. Meissen Porzellen Manufactur. Hard paste. Painted blue. 1723. (c) BRISTOL, Great Britain. Pottery, porcelain. Painted blue, gold. 1770-1781. (d) RAUENSTEIN, Germany. Porcelain. Painted blue, red, black, purple. Est. 1783. (e) MEISSEN, Germany. Hard paste. Painted blue. 1745-1763.

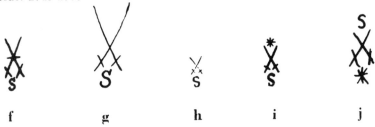

f   g   h   i   j

(f-g) PARIS, France. Samson the imitator. Circa 1873-circa 1905. (h-i) CAUGHLEY, Great Britain. Hard paste. Painted blue. 1750. (j) COALPORT, Great Britain. Porcelain. 1796.

k   l   m   n   o

(k-l) TOURNAY, Belgium. Porcelain, fayence. Est. 1751. (m) WEESP, Holland. Porcelain. Painted blue. Est. 1764. (n) MEISSEN, Germany. Hard paste. Circa 1725. (o) WORCESTER, Great Britain. Soft paste, hard paste. Painted blue, red. 1750.

a   b   c   d   e

(a-b-c-d-e) MEISSEN, Germany. Hard paste, imperfect pieces. Painted blue, scratched. 1760.

f   g   h   i   j

(f-g-h-i-j) MEISSEN, Germany. Hard paste, imperfect pieces. Painted blue, scratched. 1760.

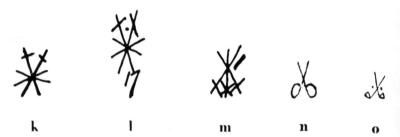

k   l   m   n   o

(k-l-m) BRISTOL, Great Britain. Porcelain. 1750. (n) WEST SMETHWICK, Great Britain. Ruskin pottery. 20th century. (o) DOROTHEENTHAL, Germany. Fayence. Est. 1707.

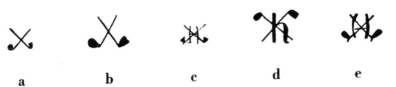

a b c d e

(a) DOROTHEENTHAL, Germany. Fayence. Painted color. Est. 1707. (b-c-d-e) VINCENNES, France. Pierre Antoine Hannong, founder. Hard paste. 1765.

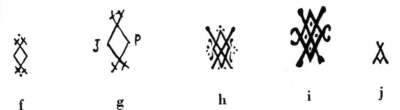

f g h i j

(f) MONTREUIL, France. Tinet, potter. 1815-1873. (g) PARIS, France. Jacob Petit. Hard paste. 1820. (h-i) MEISSEN, Germany. Hard paste. Painted blue. 1725-1730. (j) ANSBACH, Bavaria. Hard paste. Est. 1708.

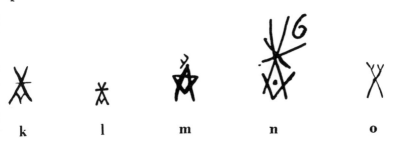

k l m n o

(k) WEESP, Holland. Hard paste. Est. 1759. (l) ANSBACH, Bavaria. Hard paste. Est. 1708. (m) SAVONA, Italy. 18th century. (n) BRISTOL, Great Britain. Porcelain. Est. 1770. (o) RUDOLSTADT, Germany. Hard paste. Painted blue. 1720.

a b c d e

(**a**) MEISSEN, Germany. Herold, manager. Hard paste. Painted blue. 1730. (**b**) WEESP, Holland. Hard paste. Est. 1759. (**c**) MEISSEN, Germany. Herold, manager. Hard paste. Painted blue. 1730. (**d-e**) RUDOLSTADT, Germany. Hard paste. Painted blue. 1720.

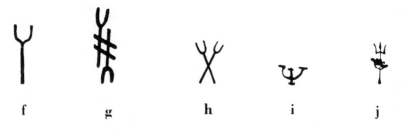

f g h i j

(**f-g-h**) VOLKSTEDT, Germany. Porcelain. 1760. (**i**) BOW, Great Britain. Porcelain. 1750. (**j**) CHELSEA, Great Britain. Porcelain. 1745-1784.

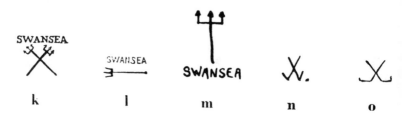

k l m n o

(**k-l-m**) SWANSEA, Great Britain. Hard paste. Impressed. 1814. (**n-o**) THURINGIA, Germany. Limbach, factory. Porcelain. Est. 1772.

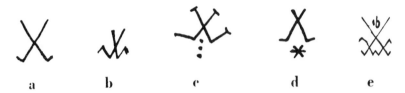

a b c d e

(a) MEISSEN, Germany. Hard paste. 19th century. (b) WALLEN-DORF, Germany. Porcelain. Painted blue. Est. 1764. (c) LONG-TON, Great Britain. William Littler, potter. Porcelain, stoneware. 1750-1760. (d) THURINGIA, Germany. Limbach, factory. Porcelain. Est. 1772. (e) WORCESTER, Great Britain. Porcelain. Painted blue. Est. 1751.

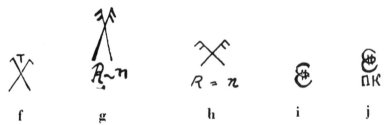

f g h i j

(f) CAUGHLEY, Great Britain. Thomas Turner, potter. Hard paste. Painted blue. 1772. (g-h) RAUENSTEIN, Germany. Porcelain. Painted blue, purple, red. Est. 1783. (i) SAINT PETERSBURG, Russia. Hard paste. Painted blue. 1762. (j) SAINT PETERSBURG, Russia. Paul Korniloffe. Hard paste. Painted. 1762.

k l m n o

(k) THURINGIA, Germany. Ilmenau, factory. Fayence, porcelain. Est. 1777. (l-m-n) TOURS, France. Fayence, hard paste. Painted blue. 1840. (o) BUEN RETIRO, Spain. Soft paste. 1759-1808.

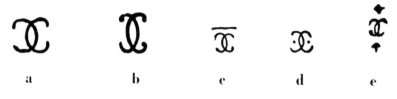

a   b   c   d   e

(a) NIDERVILLER, France. Hard paste. 1770-1793. (b) LUD-WIGSBURG, Germany. Hard paste. 1758-1793. (c-d) NIDERVIL-LER, France. Hard paste. 1770-1793. (e) NUREMBURG. Germany. Fayence. Est. 1712.

f   g   h   i   j

(f) ILMENAU, Germany. Porcelain. Est. 1777. (g) NIDERVIL-LER, France. Hard paste. 1770-1793. (h-i) STOKE-ON-TRENT, Great Britain. W. T. Copeland. Porcelain. 1833. (j) SEVRES, France. Porcelain. 1824-1828.

k   l   m   n   o

(k-l-m-n) SEVRES, France. Porcelain. 1824-1828. (o) LUDWIGS-BURG, Germany. Hard paste. Painted blue, red. 1758-1793.

a   b   c   d   e

(**a**) BUEN RETIRO, Spain. Soft paste. 1759-1808. (**b**) FON-
TAINEBLEAU, France. Hard paste. After 1875. (**c**) STOKE-ON-
TRENT, Great Britain. Minton, factory. Hard paste. Painted blue,
red. 1790. (**d**) PARIS, France. Gros Caillou, factory. Hard paste.
Painted color. 1773. (**e**) SEVRES, France. Soft paste. 1745-1753.

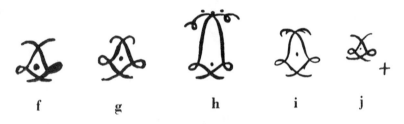

f   g   h   i   j

(**f-g-h-i**) SEVRES, France. Soft paste. 1745-1753. (**j**) COALPORT,
Great Britain. Porcelain. Est. 1796.

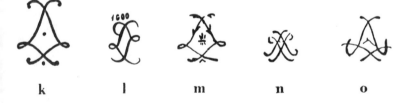

k   l   m   n   o

(**k**) SEVRES, France. Soft paste. 1745-1753. (**l**) WORCESTER,
Great Britain. Hard paste. 1751-1783. (**m**) SEVRES, France. Soft
paste. 1745-1753. (**n-o**) SAINT AMAND, France. Fayence, soft
paste. 1711-1778.

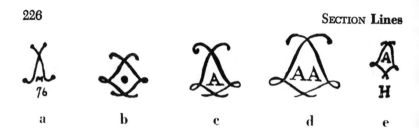

a   b   c   d   e

(a) STOKE-ON-TRENT, Great Britain. Minton, factory. Bone china. 18th century to 1831. (b) SEVRES, France. Soft paste. 1745-1753. (c) SEVRES, France. Soft paste. 1753. (d) SEVRES, France. Soft paste. 1778. (e) SEVRES, France. Soft paste. Circa 1753.

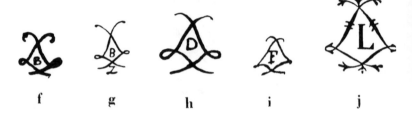

f   g   h   i   j

(f-g) SEVRES, France. Soft paste. 1754. (h) SEVRES, France. Soft paste. 1756. (i) FRANCE. Feuillet, decorator. Painted gold, black. 1820-1850. (j) SEVRES, France. Soft paste, hard paste. 1764.

k   l   m   n

(k) SEVRES, France. Soft paste, hard paste. 1790. (l) SEVRES, France. Hard paste, soft paste. 1771. (m) SEVRES, France. Hard paste, soft paste. 1821. (n) SEVRES, France. Hard paste, soft paste. 1770.

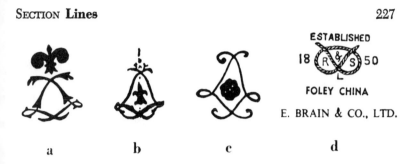

ESTABLISHED

18 R & S 50

FOLEY CHINA

E. BRAIN & CO., LTD.

a   b   c   d

(**a**) SEVRES, France. Soft paste. 1745-1753. (**b**) SEVRES, France. Soft paste. 1745-1753. (**c**) SEVRES, France. Soft paste, hard paste. 1745-1753. (**d**) STOKE-ON-TRENT, Great Britain. E. Brain and Company Limited. Foley China Company. 19th century.

e   f   g   h   i   j

(**e**) COBRIDGE, Great Britain. William Brownfield. Circa 1850. (**f-g**) TRENTON, New Jersey, U.S.A. Willetts Manufacturing Company. Est. 1879. (**h-i-j**) BOW, Great Britain. Porcelain. Painted red, blue. 1750.

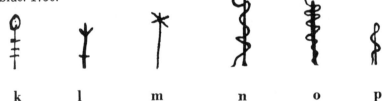

k   l   m   n   o   p

(**k**) BOW, Great Britain. Porcelain. 1750. (**l**) BUEN RETIRO, Spain. Soft paste. 1759-1808. (**m-n-o-p**) MEISSEN, Germany. Hard paste. Painted blue. 1710; or WORCESTER, Great Britain. Soft paste. Painted blue. 1753.

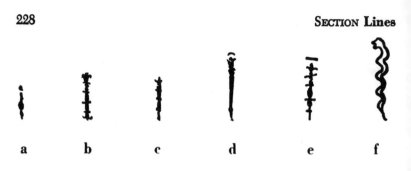

a   b   c   d   e   f

(a-b-c-d-e) BERLIN, Germany. Royal factory. Hard paste. Painted
blue. 1760. (f) RUSSIA. Fayence. 1845.

g   h   i   j   k

(g) BERLIN, Germany. Royal factory. Hard paste. Painted blue.
1760. (h) HANLEY, Great Britain. 1876. (i) NYMPHENBURG, Germany. Porcelain. Impressed or incised. Est. 1747. (j) PREMIERES,
France. Fayence. 19th century. (k) HOLLAND. Red earthenware.
1678.

l   m   n   o   p

(l) CAUGHLEY, Great Britain. Hard paste. Painted blue. 1750.
(m) BOW, Great Britain. Porcelain. 1750. (n) BOURG-LA-REINE,
France. Porcelain. 1773. (o) BRISTOL, Great Britain. Hard paste.
Painted color. 1770. (p) NIDERVILLER, France. Fayence, porcelain. 1754.

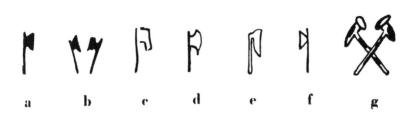

a   b   c   d   e   f   g

(a-b) BADEN BADEN, Germany. Hard paste. Painted gold, color. 1753. (c-d-e-f) HOLLAND. De Porceleyne Byl (The Porcelain Hatchet). Fayence. Delft. 1759. (g) PIRKENHAMMER, Germany. Hard paste. 1850.

SECTION **MIS-CELLANEOUS**

h   i   j

(h) BURSLEM, Great Britain. T. and R. Boote. 1890-1906. (i) BURSLEM, Great Britain. T. and R. Boote. 1842-1964+. (j) CO-BRIDGE, Great Britain. Staffordshire. Painted blue. 1800.

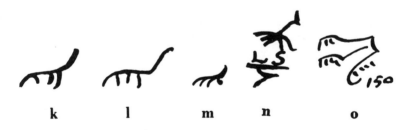

k   l   m   n   o

(k-l) HOLLAND. De Klauw (The Claw). Fayence. Delft. 1764. (m) LUDWIGSBURG, Germany. Porcelain. 1756-1824. (n-o) HOLLAND. De Klauw (The Claw). Fayence. Delft. 1764.

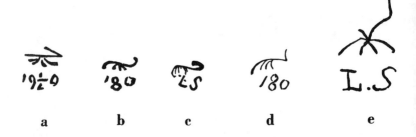

a   b   c   d   e

(**a-b-c-d-e**) HOLLAND. De Klauw (The Claw). Fayence. Delft. 1764.

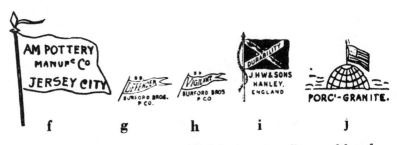

f   g   h   i   j

(**f**) JERSEY CITY. New Jersey, U.S.A. American Pottery Manufacturing Company. Printed. Circa 1835. (**g-h**) EAST LIVERPOOL, Ohio, U.S.A. Burford Brothers Pottery Company. 1879-1900. (**i**) HANLEY, Great Britain. J. H. Weatherby and Son. After 1891. (**j**) STEUBENVILLE, Ohio, U.S.A. Steubenville Pottery Company. Est. 1887.

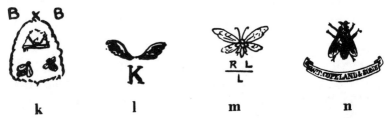

k   l   m   n

(**k**) WHEELING, West Virginia, U.S.A. Wheeling Pottery Company. Est. 1879. (**l**) KLOSTERLE, Bohemia. Porcelain, lead-glazed earthenware. 1793. (**m**) LIMOGES, France. Fayence, porcelain. 19th century. (**n**) STOKE-ON-TRENT, Great Britain. Spode, factory. W. T. Copeland and Sons. 1847-1891.

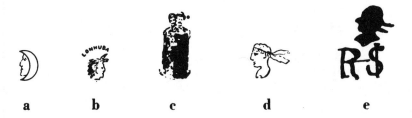

a   b   c   d   e

(**a**) WORCESTER, Great Britain. Blueware. 1751-1800. (**b**) STEU-BENVILLE. Ohio, U.S.A. Lonhuda Pottery. Est. 1892. (**c**) MON-MOUTH, Illinois, U.S.A. Monmouth Pottery Company. Circa 1890. (**d**) HOLLAND. Fayence. Delft. 18th century. (**e**) HOLLAND. De Oude Moriaan's Hooft (The Old Moor's Head). Fayence. Delft. 1680.

f   g   h   i   j

(**f**) GERMANY. 1842. (**g**) ELBOGEN, Germany. Earthenware, porcelain. Est. 1815. (**h**) VIENNA, Austria. Royal Vienna, factory. Circa 1850. (**i**) BOSTON, Massachusetts, U.S.A. New England Pottery Company. Circa 1887. (**j**) NEW YORK, New York, U.S.A. Carr and Morrison. Circa 1860.

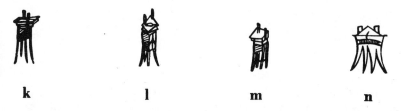

k   l   m   n

(**k-l-m-n**) DERBY, Great Britain. Hard paste. Painted blue. 1745-1848.

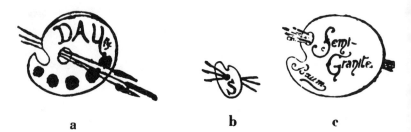

a   b   c

(a) STEUBENVILLE, Ohio, U.S.A. Steubenville Pottery Company.
Est. 1879. (b) PARIS, France. Hard paste. Painted gold. 1870.
(c) WELLSVILLE, Ohio, U.S.A. J.H. Baum. Printed. 1880.

d   e   f   g   h

(d) MONTE LUPO, Italy. Pottery. 17th century. (e-f) TRENTON,
New Jersey, U.S.A. Cook Pottery Company. Circa 1900. (g) EAST
LIVERPOOL, Ohio, U.S.A. Globe Pottery Company. Est. 1888.
(h) BOSTON, Massachusetts, U.S.A. New England Pottery Company. 1886.

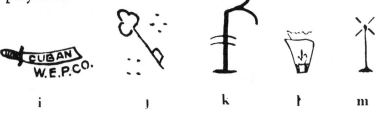

i   j   k   l   m

(i) EAST LIVERPOOL, Ohio, U.S.A. West End Pottery Company.
Est. 1893. (j) DIRMSTEIN, Germany. Fayence, earthenware. Est.
1778-1788. (k) CAUGHLEY, Great Britain. Porcelain. 1750-1814.
(l) HOLLAND. Fayence. Delft. Painted red. 1700. (m) CLIG-
NANCOURT, France. Hard paste. 1771-1775.

a   b   c   d   e

(**a**) WORCESTER, Great Britain. 1751-1783. (**b-c-d-e**) CHAN-
TILLY, France. Soft paste. Painted blue, red. 1725-1800.

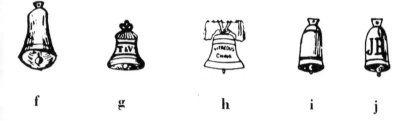

f   g   h   i   j

(**f**) SCOTLAND. J. and M. P. Bell and Company. After 1842.
(**g**) LIMOGES, France. Fayence, hard paste. 1891-1907. (**h**) TREN-
TON, New Jersey, U.S.A. Bellmark Pottery Company. Est. 1893.
(**i-j**) HULL, Great Britain. Bellevue Pottery Company. Earthenware.
1825.

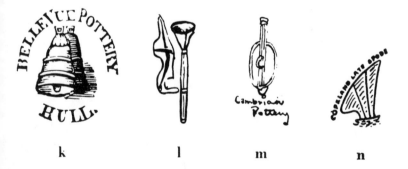

k   l   m   n

(**k**) HULL, Great Britain. Bellevue Pottery Company. Earthenware.
1825. (**l**) SAVONO, Italy. 17th century. (**m**) SWANSEA. Great
Britain. Cambrian, factory. Soft paste. 1765. (**n**) STOKE-ON-
TRENT, Great Britain. Spode, factory. W. T. Copeland and Sons.
Porcelain. 1847.

SECTION
NUMBERS
See also Section
Lines

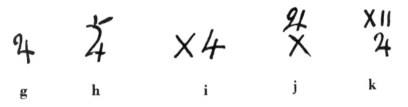

(a) BRISTOL, Great Britain. Pottery, porcelain. Painted blue, gold. 18th century. (b) PLYMOUTH, Great Britain. Hard paste. Painted red, blue, gold. 1768. (c) BRISTOL, Great Britain. Pottery, porcelain. Painted blue, gold. 18th century. (d) TRENTON, New Jersey, U.S.A. Isaac Broome. Est. 1880. (e) BRISTOL, Great Britain. Pottery, porcelain. Painted blue, gold. 18th century. (f) NEVERS, France. Pottery. Painted color. 16th century.

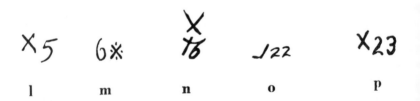

(g-h) PLYMOUTH, Great Britain. Hard paste. Painted red, gold, blue. 1768. (i) BRISTOL, Great Britain. Porcelain. 1770-1781. (j-k) PLYMOUTH, Great Britain. Painted red, gold, blue. 1768.

(l) BRISTOL, Great Britain. Porcelain. Painted blue, gold. 1770-1781. (m) TOURNAY, Belgium. Fayence. 1850. (n) BRISTOL, Great Britain. Porcelain, pottery. Painted blue, gold. 1770-1781. (o) BUEN RETIRO, Spain. Hard paste. 1804-1808. (p) BRISTOL, Great Britain. Pottery, porcelain. Painted blue, gold. 1770-1781.

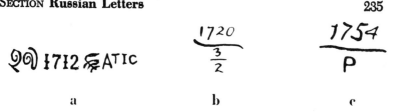

a   b   c

(**a**) YEARSLEY, Great Britain. Green-glazed earthenware. 18th century. (**b**) HOLLAND. De Ster (The Star). Fayence. Delft. 1720. (**c**) HOLLAND. De Porceleyne Schootel (The Porcelain Dish). Fayence. Delft. 1759.

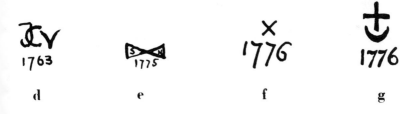

d   e   f   g

(**d**) LESUM, Germany. Fayence. 1755-1800. (**e**) BUEN RETIRO, Spain. Soft paste. 1759-1808. (**f**) BRISTOL, Great Britain. Porcelain. 1770-1781. (**g**) VINOVO, Italy. Porcelain. Painted. 1776-1820.

SECTION **RUSSIAN LETTERS**

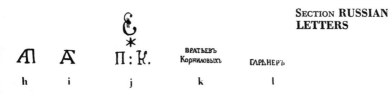

h   i   j   k   l

(**h**) MOSCOW, Russia. A. Popoff, owner. 1800-1872. (**i**) MOSCOW, Russia. A. Gardner. Hard paste. Painted color. 1750. (**j**) SAINT PETERSBURG, Russia. 1762-1796. (**k**) SAINT PETERSBURG, Russia. Hard paste. Printed. 1825. (**l**) MOSCOW, Russia. A. Gardner. Hard-paste. Painted color. 1750.

ФГ
ГУЛИНА   ПОПОВЫ   *Baranȝwka*

·a   b   c

(a) MOSCOW, Russia. Hard paste, fayence. Impressed. Circa 1800.
(b) MOSCOW, Russia. A. Popoff. Hard paste. Painted color. 1830.
(c) BARANOVKA, Poland. Porcelain. Painted black, brown. 1801-1895.

SECTION **SHIELD**
See also Sections
**Circle and Sign,
Crown and Circle,
Crown and Shield,
Square**

d   e   f   g   h   i

(d-e-f-g) VIENNA, Austria. Royal Vienna, factory. Hard paste.
Painted blue, incised. 1744-1820. (h-i) VIENNA, Austria. Royal
Vienna, factory. Hard paste. Painted blue. 1750-1780.

j   k   l   m   n   o

(j) GERMANY. C. M. Hutschendreuther. Underglaze blue. Est.
1814. (k) VIENNA, Austria. Royal Vienna, factory. Hard paste.
1850-1864. (l) ANSBACH, Germany. Hard paste. Est. 1758. (m)
GERMANY. C. M. Hutschendreuther. Underglaze blue. Est. 1814.
(n) MALTA. Pottery. Impressed. 19th century. (o) LUDWIGS-
BURG, Germany. Porcelain. Est. 1756.

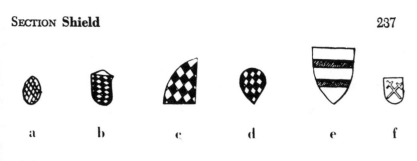

a   b   c   d   e   f

(**a**) NYMPHENBURG, Germany. Porcelain. Painted. 1800. (**b**) NYMPHENBURG, Germany. Porcelain. Painted. 1754-1862. (**c**) FRANKENTHAL, Germany. Porcelain. Painted blue. 1756. (**d**) NYMPHENBURG, Germany. Porcelain. Painted. 1800. (**e**) GERMANY. Fayence. Circa 1830. (**f**) MEISSEN, Germany. Bottger stoneware. 1724.

g   h   i   j   k   l

(**g**) MEISSEN, Germany. Bottger stoneware. 1710. (**h-i**) NUREMBERG, Germany. Fayence. Est. 1712. (**j**) SAVONA, Italy. Fayence. 17th century. (**k-l**) HEREND, Hungary. Moritz Fischer, owner. Overglaze blue. 19th-20th century.

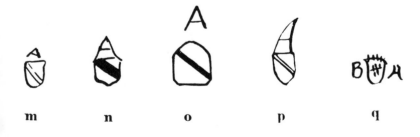

m   n   o   p   q

(**m-n-o-p**) ANSBACH, Germany. Hard paste. Painted blue. Est. 1758. (**q**) SAVONA, Italy. Fayence. 18th century.

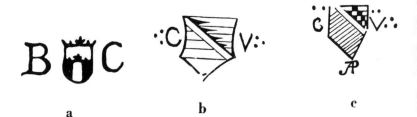

a   **b**   **c**

(**a**) SAVONA, Italy. 18th century. (**b-c**) KLOSTER VEILSDORF,
Germany. Porcelain. Underglaze blue. 1765.

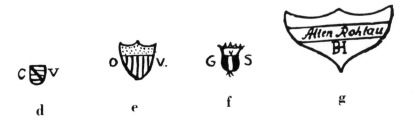

d   **e**   **f**   **g**

(**d**) KLOSTER VEILSDORF, Germany. Porcelain. Underglaze
blue. 1765. (**e**) WHEELING, West Virginia, U.S.A. Ohio Valley
China Company. 1890. (**f**) SAVONA, Italy. Fayence. 18th century.
(**g**) ALT-ROHLAU, Germany. Pottery, porcelain. Est. 1813.

h   **i**   **j**   **k**   **l**

(**h**) STEUBENVILLE, Ohio, U.S.A. Steubenville Pottery Com
pany. Est. 1887. (**i**) EAST LIVERPOOL, Ohio, U.S.A. Burfor
Brothers Pottery Company. Circa 1880. (**j**) TRENTON, New Jer
sey, U.S.A. Crescent Pottery Company. Est. 1881. (**k**) LONGPOR1
Great Britain. John Davenport, potter. Earthenware, porcelair
Printed. Circa 1800. (**l**) SEVRES, France. Mark tells year of decc
ration. 1902-1940.

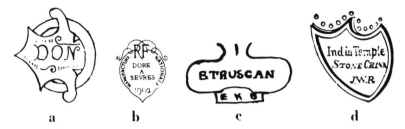

a   b   c   d

(a) STEUBENVILLE, Ohio, U.S.A. Steubenville Pottery Company.
Est. 1887. (b) SEVRES, France. Mark tells year of gilding. 1902-
1940. (c) FENTON, Great Britain. Circa 1830. (d) SHELTON,
Great Britain. 1815.

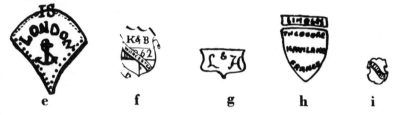

e   f   g   h   i

(e) MIDDLESBOROUGH, Great Britain. Earthenware. Impressed.
1845. (f) WORCESTER, Great Britain. Kerr and Binns. 1852-1862.
(g) SCHLAGGENWALD, Germany. Lippert and Haas. 1832-1846.
(h) LIMOGES, France. Haviland, factory. Whiteware. Painted
green. 1936-1945. (i) TRENTON, New Jersey, U.S.A. Crescent
Pottery Company. Est. 1881.

j   k   l   m   n

(j-k) BOSTON, Massachusetts, U.S.A. New England Pottery Com-
pany. Est. 1875. (l) TRENTON, New Jersey, U.S.A. Columbian Art
Pottery Company. Est. 1876. (m) DOYLESTOWN, Pennsylvania,
U.S.A. Moravian Pottery and Tile Works. Circa 1890. (n) GER-
MANY. Est. 1870.

a   **b**   **c**   **d**   **e**

(**a**) PIRKENHAMMER, Germany. Hard paste. Est. 1807. (**b**)
WORCESTER, Great Britain. Kerr and Binns. Porcelain. 1852-1862.
(**c**) GERMANY. Circa 1850. (**d**) BALTIMORE, Maryland, U.S.A.
F. Haynes and Company. Est. 1880. (**e**) BALTIMORE, Maryland,
U.S.A. Edwin Bennett. Circa 1875.

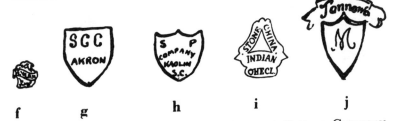

f   **g**   **h**   **i**   **j**

(**f**) TRENTON, New Jersey, U.S.A. Crescent Pottery Company.
Est. 1881. (**g**) AKRON, Ohio, U.S.A. Summit China Company.
Printed. Circa 1890. (**h**) KAOLIN, South Carolina, U.S.A. Southern
Porcelain Company. Circa 1860. (**i**) HANLEY, Great Britain. Old
Hall Porcelain Works. 20th century. (**j**) TONNOWA, Germany.
Fayence, porcelain. 1813-1880.

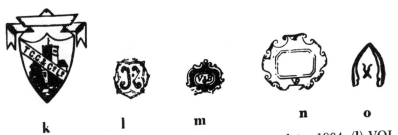

k   **l**   **m**   **n**   **o**

(**k**) CHURCH GRESLEY, Great Britain. Porcelain. 1864. (**l**) VOI-
SONLIEU, France. Fayence. Impressed. 1839-1858. (**m-n**) MET-
TLACH, Germany. Glazed earthenware. Est. 1809. (**o**) EAST
HAMPTON, New York, U.S.A. Middle Lane Pottery. Circa 1890.

a   b   c   d   e

(a) TRENTON, New Jersey, U.S.A. Greenwood Pottery Company. Printed. Est. 1864. (b) LIVERPOOL, Ohio, U.S.A. Knowles, Taylor, and Knowles. Est. 1854. (c) BOSTON, Massachusetts, U.S.A. New England Pottery Company. Printed. Est. 1875. (d) WELLSVILLE, Ohio, U.S.A. Pioneer Pottery Company. Circa 1890. (e) TRENTON, New Jersey, U.S.A. Coxon and Company. Circa 1875.

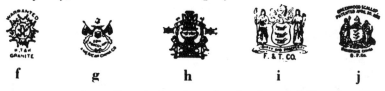

f   g   h   i   j

(f) LIVERPOOL, Ohio, U.S.A. Knowles, Taylor, and Knowles. Est. 1854. (g) TORONTO, Ohio, U.S.A. American China Company. Est. 1896. (h) HANLEY, Great Britain. Fayence. F. Winkle and Company. 19th century. (i) TRENTON, New Jersey. U.S.A. Fell and Thropp Company. 19th century. (j) TRENTON, New Jersey, U.S.A. Greenwood Pottery Company. Porcelain. Printed. 1880.

k   l   m   n   o

(k) TRENTON, New Jersey, U.S.A. Crescent Pottery Company. Est. 1881. (l) BALTIMORE, Maryland, U.S.A. D. F. Haynes and Company. Est. 1879. (m) TRENTON, New Jersey, U.S.A. East Trenton Pottery Company. Circa 1890. (n) FENTON, Great Britain. John Edwards. Circa 1880-1900. (o) TRENTON, New Jersey, U.S.A. Trenton Pottery Company. 19th century.

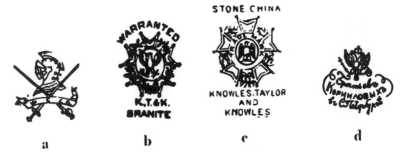

a   b   c   d

(a) WHEELING, West Virginia, U.S.A. Warwick China Company.
Est. 1887. (b) EAST LIVERPOOL, Ohio, U.S.A. Knowles, Taylor,
and Knowles. Circa 1890-circa 1907. (c) EAST LIVERPOOL, Ohio,
U.S.A. Knowles, Taylor, and Knowles. Est. 1854. (d) SAINT PE-
TERSBURG, Russia. After 1830.

e   f   g   h

(e) SYRACUSE, New York, U.S.A. Onondaga Pottery Company.
1874-1893. (f) ZELL, Germany. Glazed earthenware. Est. 1818. (g)
GERMANY. Circa 1875. (h) BURSLEM, Great Britain. Enoch Wood
and Sons. 1818-1846.

i   j   k

(i) METTLACH, Germany. Fayence. 1842. (j) ZELL. Germany.
Glazed earthenware. After 1818. (k) STOKE-ON-TRENT, Great
Britain. Porcelain. Printed. Circa 1799.

a b c

(a) SCHLAGGENWALD, Germany. Porcelain. 1793-1866. (b) STOKE-ON-TRENT, Great Britain. Spode, factory. Copeland and Garrett. 1833-1847. (c) · BENNINGTON, Vermont, ·U.S.A. Impressed. Circa 1850.

d e f

(d) LONGPORT, Great Britain. G. Phillps, potter. Earthenware. 19th century. (e) STOKE-ON-TRENT, Great Britain. Minton, factory. After 1868. (f) SHELTON, Great Britain. Porcelain. 19th century.

g h i

(g) STOKE-ON-TRENT, Great Britain. Minton, factory. 1850. (h) COBRIDGE, Great Britain. Circa 1850. (i) STOKE-ON-TRENT, Great Britain. Spode, factory. 19th century.

SECTION **SQUARE**
See also Sections
**Circle and Sign,
Shield**

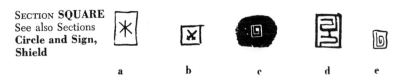

a   b   c   d   e

(**a-b**) MEISSEN, Germany. Bottger red stoneware. 1710-20. (**c**) NEWCASTLE, Great Britain. John and David Elers, potters. Stoneware. 1690-1710. (**d**) CHELSEA, Great Britain. Porcelain. 1745-1785. (**e**) HOLLAND. De Porceleyne Byl (The Porcelain Hatchet). Fayence. Delft. 1759.

f   g   h   i   j

(**f**) WORCESTER, Great Britain. Porcelain. Blue underglaze. Est. 1751. (**g-h**) MEISSEN, Germany. Bottger red stoneware. Circa 1718. (**i-j**) WORCESTER, Great Britain. Porcelain. Est. 1751.

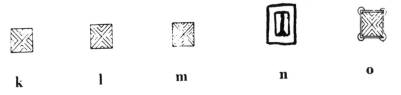

k   l   m   n   o

(**k-l-m**) WORCESTER, Great Britain. Porcelain. Blue Underglaze. Est. 1751. (**n**) DERBY, Great Britain. Painted blue. 1775. (**o**) WORCESTER, Great Britain. Porcelain. Blue underglaze. Est. 1751.

a　　　b　　　c　　　d　　　e

(a) WORCESTER, Great Britain. Porcelain. Blue underglaze. Est. 1751. (b) TUNSTALL, Great Britain. William Adams, potter. 1787-1805. (c) BOW, Great Britain. Est. 1750. (d) HANLEY, Great Britain. Impressed. Circa 1875. (e) STOKE-ON-TRENT, Great Britain. Spode, factory. Copeland, late Spode. Printed blue. 1847-1891.

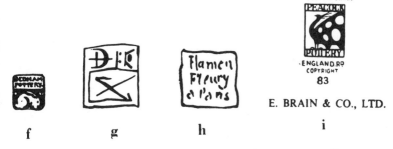

E. BRAIN & CO., LTD.

f　　　g　　　h　　　i

(f) DEDHAM, Massachusetts, U.S.A. Dedham Pottery Company. Circa 1900. (g) BOW, Great Britain. Est. 1750. (h) PARIS, France. 1773. (i) STOKE-ON-TRENT, Great Britain. E. Brain and Company Limited. Foley China Company. 20th century.

j　　　k　　　l　　　m

(j) FRANCE. Hard paste. 1860. (k) SHELTON, Great Britain. 1762. (l) TRENTON, New Jersey, U.S.A. William Young and Sons. Circa 1855. (m) PRAGUE, Germany. Kriegel and Company. Porcelain. 1836-1862.

a   b   c   d   e

(**a**) LONGTON, Great Britain. Mayer and Newbold, potters. Painted red. 19th century. (**b**) NEWBURYPORT, Massachusetts, U.S.A. Merrimac Ceramic Company. Est. 1897. (**c**) FENTON, Great Britain. 18th century. (**d**) NEW ORLEANS, Louisiana, U.S.A. Newcomb Pottery Company. 19th century. (**e**) SEVRES, France. Painted black on hard paste, blue on soft paste. 1912-1917, 1921-1927.

f   g   h   i   j

(**f-g**) STOKE-ON-TRENT, Great Britain. Spode, factory. Ironstone. Printed blue. 1815-1830. (**h**) NEW YORK, New York, U.S.A. Carr and Morrison. 1853-1888. (**i**) WORCESTER, Great Britain. Porcelain. Painted color. Est. 1751. (**j**) ZELL, Germany. Glazed earthenware. After 1818.

k   l   m.   n   o

(**k**) HOLLAND. Fayence. Delft. 1705. (**l**) COLORADO SPRINGS, Colorado, U.S.A. Van Briggle Pottery Company. Est. 1900. (**m**) STOKE-ON-TRENT, Great Britain. After 1891. (**n**) STEUBENVILLE, Ohio, U.S.A. Steubenville Pottery Company. Est. 1887. (**o**) LONGTON, Great Britain. Hilditch and Son. Est. 1830.

a   b   c

(**a**) HANLEY, Great Britain. Job Meigh, potter. 18th century. (**b**) MEISSEN, Germany. Impressed. 19th century. (**c**) FENTON, Great Britain. Myatt, potter. Staffordshire. Impressed. 18th-19th century.

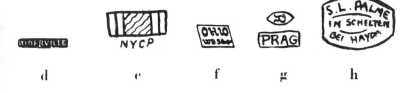

d   e   f   g   h

(**d**) NIDERVILLER, France. Fayence. Impressed. 1780-1800. (**e**) NEW YORK, New York, U.S.A. Carr and Morrison. Printed. 1855-1871. (**f**) EAST LIVERPOOL, Ohio, U.S.A. William Brunt Pottery Company. 1850-1895. (**g**) PRAGUE, Germany. Porcelain. 1810-1862. (**h**) GERMANY. 1820.

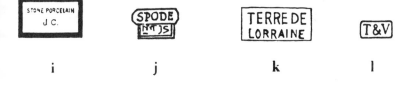

i   j   k   l

(**i**) NEW YORK, New York, U.S.A. Carr and Morrison. Printed. 1855-1871. (**j**) STOKE-ON-TRENT. Great Britain. Spode, factory. 1845-1891. (**k**) LUNEVILLE, France. Fayence. Circa 1775. (**l**) LIMOGES, France. Tresseman & Vogt. Porcelain. 1882.

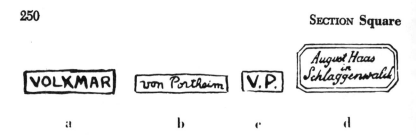

a   b   c   d

(a) METUCHEN, New Jersey, U.S.A. Charles Volkmar and Son. Est. 1903. (b-c) CHODAU, Germany. Est. 1804. (d) SCHLAG-GENWALD, Germany. Porcelain. 1793-1866.

f   g

(e) ALT-ROHLAU, Germany. 1813. (f) SHELTON, Great Britain. John and William Ridgway. 1802. (g) BURSLEM, Great Britain. Doulton, factory. After 1891.

h   i   j

(h) FENTON, Great Britain. Staffordshire. 1813-present. (i) HAVI-LAND, France. Whiteware. 1856. (j) MEISSEN, Germany. Hard paste. 1723.

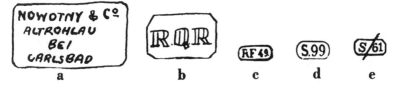

a   b   c   d   e

(a) ALT-ROHLAU, Germany. Porcelain, fayence. Est. 1814. (b) PHILADELPHIA, Pennsylvania, U.S.A. Richard Remmey (Remney). Impressed. Est. 1859. (c) SEVRES, France. Hard paste. 1849. (d) SEVRES, France. Painted green on hard paste, black on hard paste, blue on soft paste. 1848-1899. (e) SEVRES, France. Hard paste, undecorated when it left the factory. Printed green. 1861.

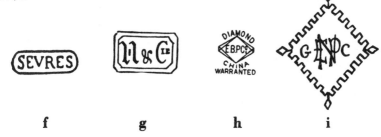

f   g   h   i

(f) SEVRES, France. Porcelain. 1860-1891. (g) SARREGUE-MINES, France. Utzchneider and Company. Fayence. Before 1890. (h) BALTIMORE, Maryland, U.S.A. Edwin Bennett. Circa 1875. (i) BOSTON, Massachusetts, U.S.A. New England Pottery Company. Circa 1887.

j   k   l   m

(j) TRENTON, New Jersey, U.S.A. Glasgow Pottery Company. 1863-1890. (k) BALTIMORE, Maryland, U.S.A. Maryland Pottery Company. Est. 1879. (l) NEW MILFORD, Connecticut, U.S.A. New Milford Pottery Company. Est. 1887. (m) WHEELING, West Virginia, U.S.A. Ohio Valley China Company. Circa 1890.

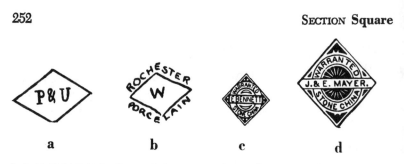

a   b   c   d

(a) LONGTON, Great Britain. Poole and Unwin, potters. 19th century. (b) WHEELING, West Virginia, U.S.A. Wheeling Pottery Company. Est. 1879. (c) BALTIMORE, Maryland, U.S.A. Edwin Bennett. 1856. (d) BEAVER FALLS, Pennsylvania, U.S.A. Mayer Pottery Company. Est. 1881.

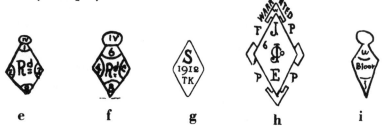

e   f   g   h   i

(e) GREAT BRITAIN, 1842-1867 (see Foreword for complete explanation). (f) GREAT BRITAIN. 1868-1883 (see Foreword for complete explanation). (g) SEVRES, France. Painted black on hard paste, blue on soft paste. 1912-1917, 1921-1927. (h) PHILADEL-PHIA, Pennsylvania, U.S.A. J. E. Jeffords and Company. Printed. Circa 1875. (i) U.S.A. William Bloor. Impressed. 1862.

j   k   l   m

(j) COLORADO SPRINGS, Colorado, U.S.A. Van Briggle Pottery Company. Est. 1901. (k) BALTIMORE, Maryland, U.S.A. F. Haynes and Company. 1882-1884. (l) PHOENIXVILLE, Pennsylvania, U.S.A. Chester Pottery Company. Est. 1894. (m) LUNE-VILLE, France. Fayence. Circa 1775.

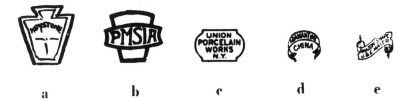

a   b   c   d   e

(a) EAST LIVERPOOL, Ohio, U.S.A. Vodrey Brothers. Circa 1875. (b) PENNSYLVANIA, U.S.A. Pennsylvania Museum and School of Industrial Art. Est. 1903. (c) NEW YORK, New York, U.S.A. Union Porcelain Works. Circa 1880. (d) WHEELING, West Virginia, U.S.A. Wheeling Pottery Company. Est. 1879. (e) BEAVER FALLS, Pennsylvania, U.S.A. Mayer Pottery Company. Est. 1881.

f   g   h   i

(f) STEUBENVILLE, Ohio, U.S.A. Steubenville Pottery Company. Est. 1887. (g) EAST LIVERPOOL, Ohio, U.S.A. Knowles, Taylor, and Knowles. Est. 1854. (h) GERMANY. Circa 1835. (i) EAST LIVERPOOL, Ohio, U.S.A. Brunt, Bloor, and Martin. Est. 1876.

j   k   l   m

(j) EAST LIVERPOOL, Ohio, U.S.A. Knowles, Taylor, and Knowles. Est. 1854. (k) SEBRING, Ohio. French china. (l) EAST LIVERPOOL, Ohio, U.S.A. Knowles, Taylor, and Knowles. Est. 1854. (m) DERBY, Great Britain. Robert Bloor. 1811-1848.

(a) SWANSEA, Wales. Porcelain. 1814-1822. (b) EAST LIV-
ERPOOL, Ohio, U.S.A. Brunt, Bloor, and Martin. Est. 1876. (c)
SEBRING, Ohio. French china. (d) BALTIMORE, Maryland, U.S.A.
F. Haynes and Company. 1880-1890. (e) EAST LIVERPOOL, Ohio,
U.S.A. Knowles, Taylor, and Knowles. Est. 1854.

(f) SHELTON, Great Britain. John Ridgway, potter. Staffordshire.
After 1802. (g) LIMOGES, France. Porcelain. After 1891. (h)
SEBRING, Ohio. French china. (i) EAST LIVERPOOL, Ohio,
U.S.A. Brunt, Bloor, and Martin. Est. 1876.

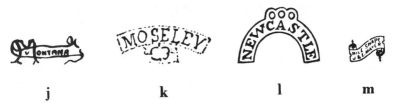

(j) EAST LIVERPOOL, Ohio, U.S.A. Knowles, Taylor, and
Knowles. Est. 1876. (k) BURSLEM, Great Britain. Moseley, potter.
Staffordshire. 1811-1857. (l) NEWCASTLE-ON-TYNE, Great Britain. Earthenware. 18th-19th century. (m) BEAVER FALLS, Pennsylvania, U.S.A. Mayer Pottery Company. Est. 1881.

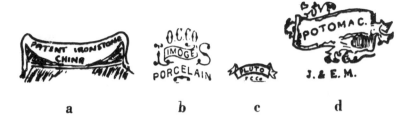

(a) FENTON, Great Britain. Joseph Myatt. 18th-19th century. (b) EAST PALESTINE, Ohio, U.S.A. Ohio China Company. 19th century. (c) SEBRING, Ohio. French china. (d) BEAVER FALLS, Pennsylvania, U.S.A. Mayer Pottery Company. Est. 1881.

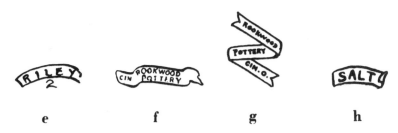

(e) BURSLEM, Great Britain. John and Richard Riley, potters. Staffordshire. 19th century. (f-g) CINCINNATI, Ohio, U.S.A. Rookwood Pottery Company. Circa 1880. (h) BURSLEM, Great Britain. Ralph Salt, potter. Impressed. 19th century.

(i) WELLSVILLE, Ohio, U.S.A. Wellsville China Company. Est. 1879. (j) EAST LIVERPOOL, Ohio, U.S.A. Union Potteries Company. 19th century. (k) STOKE-ON-TRENT, Great Britain. W. T. Copeland and Sons. Spode, factory. 1847-1891. (l) EAST LIVERPOOL, Ohio, U.S.A. Knowles, Taylor, and Knowles. Est. 1876.

a   b   c   d

(**a**) EAST LIVERPOOL, Ohio, U.S.A. Knowles, Taylor, and Knowles.
Est. 1854. (**b**) SEBRING, Ohio. French china. (**c-d**) BEAVER
FALLS, Pennsylvania, U.S.A. Mayer Pottery Company. Est. 1881.

e   f   g

(**e**) LISBON, Ohio, U.S.A. Thomas China Company. 19th century.
(**f**) BENNINGTON, Vermont, U.S.A. United States Pottery Company. Porcelain. Circa 1850. (**g**) STEUBENVILLE, Ohio, U.S.A.
Steubenville Pottery Company, Est. 1887.

h   i   j   k

(**h**) BURSLEM, Great Britain. John Walton. Earthenware. 18th-
19th century. (**i**) WELLSVILLE, Ohio, U.S.A. Pioneer Pottery
Company. Circa 1890. (**j**) EAST LIVERPOOL, Ohio, U.S.A. Vodrey Brothers. Circa 1875. (**k**) EAST LIVERPOOL, Ohio, U.S.A.
Brunt, Bloor, and Martin. Est. 1876.

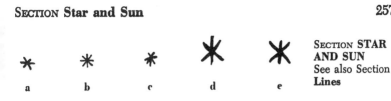

a   b   c   d   e

(a) DERBY, Great Britain. Isaac Farnsworth. 18th-19th century.
(b) GINORI, Italy. 1737. (c) THURINGIA, Germany. Wallendorf,
factory. Porcelain. 1764. (d) HOLLAND. De Ster (The Star).
Fayence. Delft. 1690. (e) BARANOVKA, Russia. Porcelain. Circa
1805.

f   g   h   i   j

(f-g-h) DOCCIA, Italy. Ginori, factory. Soft paste. Painted color.
1735. (i) CAUGHLEY, Great Britain. Porcelain. 1750. (j) HOL-
LAND. De Ster (The Star). Fayence. Delft. 1759.

k   l   m   n   o

(k) NOVE, Italy. Fayence, porcelain. Painted gold, color. Est. 1728.
(l) OUDE LOOSDRECHT, Holland. Porcelain. Painted blue, red.
1771. (m) ETRURIA, Great Britain. Wedgwood, factory. Impressed. 1765-1850. (n) NOVE, Italy. Hard paste. Painted gold,
color. Est. 1728. (o) DOCCIA, Italy. Ginori, factory. 18th century.

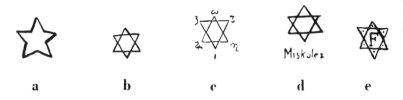

a   b   c   d   e

(a) TRENTON, New Jersey, U.S.A. Star Porcelain Company. 19th century. (b) DOCCIA, Italy. Soft paste. Painted gold. 1735. (c) NYMPHENBURG, Germany. Hard paste. Est. 1755. (d) MIS-KOLEZ, Germany. Est. 1882. (e) FAENZA, Italy. Circa 1880.

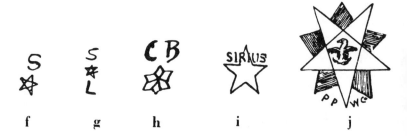

f   g   h   i   j

(f) SAVONA, Italy. 18th century. (g) SEVILLE, Spain. 19th century. (h) HOLLAND. De Ster (The Star). Fayence. Delft. 1720. (i) EAST LIVERPOOL, Ohio, U.S.A. Globe Pottery Company. Circa 1896. (j) WELLSVILLE, Ohio, U.S.A. Wellsville China Company. Est. 1879.

k   l   m   n   o

(k) EAST LIVERPOOL, Ohio, U.S.A. C. C. Thompson Pottery Company. Est. 1888. (l) TRENTON, New Jersey, U.S.A. Trenton Pottery Company. Est. 1865. (m) NEVERS, France. Fayence. 17th century. (n-o) NEW CUMBERLAND. West Virginia, U.S.A. Chelsea China Company. Printed. Est. 1888.

a   b   c   d   e

(a-b) HOCHST, Germany. Hard paste. Painted blue, red, gold. 1750. (c) BALTIMORE, Maryland, U.S.A. Edwin Bennett. Circa 1875. (d-e) SAINT CLOUD, France. Soft paste. Painted blue. 1678-1766.

f   g   h   i   j

(f) DERBY, Great Britain. Robert Bloor. 1811-1848. (g-h) NEW MILFORD, Connecticut, U.S.A. Milford Pottery Company. Est. 1886. (i-j) HORNBERG, Germany. Horn Brothers. Fayence. 1880.

k   l   m   n   o

SECTION **TOWER**
See also Section
Miscellaneous

(k) WURZBURG, Germany. Hard paste. Painted blue. 1775. (l) CINCINNATI, Ohio, U.S.A. Rookwood Pottery Company. Circa 1880. (m) VINCENNES, France. Soft paste. Painted color, 1753. (n) LA TOUR D'AIGUES, France. Fayence. Est. 1753 (may be Tournay mark). (o) TOURNAY, Belgium. Soft paste. Est. 1751.

a   b   c   d   e

(**a**) LA TOUR D'AIGUES, France. Fayence. Est. 1753 (may be
Tournay mark). (**b**) TOURNAY, Belgium. Soft paste. Est. 1751.
(**c**) CLIGNANCOURT, France. Hard paste. Painted blue, gold.
1771-1798. (**d**) SAVONA, Italy. 18th century. (**e**) GERMANY.
Circa 1840.

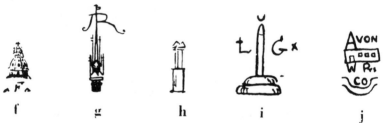

f   g   h   i   j

(**f**) FLORENCE, Italy. Soft paste. Painted color. 1580. (**g**) GER-
MANY. Circa 1840. (**h**) TOURNAY, Belgium. Soft paste. Est. 1751.
(**i**) LIEGE, Belgium. Fayence. 1752-1811. (**j**) WHEELING, West
Virginia, U.S.A. Wheeling Pottery Company. Est. 1903.

k   l   m

(**k**) COPENHAGEN, Denmark. Bing and Grondahl, factory. 1853.
(**l**) BURSLEM, Great Britain. 1795. (**m**) METTLACH, Germany.
Glazed earthenware. Est. 1809.

a   b   c

(a) HAVILAND, France. Whiteware. Painted green. 1892. (b) OLD HALL, Great Britain. Earthenware. 19th century. (c) HUNGARY, Zsolnay. Soft paste. Est. 1855.

SECTION
TRIANGLE AND HEART
See also Sections
Circle and Sign, Shield

d   e   f   g   h   i

(d) CHELSEA, Great Britain. Soft paste. Painted gold, red. 1745-1750. (e) BOW, Great Britain. Incised, painted blue, red. Est. 1750. (f) DERBY, Great Britain. Hard paste. Painted blue, impressed. Est. 1745. (g) CHELSEA, Great Britain. Soft paste. 1745-1750. (h) BOW, Great Britain. Porcelain. Incised. Est. 1750. (i) KORZEC, Poland. Porcelain. 1790-1797.

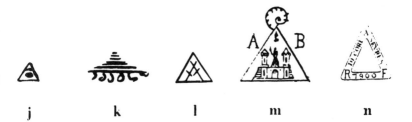

j   k   l   m   n

(j) KORZEC, Poland. Porcelain. 1790-1797. (k) PERSIA. 19th century. (l) BRISTOL, Great Britain. Hard paste. Impressed. 18th century. (m) MAGDEBURG, Germany. 1894-1907. (n) SEVRES, France. Mark tells year of decoration. 1900-1902.

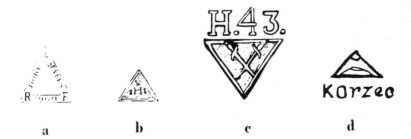

a   b   c   d

(**a**) SEVRES, France. Painted red. Guilder's mark. 1900-1902. (**b**) QUIMPER, France. Fayence. 1782-1872. (**c**) MEISSEN, Germany. Porcelain. Impressed. 1766-1780. (**d**) KORZEC, Poland. Porcelain. 1790-1797.

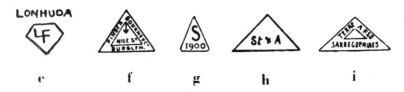

e   f   g   h   i

(**e**) STEUBENVILLE, Ohio, U.S.A. Lonhuda Pottery Company. Est. 1892. (**f**) BURSLEM, Great Britain. 1862-1882. (**g**) SEVRES, France. Hard paste painted black, soft paste painted blue. 1900+. (**h**) GERMANY. Est. 1889. (**i**) SARREGUIMINES, France. Porcelain, fayence. 1935+.

j   k   l   m

(**j**) HANLEY, Great Britain. 19th century. (**k**) NEWCASTLE, Great Britain. 1875-circa 1908. (**l-m**) ORLEANS, France. Hard paste, soft paste. Painted color. 1753-1812.

a   b   c   d

(a) TOURNAY, Belgium. Est. 1753. (b) BRUGES, Belgium. 18th century. (c) PARIS, France. Rue Popincourt, factory. Porcelain. 1782-1835. (d) Liverpool, Great Britain. Richard Chaffers. 1740-1765.

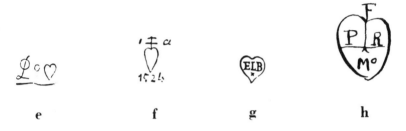

e   f   g   h

(e) MOUSTIERS, France. Fayence. Painted color. 17th century. (f) NAPLES, Italy. Painted color. 16th century. (g) FRANCE. Fayence. Impressed. Circa 1830. (h) MILAN, Italy. Fayence. 18th century.

i   j   k

(i) GERMANY. Fayence. 19th century. (j) GERMANY. Benedikt Brothers. Est. 1884. (k) LIVERPOOL, Great Britain. Richard Chaffers. 1740-1765.

INDEX OF MARKS

INDEX OF MANUFACTURERS